Languages and Their Territories

J.A. LAPONCE

Translated by Anthony Martin-Sperry

Bilingualism is a fact of life in many areas throughout the world; in some areas, including Canada, it is also a political issue of great contention. In this thoughtful analysis J.A. Laponce explores the phenomenon of bilingualism from historical, geographical, political, and psychobiological perspectives.

Beginning with a study of how we learn language, he explains how the human brain resists bilingualism because it is reluctant to store a multiplicity of signifiers for a single object or concept. Perfect bilingualism is thus virtually impossible to achieve, and so it is only with great difficulty, and at considerable cost, that languages coexist within a population.

This impulse for unilingualism translates into the creation of territorial niches based on unilingual commonality. Each language group strives to establish its domination and exclusivity in a given territory, goals much more easily achieved if a language has control of the machinery of government and in particular the control of an independent state. In multilingual societies the dominant language forces the subordinate to assume the costs of sustaining more than one language and to operate in fewer and fewer areas of activity.

The applications to Canada are obvious. Laponce also applies his theory to a number of other multilingual societies and governments and draws provocative conclusions about minority language rights and options.

This book was originally published in French as *Langue et territoire*.

J. A. LAPONCE is a professor of political science, University of British Columbia.

J. A. LAPONCE

Languages and Their Territories

Translated from the French by
Anthony Martin-Sperry

UNIVERSITY OF TORONTO PRESS
Toronto Buffalo London

© University of Toronto Press 1987
Toronto Buffalo London
Printed in Canada

ISBN 0-8020-5703-9 (cloth)
ISBN 0-8020-6631-3 (paper)

Canadian Cataloguing in Publication Data

Laponce, J.A., 1925-
  Languages and their territories

  Translation and new ed. of: Langue et territoire.
  Includes bibliographical references and index.
  ISBN 0-8020-5703-9 (bound) ISBN 0-8020-6631-3 (pbk.)

  1. Languages – Political aspects.   2. Bilingualism.
  3. Multilingualism.   I. Title.

  P106.L3616 1987   400   C86-095101-4

This book has been published with the help of a grant from the Social Science
Federation of Canada, using funds provided by the Social Sciences and
Humanities Research Council of Canada.

Cet ouvrage est dédié à ma mère

en souvenir de nos leçons d'anglais

et de ses cours de français.

Contents

Preface

This is both a translation and a second edition. It differs from the original not only in its language, hence to some extent in its style, but also in its content. Some sections have been revised, that dealing with Yugoslavia in particular; some classifications have been modified because of changes in political regimes, for example, in Argentina and the Philippines, or because of changes in language legislation, notably in Luxembourg and Singapore. I have tempered or qualified some judgments – mostly on the importance of biological factors as underpinnings of language conflicts; and I have, of course, corrected the factual inaccuracies that colleagues have kindly brought to my attention, particularly in Appendix 1.

None of these changes modifies any of the original conclusions. Now, as before, I am convinced that languages have a specific territorial behaviour that needs to be taken into consideration when we analyse ethno-linguistic contacts and when we engage in language planning. I remain convinced that, in the competition in which they are caught, languages defend themselves best by means of territoriality and statehood.

So many conversations, interviews, seminars, congress panels, and round tables lie at the origins of each of the chapters that I cannot possibly thank individually the many colleagues and civil servants who offered me documents, information, suggestions, and criticisms. May they find here my deep appreciation. I have a very special debt to Jean Gottmann, and also André Siegfried – teacher to both of us; I owe to them a liking for political geography. To Roland Breton and William MacKey I owe a research suggestion that I have attempted to operationalize in chapter 3, where I measure the relative power of various languages. My colleagues at the University of British Columbia – notably Ivan Avakumovic, Alan Cairns, Peter Chamberlain, David Elkins, Diane Mauzy, Stephen Milne, Bernard St

Jacques, Paul Tennant, and John Wood – have given me valuable information and advice. So did colleagues and friends at nearby or distant universities: Maureen Covell and Heribert Adam at Simon Fraser; Anthony Birch at the University of Victoria; Pierre van den Berghe, Paul Brass, Jonathan Pool, Margaret Levi, and Michael Hechter at the University of Washington in Seattle; John Meisel at Queen's University; John Trent and Paul Lamy at the University of Ottawa; Kenneth McRae at Carleton University; Léon Dion, Gérard Bergeron, Jean-Denis Gendron, and William MacKey at Laval University; Jayaratnam Wilson at the University of New Brunswick; Karl Deutsch at Harvard University; Claude Raffestin at the University of Geneva; Paul Claval at the University of Paris IV; Georges Goriely at the Free University of Brussels; André Philippart, secretary of the Belgian Political Science Association; Francis Delpérée at the University of Louvain; H. van Hassell at Leuwen University; Erick Allardt at the University of Helsinki; Rango Burgaski at the University of Belgrade; Jack Hayward at the University of Hull; and the anonymous readers of the Social Sciences Federation of Canada. I deeply regret that Val Lorwin and Stein Rokkan did not live long enough to find here the recollections of our discussions on a subject that fascinated them.

At the crossroads of psychology, biology, sociolinguistics, geography, and political science, this work needed foundations in a variety of disciplines and subfields. These foundations might have often been built on quicksand without the help of the well-organized Social Sciences division at the Library of the University of British Columbia, where reference librarians specialize in specific disciplines. I am particularly grateful to Jacqueline Hooper and Iza Laponce. Their help in searching the Library collection was essential. The works that I consulted are nearly all written in English or French – 80 per cent are English, 18 per cent French – the only two languages I can read easily. This distribution will no doubt look unbalanced to those who have different first or second languages. The disequilibrium would have been even greater without the assistance of Laine Ruus for translation from Swedish and that of Petula Muller for translation from German. Additionally, Petula Muller, who had typed the French manuscript, typed the revisions of the English text, not objecting to a succession of drafts and redrafts. Her speed and accuracy were much appreciated.

I am grateful to the Social Science Federation of Canada for assuming the expense of the translation and grateful to Anthony Martin-Sperry for doing a translation that pleases me very much – as much as a flattering portrait. In addition to translating, Anthony Martin-Sperry made welcomed suggestions for improving the original. Finally, but not least, my thanks are due to John Parry for his efficient final editing and to Rik Davidson for steering the book to publication.

LANGUAGES AND THEIR TERRITORIES

Introduction

Bilingualism is common, but it is abnormal – common because man is a born exchanger of information, and because one's neighbours often do not speak the same language as one does; abnormal because we reject true synonymy and tend naturally toward unilingualism, at least in a closed communication system.

Whether language be innate or not, the sociologist has no need to explain why the unilingual speaks his mother tongue; but in the case of a bilingual, and even more so in that of someone who is multilingual, an explanation is called for – almost always social rather than psychological or neurological. We do not have two languages in the way that we have two hands or two eyes. Multilingualism is explained by geographic mobility, the pressure of history, ethnic allegiance, and the ratio of asymmetrical force between the dominant group and the subordinate group; multilingualism is thus a condition particularly favourable to the study of the relations between ethnic groups and states and hence an area of privileged research for the political scientist who defines his approach as the study of communication, co-operation, and conflict resulting from the creation, maintenance, and modification of social hierarchies.

Languages, like individuals and states, are constantly involved in the conflicts of precedence and domination which arc a ceaselessly repeated feature of the hierarchies in which they exist. In so far as these languages exist only by communication, if they are to survive and flourish they need territorial niches that belong to them alone – niches in which communication will take place in one single language that can bind together the various individuals in a given society and satisfy the various roles of any given individual therein. There are of course exceptions, which we shall mention in due course. Sometimes the need for internal segregation within a given society – by role or by group – is better fulfilled with the assistance of several languages than of one alone; but it is normal among languages – and here they differ from the various species of the animal kingdom – for each language to establish its domination and then to seek exclusivity in a given territory. This domination and this exclusivity will be obtained all the more easily if a language has control of the machinery of government, and in particular the control of an independent state.

This work will be essentially an exercise in political linguistics and in political geography. Its themes are, quite simply, that languages protect themselves by territoriality; that today this territoriality is assured first and foremost by the state; and that the modern state, which requires the active participation of the masses through both the spoken and the written word, is 'glossophagic' (Calvet 1974) – destructive of its minority languages.

1

The brain as the battlefield
of languages

If languages intermingle but poorly in a given geographical area, the prime reason is mutual strife within the individual. It is as though the signifiers of different languages were engaged in a fight to the death or at least a fight for precedence, within both our individual and our collective memories, seeking to become the foremost, if not the only, vehicles of meaning.

We avoid bilingualism as we avoid true synonymy, which would endow one and the same signified with multiple designations of strictly equivalent semantic content (Genouvrier 1970). We can learn and store more than one language, at variable costs – the younger the student the less the cost. The battles of language are thus typically for children's minds, which is why I attach such importance in this chapter to works dealing with bilingualism in schools.

Neuropsychological limitations to the acquisition of several languages

The capacity for social contact by means of signs is not reserved for man alone; dolphins, whales, and apes all have symbolic systems of communication, but these communication systems are not the equivalent of human speech. Despite years of intensive education, the chimpanzee Washoe – one of the most highly educated animals – has assimilated no more than 200 signs and cannot put more than three or four of these together to form coherent phrases. Washoe learned to 'read' in 1966; and some ten years later she passed her knowledge on to her adoptive baby (Keerdoja 1979; Walker 1978). However, even with human assistance, Washoe has transmitted to her baby only part of what she has learned; and the baby is unlikely to pass on to his own offspring more than a small part of Washoe's artificial language. Thus although certain animals can acquire some primitive forms of language, speech and nomenclature are the prerogatives of man alone.[1]

The human memory has limited retention when compared with the artificial intelligences that surround us, such as books and computers. I could not reproduce this page in the form in which I have just written it unless I learned it by heart – a tiresome effort. In an industrial society, the everyday vocabulary comprises some 6,000 words (Macnamara 1967b). It takes time to learn 6,000 words, and even longer to learn how to use them. If we wish to be understood we have to know how to put these words in the proper order, in accordance with rules over which we have little influence. How many words can we learn? Certainly many more than 6,000; doubtless tens of thousands can be learned, but there is a limit. Bilinguals are not rare; there are fewer trilinguals and quadrilinguals; but those who speak more than four languages are exceptional.

If we were to surround a child with the 5,000 or so languages now spoken and arranged for each language to have equal access to this child, what would happen? Probably almost complete paralysis of understanding and the power of speech, since the understanding of a concept and the production of the corresponding reactions are achieved by repetition. The brain is not just a simple piggy-bank – a degree of organization is required for it to understand the information it receives. Our child would possibly reach puberty knowing how to say 'Mama' in 5,000 different languages, but little else; or more probably he would add his own personal language to the 5,000 surrounding him – a language formed of his own particular gestures and sounds.[2] Between one single language and 5,000, where does the point of unbearable overload lie? The answer varies with the individual; but generally speaking it is close to unity, for languages learned directly by imitation as for those learned indirectly by a process of analysis.[3] The cost of learning a language is greatly increased when the student changes from one method to the other, since each of them corresponds to different stages of

1 According to Geschwind (1964), the power of naming – a power peculiar to man – depends on the capacity for establishing associations between different modes of cognizance such as the visual and the auditory or the tactile and the auditory. Unlike man, the monkey lacks certain neural circuits essential for such operations: there are plenty of transmission circuits between the auditory and the visual but not enough circuits in the opposite direction.

2 Natural languages currently spoken in the world have not been the object of systematic enumeration. On this subject, see chapter 3, p. 54. Five thousand is a very approximate total.

3 By and large, these two methods correspond to two different codings: the perceptive and the semantic (Champagnol 1974).

development. According to Gesell and Ilg (1949), the development of language in the child follows a well-defined progression: first month – undifferentiated sounds; second month – better differentiation in the sounds; then incoherent babbling; then acquisition of vowels followed by consonants (first gutturals, then dentals, and finally nasals). In this way the child's grasp of the language improves, till at the age of one he can pronounce a few words. He forms simple phrases during his second year and is talking coherently before the age of 4. Between 6 and 8 he acquires a complete understanding of the linguistic 'shape' of his language; between 8 and 9 he begins to get a grasp of its structure; and from the age of 9 onward (and especially after puberty) he becomes increasingly analytical. Now he has to understand in order to learn.

Lenneberg (1967, 58) sums up the interaction between physical development and linguistic capability as follows:

Between the ages of three and the early teens the possibility for primary language acquisition continues to be good; the individual appears to be most sensitive to stimuli at this time and to preserve some innate flexibility for the organization of brain functions to carry out the complex integration of subprocesses necessary for the smooth elaboration of speech and language. After puberty, the ability for self-organization and adjustment to the physiological demands of verbal behavior quickly declines. The brain behaves as if it had become set in its ways and primary, basic language skills not acquired by that time, except for articulation, usually remain deficient for life. (New words may be acquired throughout life, because the basic skill of naming has been learned at the very beginning of language development.)

Larew (1961) showed that among anglophones 7–14 years of age the capability of reproducing Spanish phonemes decreases as they grow older. Masson (1964) made a similar finding when he compared the results of French instruction received by children aged 5–6 with those of children aged 11–12; those in the younger group made much more rapid progress. Similarly, Asher and Garcia (1969), in a comparative study of Cuban immigrants to the United States, noted that those who immigrated before the age of 6 were considerably more likely to speak English without an accent, while those who arrived after the age of 13 were more likely to speak it with an accent.[4]

---

4 Languages learned after puberty interfere with each other more than those learned in early childhood (Imedadze 1960). However, a minority of adults seem capable of reproducing the sounds of newly learned languages without accent, at least in the laboratory (Neufeld 1977).

A language does not, of course, boil down to its pronunciation; but the partial rejection of new sounds is merely one aspect of the linguistic matrix of the individual.

Do languages have a genetic basis?

Darlington in 1947 suggested that the sounds of natural languages are due to individual preferences stemming from genetic origins. Basing himself on this theory, Brosnahan (1961) noted that the sound 'th' in English is also found in languages as diverse as Finno-Ugric and Basque; this sound, which formerly covered the whole of central Europe, is today found only on the periphery of the continent. He concluded that the reason for its gradual disappearance was probably the spread of genes unfavourable to this particular sound, along an east-west axis – the dominant axis of European migrations. This theory is still merely a hypothesis. Speaking calls for the co-ordination of more than a hundred muscles, and differences of sound depend on complex muscular adjustments carried out fourteen times per second. Can differences of a genetic nature in the condition and control of these muscles affect large population? This is possible, but remains to be proved (Lenneberg 1967, 97). However, these genetic differences could not be other than minimal and could not obscure this fundamental phenomenon – proof, if proof be needed, that man forms but one species; a normal baby, taken from any linguistic group and brought up in another, will have no difficulty in learning the language of the latter group and will speak it without an accent.

There is no biological obstacle that prevents an individual from learning one language rather than another, and no serious neuropsychological obstacle to his learning two languages (perhaps even three or four) instead of only one – at least while he is still quite young and capable of learning several languages by the direct method at a relatively modest cost; but there *is* a cost, and this will increase as the individual grows older. Bilingual adults who learned their two languages in infancy often claim that they were not conscious of learning two different languages. Is their memory sound? Childhood was such a long time ago. Do they remember their rejection of certain baby-foods, or their disgust when newborn brothers and sisters appeared on the scene? Generally not. When young bilingual children of my acquaintance realize that the person talking with them is bilingual, they try to impose one particular language on the conversation, as though one of their two languages demands less effort on their part than the other. Further, if these same children are forced to speak their second language, they show irritation. One thing seems clear: the child does not accumulate several signifiers for one and the same signified just for the fun of it. Try to convince him that if he is 'Jean' he is also 'John,' or that 'Cendrillon' is no more of a drudge than 'Cinderella' (or vice versa, in both cases). You might just as well give up trying in the former case, and success in the latter case will take time and will not be easily achieved. The child seeks constantly to enlarge his vocabulary, not 'vertically' by piling up signifiers one on top of the other but 'horizontally' by extending his grasp over more and more signifieds.

Bilingual memory

How does the bilingual brain store the signals it receives? More precisely, how does the brain distribute the code-signs of two different languages within the memory? The simplest theory, that of Penfield (1959), postulates a single central switch that gives access to the language being used and simultaneously blocks off that part of the memory that stores the code-signs of the language not being used. However, this theory does not satisfactorily explain the commonly reported observation that among even the most gifted bilinguals, even professional interpreters, one language intrudes upon the other, at the level either of structure or of vocabulary. A typical intrusion might have the French-English bilingual saying 'coercion' when speaking French, instead of 'coercition' (Mackey 1962; Hamers and Lambert 1974; Durga 1978; Mägiste 1979). The other current interpretation, the tag theory, is in my opinion preferable to Penfield's. Observation of the verbal behaviour of bilinguals, supported by laboratory tests, indicates that linguistic codes are probably grouped according to meaning, i.e. in terms of the signified.

As Macnamara (1967a; 1976b) and Macnamara and Kushnin (1971) note, bilinguals differ markedly in their capacity to maintain two separate languages. Certain bilinguals with twin mother-tongues – for example, Pierre Trudeau – can change rapidly from one language to the other as though they possessed a central switch to block off interferences. However, most laboratory experiments contradict the hypothesis of separate linguistic memories. In a typical experiment (Anderson and Bower 1972), subjects were asked to recall, after a certain lapse of time, the concepts that had been presented to them in two different languages. The results showed that the concepts remained grouped in the memory according to their meaning, i.e. according to the signified, and were matched with linguistic tags. For example, the signified 'cat' forms part of a group containing concepts such as kitten, tomcat, alley cat, he-cat, and she-cat, in which each term has one or more tags to mark the linguistic and semantic differences separating that particular term from the other terms in the group.[5] Saegert, Hamayan, and Ahmar (1975) showed that their multilingual subjects had no difficulty in remembering the language of a bilingual series of words having no relationship to one another, but they were more likely to make a mistake when asked to remember in which tongue words of different languages integrated into the logical context of a sentence had been presented to them. The linguistic tag prevails in the absence of specific meaning but loses its importance when the aggregate of the words forms a meaningful whole.

If the bilingual's brain is a battlefield, the battle is not a pitched one – language versus language. The conflict is more likely to be a series of duels in which the first casualties are concepts used rarely in one language but often in the other. Other early casualties are linguistic tools with no obvious logic to them (the bilingual anglophone asks himself: does one say 'penser à' or 'penser de'?). Next, entire groups of signifiers drop out; and finally – before they too disappear – there remain only everyday words, odds and ends of sentences in current use, impoverished constructions, and shabby little vocabularies.[6]

The single-switch theory (which I feel to be inadequate) has not been entirely abandoned, but its adherents are clearly in the minority. Barnett (1977) counted, among 26 recent studies of the bilingual memory, only 5 supporting linguistic separation, while 13 supported semantic organization with linguistic tags, and 3 held that such organization develops as a function of both meaning and language together.[7] Barnett has an eminently reasonable explanation for these divergent conclusions: the balanced bilingual

5 Measurements of semantic distance between concepts grasped in two different languages, which according to the dictionary should have the same meaning, reveal noticeable differences in bilinguals of the convergent type, as in those of the divergent type – perhaps somewhat larger among the former than among the latter (Stafford and van Keuren 1968). For the distinction between these two types of bilinguals, see chapter 2, p. 29.

  Paradoxically, the difficulty in finding true synonyms, not only among different languages but even more so within a single language, stems from the fact that words – at least those most frequently used – rarely have only one single meaning (Alston 1964, 44; Mackey 1971).

6 Young and Navar (1968) report that the acquisition of new associations of ideas in one of the languages of their bilingual subjects is connected with the forgetting of associations in the other language.

7 Studies done after Barnett's survey confirm on the whole the hypothesis of a common semantic memory (Caramazza and Brones 1980). Wiens and his colleagues (1976) put forward a compromise theory midway between the single switch theory and the tag theory. Bilingual memory, they held, is composed of two distinct ensembles with considerable overlapping.

groups concepts in his memory primarily according to meaning and second-
arily according to language.[8]

The mental cost of bilingualism: interference

If the bilingual does not have separate linguistic memories, then are not languages a source of enrichment, even when they are engaged in a battle in the
partisan war postulated above?

In one of his essays, Queneau poses the question: once I know the word
'escargot,' what advantage is there in my also knowing the word 'snail'?

8 Measurements of the cerebral activity of bilinguals show that they use the right side of
their brain more than unilinguals do in some experiments. According to Bever (1974) the
mother-tongue is more to the left than is the second language. Sussman et al (1982)
report a higher level of right-brain lateralization of the second language, especially when
that language has been acquired early in life. Mishkin and Forgays (1952), like Orbach
(1953), report that in Anglo/Yiddish bilinguals, English is systematically to the left,
while Yiddish is more to the right. In similar fashion, Rogers, TenHouten, and their
colleagues (1977) note that among Hopi children the Indian language is more to the
right. More generally, Critchley (1974) considers that ideogrammatic Asiatic languages
use the occipital/parietal area of the right brain more frequently than European languages do, and Tsunoda (1978) – whose findings remain to be duplicated – considers
that the characteristic sounds of Japanese, due in particular to the way the vowels are
used, produce a cerebral structure different from that produced by other languages
(except for the Polynesian group, in which the vowels are used in the same way); in consequence, bilingualism would be more 'foreign' and difficult between Japanese and English than between English and French. Albert and Obler (1978) note that the two systems of Japanese writing, the ideographic kanji and the alphabetic kana, are coded one
by the right brain, the other by the left. Other authors, in contrast, report identical cerebral processes in the two languages of their bilingual subjects: Kershner and Jeng (1972)
in the case of Chinese/English bilinguals, Walters and Zatorre (1978) in the case of
Spanish/English bilinguals, and Soares (1982; 1984) in the case of Anglo/Portuguese
bilinguals.

   Verification that cerebral processes differ in different languages would probably
strengthen the bond between bilingualism and biculturalism. For example, if the Hopi
language entails the more frequent use of the right brain (as TenHouten thinks) because
it brings the speaker into closer contact with his physical environment, then passing to
this language from English would involve not only a change of role but a profound
change of personality. The results of studies on the cerebral lateralization of languages
indicate, by their contradictions, that from the neurophysiological point of view there
are probably different types of bilinguals. The particular languages, the age at which
these languages were acquired, the social environment, and the ways in which they were
acquired and are used are no doubt among the differential factors to be considered
(Luria 1974–75); (Lambert 1978; Laponce 1985). Studies on the recovery of speech
among bilingual aphasiacs confirm the diversity of types of bilinguals, since it is not
possible to predict which language will be the first to be recovered (Lambert and Fillenbaum 1959; Paradis 1977).

From the viewpoint of communication with others who know only the word 'snail,' the question loses its interest – the answer is too obvious. But from the viewpoint of comprehension, of ease of conceptualization, of rapidity of reaction to verbal stimuli, and of linguistic creativity, the question raises fundamental problems with no simple solution. Studies comparing unilinguals with bilinguals, and more particularly communication between individuals, indicate that even if bilingualism aids conceptualization, it is an obstacle to rapidity of reaction.

There have been three main forms of research on the cost of memory and on the reaction time of the bilingual who registers, encodes, and decodes bilingual messages. The first sets out to determine whether the use of one language rather than another involves a greater psychological cost; the researcher seeks to establish whether one language tends always to dominate the other in a given social role – as claimed by the theory of the hierarchy of codes. The second type of research compares bilingual communication with unilingual; the researcher seeks to assess the cost of switching from one language to the other. The third type seeks to determine whether the bilingual or the unilingual has a greater facility for memory, conceptualization, and communication.

Research of the first type is conclusive. Appropriate tests can easily determine a bilingual's dominant language. In this language the subject reacts faster and is more creative (Wakefield 1975). Such differences are not apparent, however, if the test being used is too easy. An English-French bilingual's time of response – 'yes' or 'no' – to a simple question such as 'Is a cat an animal?' may for both languages be the same to within a hundredth of a second. But a difference becomes apparent when the question and its answer are more complex, for example, when the subject is asked to name, by association of ideas, as many concepts as possible within a given time. The same will happen when he is asked to dissociate conflicting stimuli – for example, to react to the name of a colour printed in a colour different from the one the name describes.

Experiments carried out by Dornic (1975) show clearly that the harder the linguistic task, the greater the difference of reaction time in the two languages of fluent bilinguals. In a typical example, bilingual subjects are asked to find first one, then two, then three correct answers to mathematical problems that grow increasingly complicated – problems posed first in one language, then in the other, with the subject being required to answer in the language in which the question is posed.[9] The time needed to solve the

9 See also the experiments of Marsh and Maki (1976) and Hardycz (1978). The dominant language, the one better established at the level of the central nervous system, is not

problem is always shorter in the dominant language, but the curves are not parallel – the harder the question, the wider the gap between the curves, as in Figure 1.

The consequences of increasing inequality are important, both psychologically and socially. The bilingual tends to define his problems – whether set by himself or by others in his subordinate language – in terms of the increased cost involved in the use of that language. At a certain point, which varies with the individual, the cost of using the subordinate language seems too high, and the person either switches to the dominant language or avoids a problem regarded as too difficult. This explains the silence or lack of participation at meetings by some bilinguals when certain problems are under discussion; they are avoiding situations in which the language cost is prohibitive.[10]

Research of the second type – comparing unilingual communication with bilingual – indicates, as does that of the first type, that the cost of bilingualism increases with the complexity of the problems posed. An experiment caried out by Tulving and Colotla (1970) showed that trilingual students asked to recall a list of words previously presented to them in writing recalled a bilingual list as well as they did a unilingual one, when the list contained no more than seven concepts; but above seven, these same subjects found it easier to recall a unilingual list. In their interpretation of the results, the authors distinguished between primary and secondary memories: for up to seven concepts the subjects had used only their primary memory; but beyond seven, they must have passed the data into their long-term, secondary memory. Other authors, such as Lambert, Ignatow, and Krauthamer (1968) and Nott and Lambert (1968), found in their bilingual subjects the same facility for retention of lists of words, whether unilingual or bilingual, even though such retention implied the use of the secondary

---

necessarily the mother-tongue, even if this is still in current use (Lebrun 1971). The dominant language of a bilingual is not only the one he will prefer to use when the problem to be solved is complex; it is also the one that tends to define the nominal categories of the two languages when these categories do not coincide – the categories of colour, for example (Ervin 1961). But in the case of different classifications in the two languages (probably when the dominance of the first language is less clear), the categories of the bilingual in his two languages become less sharply defined, as though he were trying to amalgamate the two differently classified systems (Caskey-Sirmons and Hickerson 1977). This is probably a source of imprecision in both languages.

10 Jaakkola (1976) reports that some Finnish-speaking Swedes keep silent when they answer the telephone; at their ease neither in Finnish nor in Swedish, they bury themselves in a 'silent minority.'

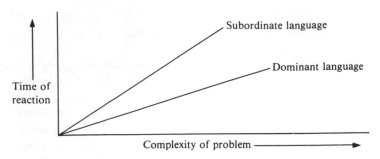

FIGURE 1
Reaction time in 'fluent' bilinguals

memory.[11] However, here again the difficulty of the task should not be overlooked. To remember lists of separate words is one thing; to remember a more complex symbolic system such as a sentence or a poem is quite another. Dornic (1975) drew attention once again to a phenomenon familiar to every bilingual – telephone numbers stored in one's long-term memory are usually couched in a single language, and translation is not automatic. Typically, the bilingual wishing to switch a telephone number from one language to the other must first pass the number from the long-term to the short-term memory, in which the translation takes place. A unilingual code in the long-term memory is more economical than a bilingual code.

Numerous experiments – for example, those of Kolers (1966), Macnamara and Edwards (1968), Marsh and Maki (1976) – show that changing language during communication takes time, and that it is more efficient to operate in one single language than in two. Dornic (1975) showed in addition that it is not only the switch from one language to another that is inefficient; the lack of language identity between the subject and his surroundings is also a factor. The bilingual's times of reaction to unexpected stimuli are shorter not only when he is free to react in the language of his choice but also when this same language is that of his environment. The retarding and paralysing effect of surroundings in which a language other than that of the subject's choice is in use is seen in the agonizing mental gymnastics known as 'passive bilingualism' (more accurately 'depressive bilingualism'). In passive bilingual conversation, the parties talk in different languages. Con-

11 Perhaps this lack of difference stems directly from the experiment's use of the second memory. McCormack (1976) reports that even when his bilingual subjects had identical reaction times in the long-term memory, the dominant language had the advantage in reaction times in the short-term memory (see also McCormack and Novell 1975).

versation becomes opaque, dull, and morose and gets tangled up in interferences – or freezes in clichés. [12] Communication is paralysed by the non-congruence of the two systems; the speakers understand but cannot help each other; finally they speak their own language as though it were a translation.

Bilingualism is costly, in terms of both memory and reaction time. Thus for an individual to become or to remain bilingual, the social benefit must outweigh the mental cost; and this mental cost explains why the tendency toward unilingualism never entirely disappears. Certainly, there are people who 'learn languages' easily, who keep acquiring other languages, not from any real social necessity but solely for pleasure; these are indeed fascinating cases but rare and merely confirm the norm: the mind works more quickly and with less effort in a unilingual semantic system; its natural inclination is toward unilingualism.

Is there then no intellectual advantage in bilingualism other than communication with others? Does not bilingualism help in the understanding of the signified? We shall examine this question with the help of a review of works dealing with scholastic bilingualism.

Scholastic bilingualism

The numerous studies on the effects of bilingualism in the school are not as conclusive as one would wish; it is difficult to find a unilingual control-group whose intellectual quotient, social category, and motivation are identical with those of the bilingual group being studied. It does not help either that the instability of the results obtained during the past 50 years correlates so closely with changes of societal values. When it was believed that bilingualism was bad for the intellectual development of the child, in an era in which the dominant linguistic groups felt completely sure of themselves and their educational mission, students of bilingualism more often than not found bilingualism to have a retarding effect on a child's education. In more recent times – characterized in the West by an attack of conscience in the dominant groups and their concomitant sympathy for subordinates – it was generally found that bilingualism had beneficial effects. The studies carried out in this later period were of higher quality than the earlier ones,

12 The strangest passive bilingualism is the one that induces participants to use their second language, in order to be seen in a more favourable light by the person with whom they speak (Simard and Taylor 1976). Speaking the other's language means refusing to use the power one might have to impose with one's own language and preferring fellowship to power even if communication suffers thereby (Brown and Gilman 1968; Myers and Vry 1977).

but the choice of tests may have been influenced by the results that seemed to be expected. Before we examine the question, let us review the most important of these studies.

Harmful bilingualism

Shortly after the First World War, Saer (1922) carried out a study of scholastic bilingualism with a view to comparing the knowledge of words possessed by both unilinguals and bilinguals in Wales. His sample consisted of 140 children taken from both an urban and a rural environment. Comparison of the intellectual quotient of unilingual anglophones with that of Welsh-English bilinguals whose mother-tongue was Welsh showed that in a rural environment the IQ of the anglophones was 96 when tested in English, while the IQ of the Welsh children was 10 points lower when tested in Welsh. In an urban environment, the author found no difference between unilinguals and bilinguals (100 and 99, on average). Further, in the rural environment Saer noted a remarkable increase in the vocabulary of unilingual anglophones from the age of 8 onwards, an increase that did not occur in bilinguals until the age of 10. Generally speaking, the average vocabulary of unilinguals was larger than that of bilinguals, and the reactions of bilinguals were slower. A test of dexterity that required the child to show his right hand, and then his left ear, and to identify the right and left sides of a picture, showed that bilinguals hesitated more frequently and for longer periods than unilinguals. The author concluded from this that bilingualism was the source of an intellectual confusion occurring at the levels of language and of non-automatic motor activity. Saer's study was, for those days, particularly systematic, but it raises serious difficulties in interpretation. The tests were administered in different languages and revealed differences within the rural environment that did not exist in the urban and thus could have been due to variations in intellectual development or in social background, and hence in motivation to study. The language of the test was a distorting factor when answers to a school question were required in the language of the home, or vice versa.

In the same period – still in Wales – F. Smith (1923) followed the progress of both unilinguals and bilinguals between the ages of 8 and 11 in a rural environment, over a period of two years. The tests used for the comparison were of the following nature: free composition, reconstruction of mutilated sentences, richness of vocabulary, analogical capacity. Smith noted that on average the unilinguals did better than the bilinguals over the series of four tests. Once again, however, the study lacked even a partial control of factors such as intelligence and social background.

The need to use controls of intelligence became evident from the work of American researchers in the 1920s, who showed what numerous subsequent studies would confirm: verbal measurements of the coefficient of intelligence are inextricably bound to the language, and hence to the culture, of the subject. According to Wang (1926) and Graham (1925), it is impossible to draw any conclusion whatever as to the relative intelligence of different ethnic groups if no account is taken of the linguistic factor. However, these same authors noted that their bilingual subjects were less successful at English schools than their unilingual subjects. They concluded, as had Saer and Smith in Wales, that bilingualism slowed scholastic development in the child. Jamieson and Sandiford (1928) showed, almost at the same time, that bilingual Indians in Ontario were unable to use English as easily as unilingual anglophones of a similar social status.

Barke (1933) used more precise measurements than his predecessors and in a study dealing with Wales showed that the comparison of unilinguals with bilinguals gave dissimilar results, depending on whether verbal or spatial aptitude tests were used. His study – the first to offer systematic examination of verbal and non-verbal intelligence – indicated that a group of bilingual children aged 10–14, although six months ahead of unilinguals non-verbally, were almost a year behind verbally. He concluded that when the language used at school does not reinforce and enrich the language of the home the bilingual is at a disadvantage, at least in speech.

Darcy (1946) confirmed the observations made by Barke, Graham, and Wang. He used verbal and spatial tests to compare children brought up in a unilingual environment (family and kindergarten) with those brought up in a bilingual environment (Italian at home, English at school). The unilinguals were clearly superior in the verbal aptitude test; the bilinguals were superior (and in exactly the same proportion as in the former test) in the spatial test – even after the influences of age, sex, and social status were eliminated. The gap noted in aptitude, both verbal and non-verbal (notably spatial), led to speculations as to whether bilingualism might actually improve spatial control. If bilingualism frequently caused verbal retardation, there was possibly compensation. In fact, several studies carried out before 1960 – those of Ronjat (1913), Pintner and Arsenian (1937), Leopold (1939–49), Spoerl (1943), and O'Doherty (1958) – had already concluded that there was no negative correlation between intelligence and bilingualism.

Ronjat's (1913) case study showed that parallel development of two languages in the young child did not retard the acquisition of correct pronunciation. Leopold followed the linguistic development of his own daughter in a most detailed study from 1939 to 1949; he concluded that bilingualism had a beneficial effect, since it forced the child to separate the signifier from the signified. 'As she kept hearing different words referring to the same things, her attention was drawn to the essential – to the content rather than the form' (1941, 121). O'Doherty (1958) criticized the studies of his contemporaries, holding that they made no distinction between pseudo and true bilinguals and did not separate those who knew one language much better than the other from those who knew both languages more or less equally well. Without giving any proofs, he believed the true bilingual to be better endowed intellectually than the unilingual.

These reports of positive correlation, or of complete absence of correlation, between intelligence and bilingualism remained clearly in the minority until the beginning of the 1950s (Darcy 1953). Psychologists and educationalists interested in the problems of the bilingual child concluded that bilingualism retarded, if not the intellectual development of the subject, then at least his verbal development.

Peal and Lambert: beneficial bilingualism

Peal and Lambert's (1962) subjects were 10-year-old children from six francophone schools under the jurisdiction of the Catholic School Commission of Montreal. In each school all 10-year-olds were tested. Instructions were given in French by a francophone, except for the English vocabulary test, which was administered by an anglophone. These tests made it possible to separate unilinguals from 'balanced bilinguals,' whose knowledge of French and English was almost equal. The subject's intelligence was measured by both verbal and non-verbal tests. The authors also obtained measurements of their subjects' attitudes toward French Canadians and English Canadians, by means of a self-administered questionnaire. Osgood's semantic grid (1957) was used to measure self-perception as regards the English- and French-Canadian ethnic groups; the children were asked also to give their opinion, favourable or unfavourable, of unseen people who read alternate passages of French translated into English and vice versa. Finally, the authors obtained data from these pupils and their teachers about the parents' occupation and social standing. When this last variable is controlled (the article unfortunately does not give the text of the question used to measure social class), the study shows that the bilinguals did better in both verbal and non-verbal tests; even in French dictation they outscored the unilinguals. Thus bilinguals apparently have the advantage in both languages.

But what is the chain of causality? Are bilinguals more successful because they are bilingual? Or are they bilingual because they are more successful? Do the tests measure innate or acquired intelligence? Francophone parents who encouraged their children to learn English probably had high social ambitions for them; perhaps the parents of unilingual children did not have such ambitions. Indeed, the authors reported that the francophone parents of their bilingual subjects did encourage their children to speak English. In the spatial tests there was almost no difference between the two groups, but the bilinguals did better in concept formation and in disaggregation and reaggregation of symbolic associations. Peal and Lambert thought that this could be because the bilingual pupils were the balanced type of bilingual; if they had two signifiers of the same meaning for a given signified, the dissociation which that implied between signifier and signified gave them a mental flexibility that the unilinguals did not have. The authors concluded from this that the intellectual structure of the bilingual is probably more diversified than that of the unilingual, but they admitted that they had not been able to determine whether the bilinguals had become bilingual because they were more intelligent or more intelligent because they were bilingual. Be that as it may, Peal and Lambert's conclusions ran counter to those of Saer and of most of the authors of the preceding period.

Other studies favouring bilingualism

The studies that followed Peal and Lambert's produced similar results; only a few need be summarized here.[13]

A test carried out in Brampton, Ontario, during the 1970s indicated that anglophone students 14–15 years of age who were being taught not only French but also mathematics, history, geography, and science, all in French, were not falling behind in their ability to express themselves in English, in comparison with those who were receiving a unilingual education in English. The comparison was carefully made between pupils of the same age, the same sex, and the same IQ. The authors (Barik and Swain 1976a, b) concluded that teaching for 70 per cent of the time in the second language (in this case, French) had no harmful effect on the knowledge and use of the first language. However, in the interpretation of these results the authors did not take into consideration the so-called 'Hawthorn factor,' which gives the group being tested an advantage over the control group, when the participants know they are taking part in an unusual and prestigious experiment. The test group is more productive and more creative because it is better integrated and thus has a higher morale. The presence of

---

13 Among the bibliographical guides to the numerous studies on bilingual education, see the résumé and bibliography of Paulston (1980).

this factor was likely in the Brampton case: the students in the bilingual program had been chosen not at random but on the basis of above-average IQ; also, their parents wanted them to participate in such a program. Given equal intelligence, a pupil in the test group thus had an advantage over one in the control group, since his educational environment was of a higher-than-normal intellectual level and he knew himself to be part of an élite group.

Tests were carried out also at St Lambert in Montreal in the 1960s (Bruck et al 1977; Lambert et al 1973). Ten-year-old anglophone children from English-Canadian circles had received their education in French from grade 1 onward. After five years' schooling, they did almost as well, both in French and in English, as the unilingual control group.

The research work of Barik and Swain in Toronto (1976); Carringer in Mexico (1974); Bain and Yu (1976, 1978) in France, Germany, and Canada; Landry in the United States (1972); Skutnabb-Kangas in Sweden (1976); Ianco-Worrall in Finland (1972); and Okoh in Nigeria and Wales (1980) confirmed Leopold's findings – bilingualism does not retard intellectual development in the child. On the contrary, it facilitates dissociative thought (which dissociates the signifier from the signified) and thus facilitates the solution of unusual problems, such as the one that Ianco-Worrall set his young subjects: 'Let's call a dog a "cow." Does this "cow" have horns?'

Bilingualism in the child: a summary

How can the difference between the results of pre-1960 studies and of those after 1960 be explained? Were such factors as social background, scholastic success, and intelligence better monitored in the recent studies? Partly so – but it seems to me that the difference is due mainly to the fact that most of the pre-1960 studies dealt with children whose mother-tongue was neither well rooted nor well protected, either in the child or in his social or family surroundings. Welsh children in Great Britain, or Puerto-Ricans in the United States, have to work with a mother-tongue of limited scope; they stumble in each of their two languages. The language of the home and the language of the school are both weak and support each other but poorly. These so-called bilingual children should more accurately be described as semi-lingual; they work with two partially developed languages. The post-1960 studies dealt with subjects who – except in the Swedish study – came from well-to-do circles whose mother-tongue was protected by family, social, and educational background. In the Swedish study, at Gothenburg, the Finnish immigrants who did best were those whose primary education had been in their mother-tongue – those who had grasped one language thoroughly before learning another.

If we add the difference of attitudes toward multiculturalism in Canada, Great Britain, and the United States, both before and after 1960, we can explain most of the contradictions apparent in the works cited above. From the concept of bilingualism obtaining before the Second World War, as being a minor evil and a transitional phenomenon, these three societies moved toward the concept of bilingualism as a source of enrichment. Teachers, parents, and students may well have reacted in consequence. Success is more likely if one believes that what one is doing is success-oriented.

From these studies we can draw some conclusions. The acquisition of a second language does not retard mental or verbal development. On the contrary, it is generally conducive to the dissociation of the signifier and the signified and thus aids comprehension – but only when the two languages do not produce identity conflicts, which implies, in most cases, a well-established order of precedence between the dominant and the subordinate languages.

If two languages learned at the same time cause conflicts of ethnic identity – if neither establishes clear dominance – tensions will often result between languages and between social roles. Bilingualism may then retard intellectual development. The bilingualism of the anglophone in St Lambert is not that of the son of Welsh peasants. There are two sorts of bilingualism; one of them puts marbles in your pocket, the other puts pebbles in your mouth. Positive bilingualism calls for the collaboration of parents, teachers, and children. These children do not choose to become bilingual; society forces them to do so. If society and parents collaborate in an undertaking perceived by the child to be socially advantageous, success will probably be achieved; but if the child sees no important social advantage in the undertaking, he or she will probably fail in it. The biological and mental obstacles to the acquisition of two languages can be overcome only with a heavy expenditure of social and psychological energy. The social cost may be extra homework and extra classes, parental bilingualism on a 'one parent –one language' basis, or bilingual schools. The psychological expenditure exists typically in the form of motivation and acceptance of the need to reduce the distance between oneself and the other person whose language one is learning to speak. [14]

Within a bilingual society, the minority group tends to learn the language of the dominant group, rather than vice versa. When studies claimed to show that this bilingualism was a likely source of intellectual retardation, this seemed to offer an explanation of the reluctance of the dominant group

14 Unless one is obliged to learn a second language, to do so implies tolerance or a rare degree of masochism. As Stengel (1939) observes, it is the equivalent of reverting to childhood.

to acquire a minority language. When it was established that bilingualism facilitates comprehension, and further that the advantage was more apparent in a member of the dominant group whose mother tongue was well protected, then the observed asymmetry became even more interesting. It led to the conclusion that the psychological advantages arising from bilingualism were not sufficient to compensate for the social cost (acquisition and memory) and the psychological cost (the 'prolapse,' the lowering process implied in bringing oneself down to the level of the subordinate ethnic group).[15]

We can now answer Queneau's question – what advantage is there in learning 'chat' if one knows 'cat'? It probably makes it easier – at least for the young child – to reject a certain type of primitive thinking which confuses the word with the thing. But this advantage is often accompanied by disadvantages (interference and stereotyping of expression) and is not a sufficient explanation of why a monolingual becomes a bilingual. The explanation of this transition from one state to the other cannot be either biological or psychological – it can be only social and political. We do not say 'chat' and 'cat' purely for the pleasure – or for the 'advantage' – of having two names for the same thing. The flight from synonymy prevents this being so.

The norm is to have only one or the other of these two signifiers. Cases of purely artificial and personal languages are rare, as are cases of gratuitously synonymic languages; Psalmanazar's language will serve, in short, as 'the exception that proves the rule.' This little sideline of history describes the entirely atypical case of an individual who not only had the gift of inventing foreign tongues that nobody else spoke, but could also convince his contemporaries that his creations were real living languages of which he was the interpreter (Steyn 1972). This was Psalmanazar, who in the seventeenth century deceived not only a credulous bishop, but even some erudite members of the court of the king of England. Psalmanazar – the name given him in the history books, for his real name was unknown – was of French origin, born in 1697. He travelled in Germany, passing himself off as Irish; then he joined the Dutch army – saying he was of Japanese origin. In his spare time, he invented a language and wrote the grammar for it. An army chaplain who became aware of his talents suggested he call himself a Franciscan friar; thanks to the chaplain, Psalmanazar was invited by the bishop

---

15 The social and psychological advantages of bilingualism are summed up well by Hancock (1977) and Fishman (1978b). Christophersen (1952) places more emphasis on the disadvantages. See also Adler (1977) and Jensen (1962). On the importance of taking into account the status of the languages in contact – dominant or subordinate – see, among others, Haugen and Bloomfield (1976), Fishman (1972a, b), and Cherry (1980).

of London to translate the Anglican catechism into 'Formosan.' At Oxford, he taught this language which he had invented, and in 1704 he published a history and a geography of Formosa – which of course he had never seen. The reviews of this work marked the beginning of his downfall.

Jessner (1931) describes the contemporary case of a schizophrenic who also had invented a language bearing no relation to any other known tongue; and Stuchlik (1957) reported the case of a megalomaniac paranoiac who in addition to speaking several languages had invented several others. According to Steyn, this type of artificial language appears in particularly well-gifted abnormals and forms part of a mythical system of relationships with imaginary beings. These cases belong to the realm of charlatanry and mental pathology. The normal man can speak several languages, but this runs counter to his natural tendencies.

2

Bilingualism and identity

During an inquiry into the Shona language in what was then Rhodesia, John Hofman (1975) received this revealing answer: 'To be human one must have a tribe; to be a tribe one must have a language.' This is not a universal truth; however, it will serve to state for us the problem of the bilingual's identity – especially that of the individual who lives in a geographic area in which languages overlap. Before addressing this problem, I shall clarify the terms I use, so great is the confusion surrounding the words 'bilingual' and 'unilingual.' To avoid a top-heavy classification, I shall speak only of the problem of bilingualism. Indeed, in this chapter, as in the rest of the book, I shall adopt the abridgment commonly used in sociolinguistic studies: I shall often say only 'bilingual,' when it would be more accurate to say 'bilingual and multilingual.'

Different types of bilingualism

Languages of words, sentences, paragraphs, and speech

What is a bilingual? Someone who calls himself bilingual? Someone whom we call bilingual? And if we are the ones to decide, what criteria shall we use? A scholastic type of criterion might enable us to allot marks for knowledge, and to lay down quite arbitrarily that a bilingual, to be so considered, must obtain (for example) a minimum of 40 out of 100, or 10 out of 20. Should this criterion measure understanding, elocution, or writing? Should it measure ability in translation, or perhaps in improvisation? According to the degree of difficulty of the test, we shall establish whether bilingualism is a universal or a very exceptional phenomenon.

One author may tell us that such and such a housewife of such and such an African tribe is multilingual because she can do her shopping in several dialects; she buys her vegetables in Kikuyu, her poultry in Galla, her fabrics in Swahili, and her household furniture in English. Another author may tell us that this same housewife knows only one language adequately – only in Galla can she tell her children a story, or explain to her neighbours some complicated family affair. This hypothetical housewife would probably call herself multilingual, though her contacts with other languages may be very specialized, without any broad human or social spread. From the linguistic point of view these contacts would probably appear devoid of paragraphs, often even of sentences – in short, exchanges limited to words, used very much as small change is used.[1] The more unforeseeable the linguistic exchange, and the longer and more complex it is, the rarer will we find bilingualism.

Multilingualism is the norm in pre-industrial, oral civilizations; unilingualism is the norm in industrial, urban, literate civilizations. In primitive societies multilingualism sometimes extends over the whole social group; in literate civilizations it becomes a matter for specialists. In the first case, the content of the exchange is generally poor from the semantic point of view, while in the second it is particularly rich. Passage from the bilingualism of words to that of sentences, and then to that of paragraphs, involves increases in the costs – in acquisition, memory, and upkeep – of supplementary languages to the point where it becomes necessary to specialize the task of contacts with foreign tongues.

These differences between primitive and literate societies are to be found in the very heart of contemporary cities. Let us examine the linguistic exchanges in a so-called bilingual association such as the Canadian Political Science Association, or in an office such as Canada's Ministry of Finance. Let us distinguish exchanges of words, of sentences, of paragraphs, and of conversations.

Word-exchanges such as 'Bonjour,' 'How are you?' 'Ça va bien,' 'And your wife?' correspond to the few words needed by the Galla woman when she buys her vegetables. They go scarcely beyond a gesture and a smile; they create an atmosphere that is all the more pleasing to the literate person in that it recalls the atmosphere of the tribal market and the kindergarten; they satisfy the myth of the return to the source, the return to an idyllic primitive life. Typically, such exchanges take place in informal situations. The typical

---

1 Knowledge of a second language is often tied to the frequency of its use. In any study of the effects of this second language on the identity of the speaker, account should therefore be taken of the frequency of use, as well as of the degree of knowledge of the language (Houis 1976).

sentence-exchange takes place in formal contexts of known or foreseeable content: 'Ladies and gentlemen' (or 'Chers collègues') 'I declare this meeting open.' But when it comes to the use of more complex language – paragraph- and conversation-language – bilingualism becomes something to be avoided, and people try to use one language only and to rid themselves of the effort and the embarrassment of translation.

Simultaneous translation is merely an approximation; thus, in modern civilizations – typified by impatience – the dynamics of conversation call for a lingua franca, chosen by the group in control of the situation. In the two examples we selected as an illustration, the controlling group is the anglophone. Word-language accepts bilingualism, conversation-language rejects it. This leads to situations that seem paradoxical. One such situation led Quebec political scientists of the 1970s to request that the Canadian Political Science Association, of which they were members, declare itself to be avowedly unilingual – in English. Their anglophone colleagues, especially those who did not understand conversational French, held that the association should continue to call itself bilingual. The French word-exchanges practised in this association were, for most anglophones, a 'good-will,' 'friendly-gesture,' 'smiling' French; these anglophones could not understand that anyone should wish to deprive them of the pleasure of extending the hand of friendship. To the francophone, this 'politeness' French – even when the good intentions of the speaker were appreciated – remained a 'small-change,' kindergarten French. For the francophone, word-language – a language still in its infancy – conjured up a picture not of the noble savage and the golden age of long ago, but of tutelage, of colonial status, of domination that called itself egalitarian and wished to be considered affectionate, but remained oppressive none the less.

Inclusive and exclusive languages

To speak is to communicate; but in the absence of one universal language, to speak one language rather than another is simultaneously to include (those who understand the message) and exclude (those who do not). Nevertheless, provided the context is precisely stated, it is possible to distinguish languages that tend more to the inclusive from others that tend more to the exclusive. The use of Latin by the Roman Catholic church sprang from an orientation toward international universalism – though the effect at the national level eventually became one of exclusion. The sacred language, Latin, brought the clerical élite of different cultures closer to one another; but within the very same culture it separated the clerical élite from parishioners. Like the cassock, Latin was a means for the less learned country priest to distinguish himself from the common herd; it gave him a means of making himself truly inaccessible. To pass from one language to the other – from the sacred tongue to the common tongue and back again – was to celebrate semantically the movement downward, then upward, expressed by a belief in an incarnation followed by the ascension into Heaven. When the Catholic church chose this world rather than the next – incarnation rather than transcendence, the masses rather than the élite – Latin fell out of favour as did the cassock, and the everyday language was joined by the pull-over even at divine service. Now that the father had been demoted to brother, he had to dress himself and speak the same language as everyone else.

Use of language to define a privileged audience is a common practice among many secret and not-so-secret societies – those of the scholars and the doctors as well as those of schoolchildren – which use a technical argot or a peculiar vernacular. The argot shuts out the ignorant and the unini-tiated.[2] Some of the élite at government level behave in the same way when they reserve for themselves access of languages, such as Latin in eighteen-century Europe, or English and French in twentieth-century Africa (Calvet 1974).

Languages as instruments, 'flags,' and recognition symbols

The excluding role of a language is particularly obvious in 'flag' or 'recogni-tion' languages, since they serve less as instruments of communication than means of recognition and assembly. The objective of the movement to resurrect Occitan, which was started during the 1960s by totally assimilated Languedocians, was not to replace French by a regional language but to add an exclusive language – Occitan – to an inclusive language – French. If the intellectual of Aix-en-Provence went to the considerable trouble of acquiring the regional language of his ancestors (well short of forming a language of conversation), it was not in order to communicate with his grandparents in Occitan but rather to exclude the Parisian, the tourist, and the foreigner. He used French as the language of national equality and Occitan as the language of regional privilege in order to exclude competitors

---

2 The use of exclusive codes within a given language can usually be found in the form of argots or ways of expression that differentiate, for example, profession, social class, or age group (Labov, 1968; Drake, 1980); some natural languages, under the heavy pres-sure of a dominant language, may also survive only as secret languages, as in the case of certain Romany tongues.

seeking access to local appointments – as businessmen, teachers, councilmen, or mayors, for example.[3]

The same reasoning holds within any language that has several accents. A Frenchmen from Paris or Orléans generally speaks a French with one single accent; by contrast, the educated Haitian has both French and Creole at his disposal, and many Québécois can pass easily from regional accents to the French of the Radio-Canada announcer. However, unlike the Haitian or the French Canadian, the Franco-Occitan intellectual, who has reacquired his regional language in the same way one learns a foreign tongue, will be more frequently aware that he is using it as an exclusive language than if he had learned it as his mother-tongue. In as least one case – that of Ireland – an exclusive language might have become a 'recognition' language in the true sense of the word. In its report dated 13 July 1963, the Committee for the Restoration of the Irish Language recommended that Irishmen who could speak Gaelic should be able to recognize each other by a distinguishing badge to be worn on their clothing.[4] As far as I know, this suggestion remained a dead letter; but the fact that it was put forward showed that Gaelic had become merely a badge for the great majority of the Irish.

The object of languages is more frequently to make communication and co-operation more easy than it is to exclude. Most languages, even if they are not lingua francas are open languages – languages of universal appeal, open to anyone who wishes to learn them. In consequence, language sets itself apart from the other criteria of ethnicity; language is more often 'catholic' than is religion, race, or national origin. Through the instrumentality of ethnicity and the correlation between language and religion, or again between language and national origin, some languages have at some time in their historical evolution been more or less closed than others. French and English are no longer as tied to specific religions as they used to be and the ties between English and national origin are becoming more and more indistinct. However, Arabic has an intimate bond to Islam. The openness or exclusiveness of a language will vary according to the attitude taken toward ethnicity. The Israeli has no missionary vocation either in his

---

3 On the movement for Provençal and Occitan renewal, see, among others: Lafont (1967), Tabouret-Keller (1972), Beer (1977), Berger (1977), Schlieberr-Lange (1977), and Morin and Pouget (1978). For a more general view, see Eastman (1975; 1979) and W. Ross (1979).

4 Article 33.1 recommends that the Irish use their language as a means of ordinary communication 'and, towards this end, to promote the wearing of an appropriate badge by all Irish speakers in the locality and to provide a meeting-place and social centre for them' (Commission 1963, 99).

religion or in his language; the Frenchman, in contrast, even when he does not believe his language to be superior to others, often feels himself responsible for spreading its flavour and its benefits throughout the world.

Subordinate, convergent, and divergent bilingualism

Since Ferguson and Weinreich, semanticists have distinguished three types of bilingualism according to the relationship between the signifier and the signified: subordinate, compound, and co-ordinate bilingualism.[5] But the distinction between compound and co-ordinate has become so blurred by the variety of usages made of the two terms (Skunabb-Kangas 1981) that I prefer the trilogy subordinate, convergent, and divergent. In subordinate bilingualism, the signifier of the second language, for example 'cat,' refers to the signified – the animal which through the instrumentality of the signifier of the dominant language (in this example French) is called by the name 'chat.' In this case, the specific impact of the term in the second language will be rather feeble; it will be that of a reference in a dictionary. Convergent bilingualism describes a state of similitude between meaning and context; the words 'chat' and 'cat' are then truly interchangeable, for besides referring to the same animal, they conjure up the same associations of ideas; Ferguson held that this would be the case in children who were learning two languages simultaneously, in the same family, scholastic, and social context. The third type of bilingualism – that I call divergent – describes a situation of dissociation, either of meaning or of context, or of meaning and context simultaneously. Then – whatever the dictionary may say – a 'chat' is not completely a 'cat.' Symbolically, we have subordinate, convergent, and divergent bilingualism, as represented in Figure 2.

Although synonymic bilingualism is common enough for words taken out of context – 'wine' for example – it is quite exceptional when a language is taken as a whole.[6] It is very rare that two languages are learned in the

5 For a historical account and a critique of the use of these distinctions see Diebold (1965), Macnamara (1967a), and Shaffer (1976). For an example of an experiment to measure the effects of satiation (the effect of repetition of the same concept in one language on its classification in the other language), see Jacobovits and Lambert (1961), who noted more profound effects among convergent bilinguals than among divergent. Other authors, Olton for example, do not report any difference (Lambert 1969, 103).

6 For a typology of the bonds between signifier and signified, see Marcos (1976a). Saegert and Young (1975) think that abstract concepts are coded in the form of words, while concrete concepts are coded in the form of images. This would explain why semantic variations are more pronounced, in a bilingual, on abstract concepts than on concrete concepts (D.G. Mackay 1980). To put it another way, convergent bilingualism, which is synonymic in type, will be more probable when the vocabulary is more concrete.

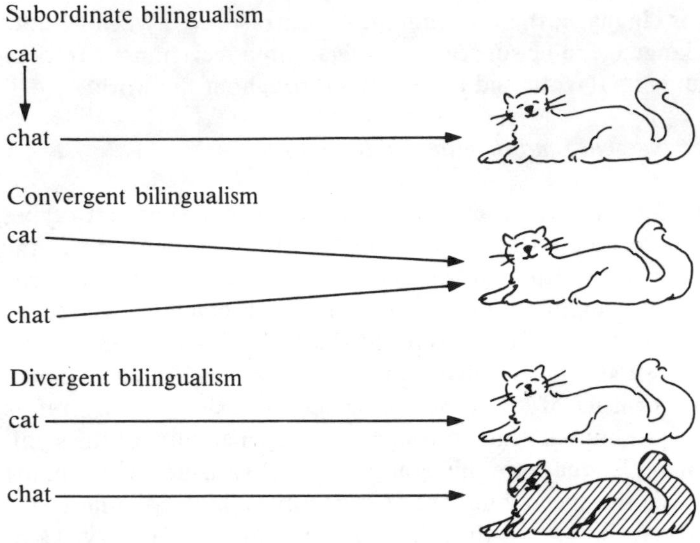

Subordinate bilingualism

cat

chat ——————————————————————→

Convergent bilingualism

cat ——————————————

chat ——————————————

Divergent bilingualism

cat ——————————————————————→

chat ——————————————————————→

FIGURE 2
Three types of bilingualism

same context; and even if they are, it is exceptional that the words and sentences and sounds of the two languages should evoke the same images, the same associations of thought. It is extremely rare for a bilingual – even if he is close to being perfectly bilingual – not to consider one of his two languages as his mother-tongue. Even among bilinguals brought up in a bilingual family it is rare that the tongues learned simultaneously from infancy are not associated with different roles. In such a family in Sri Lanka the child speaks English to his parents but Tamil to his brothers and sisters; in certain aristocratic families in St Petersburg, before the Revolution, the children spoke French among themselves, but used Russian when speaking to the servants. Louis St Laurent, one-time prime minister of Canada, who had an English-Canadian mother and a French-Canadian father made his political career as a 'French Canadian' but he usually said his prayers in English. Even among those who are bilingual at conversational level, synonymic convergent bilingualism is undoubtedly fairly rare.

Research into the degree of relative synonymy between languages – and more particularly the languages of the bilingual – reveals differences that are sometimes quite considerable. Mackey (1971) calculated that on the basis of the use of the words 'man' and 'homme' in the numerous commonplace expressions to which these words lend themselves (strong man, ladies' man, man of straw, etc) there was no more than about 40 per cent concordance between the two terms.[7] It is thus normal that with these words – as with many others, and in particular with abstract rather than concrete words ('constitution' rather than 'fork,' for example) – there should be a change in the groups of associations of ideas when one language is exchanged for the other, even when the translation is exact. Further, it is not only the semantic context of the language that varies, but also the context of the language itself where one of the languages evokes certain social roles rather than others, as, for example, where one language evokes the family while the other evokes the school. Indeed, the use of Osgood's measurements of semantic disparity shows quite clearly that the commonest terms do not have the same value (in the sense of good or evil), the same power, and the same degree of activity, according to whether the bilingual subject is tested in one language or the other – especially in the case of bilinguals of the divergent type. Tests carried out by Jacobovits and Lambert (1961) and by Stafford and van Keuren (1968) show that in the convergent bilingual the repetition of a word in one language produces an effect of satiety in the measurements of semantic disparity (the effect being measured by the tendency toward parity: neither hot nor cold; neither handsome nor ugly), while in the divergent bilingual this effect is not so pronounced. Repetition of the word 'bottle' does not have the same effect as the word 'bouteille' for the divergent as for the convergent bilingual. Thus, in the one more than the other, but appreciably in both of them, there is a change in semantic context on moving from one language to the other.

Does this shift affect behaviour and, beyond behaviour, personality and identity? Without any doubt, there are considerable variations, depending on the individual and on the culture. The subordinate bilingual is probably affected only on the behavioural level, while the divergent bilingual will be affected at the deeper level of his personality and his identity. Ervin-Tripp (1964) finds differences of reactions to thematic apperception tests (TAT) according to whether bilingual subjects answer in French or in English; the psychiatrist Marcos (1976) reports cases of bilinguals whose symptoms and diagnoses varied according to the language of analysis; and Rousey et al (1967) report that balanced bilinguals to whom he played back recordings of their own voices reacted in a more detached, more intellectual fashion when they heard themselves speaking in their second language than in their first,

---

7 There is concordance when the word 'home' appears in the French expression that corresponds to the English expression in which the word 'man' appears. The translation of 'homme à femmes' ('ladies' man') by 'lady-killer' is an example of non-concordance.

as if their second language were merely an outer tegument, while their first language were closer to their inmost heart. I have the impression that the associative images of the bilingual tend to become less definite on the common denominator of his two languages. This is perhaps why bilingual scholars write sometimes in one of their two languages and sometimes in the other, while novelists and poets almost never do so. Nabokov had a Russian phase, and then a German phase, and finally an English period; but the languages of his literary work followed one after the other, rather than mixing.

I have noticed – and several colleagues who occasionally translate their work also have – that it is harder to say the same thing in two languages when translating one's own work than when translating someone else's; and that in both cases translating accurately is a painful constraint. Each language has its own association of ideas, each pulls in a different direction – not so much by its signifieds as by their sets of signifiers.[8]

Languages of the heart and of the mind

Bilingualism by juxtaposition often dissociates a mother-tongue – the privileged language of the emotions – from the language of the school, an instrumental language which may very well develop privileged means of communication, but which rarely acquires the joyous or disturbing vibrations that permeate the language of childhood. It is not clear whether the languages of a bilingual are as lateralized as that of a unilingual. Some authors find greater involvement of the right hemisphere among bilinguals, others do not (Sussman 1982: Soares 1984; see discussion in Laponce 1985); but, irrespective of the neurophysiological situation, we may, speaking metaphorically, note that the second language has, typically, a more rational, more instrumental, a kind of 'left-brain' quality. Languages, which, in addition to being 'left-brain' languages, are also of the 'right' – the side of intuition, of context, of emotion, and of music – are generally found to be mother-tongues (Kelman 1972). Instrumental language is the language of writing; the mother-tongue is also the language of song. In some parliamentary assemblies, chanting sometimes takes over from speaking when emotions get the better of the mind. I know of no research into emotional chanting in parliaments, or of any comparisons between chanting in unilingual assemblies and chanting in bilingual ones. It would be of interest to know what happens in these latter assemblies when speech gives

---

8 Verescagin (1969) distinguishes receptive, reproductive, and creative bilingualism. In the last case friction between the two languages is most pronounced. See, in the same work, a series of psychological, sociological, and linguistic typologies of bilingualism.

way to chant, at the moment when simultaneous translation falters to a halt.

Bilingualism: perfect and uneven, by superposition, and by juxtaposition

As I have already said, perfect bilingualism is an ideal that is sometimes approached but almost never attained – all the less so when a change is made from 'word' bilingualism to 'conversation' bilingualism, and even less so when temporal and sociological dimensions are introduced into the picture. Let us consider the simplest of states – that of an individual's bilingualism at some point in his life. Before we can say that his bilingualism is perfect, we must be sure that his two languages have the same power of communication over the whole gamut of social roles. When we say of Pierre Elliott Trudeau or Brian Mulroney that they are almost perfectly bilingual – which could not have been said of Louis St Laurent – we mean that as a father, a friend, a writer, a politician, in any given situation, they are able to use English or French with equal ease; in these two languages they have the same rapidity of mental recall, the same quality of expression, the same creative ability. I cannot say whether this is really the case; only a meticulous study – such as that carried out by Gumperz (1970) when he required his subjects to wear hidden microphones that recorded their every word throughout the day – only a study of that nature would enable us to judge; it is quite possible that Pierre Trudeau would come out of such a study with exceptionally high marks – higher than Joseph Conrad's, and perhaps equal to Vladimir Nabokov's; but it is equally possible that a meticulous study of his use of French and English would reveal appreciable differences of quality in his use of the two languages. Bureaucrats in Ottawa say that although he was very fastidious about the style of documents submitted to him in French, he took little interest in the stylistic quality of English documents. Another top bureaucrat in Ottawa, who is generally regarded as bilingual – and who is indeed so at the conversational level – has a professional translator go through the letters he writes in French. I myself, after twenty years of teaching in English, have my work checked in both of the two languages I use – but especially in French (at least where my text deals with political science), although French is my mother-tongue and was the language I used almost exclusively until I was twenty-five.

To measure the order of precedence in a bilingual's two languages, we must first list the principal social roles that characterize his or her life in society. At least six are of universal application: family, work, play, religious observance, acquisition of knowledge (schools, reading), and politics. Each role has subdivisions, and there is often overlapping. Within the family, the roles of father and husband may be quite different yet overlap. Within the university some scientists hold that work and play are inseparable. Sometimes the sphere of local or tribal politics is distinct from that of national or international politics, sometimes it is not.[9]

Whatever the sphere of activity, the perfect bilingual will obtain the same marks (though not necessarily high ones) in his two languages. As an illustration, let us suppose that the whole gamut of social life were reduced to two roles only, family and work. A perfect bilingual's marks would follow the pattern shown in Table 1. Variations on this perfect equality can present three cases of differentiated bilingualism – variations of precedence in the two languages, according to social role. Let us begin with an extreme case – 'bilingualism by juxtaposition' (sometimes described as 'diglossia'). This is a bilingualism of segregation according to social role. Only one of the two languages is associated with a given role, as shown in Table 2.

Of course, Table 2 shows an extreme case; it is very rare for the roles to be so dissociated that there is no overlap. This theoretical case becomes more likely when one of the two juxtaposed languages is in the everyday sphere and the other in the religious sphere – as Arabic and Coptic in modern Egypt, Yiddish and Hebrew in nineteenth-century Germany, or Latin and the vernacular in Catholic communities.

Finally, let us examine two cases of bilingualism by superposition – one unidominant, the other alternating. In unidominant bilingualism, one of two languages used in any social situation always dominates the other. (See Table 3.) In alternating bilingualism, precedence does not always lie with the same language; the dominant language in one role becomes subordinate in another, as shown in Table 4.

The best way for a language to be assured of survival is for it always to be as close as possible to a situation of unilingualism – to dominate in all social roles, or at least in the most important ones – in short, to avoid conflicts of identity. The different social roles of a bilingual act in effect as more or less strategic positions – positions that languages 'use' for defence, retreat, or conquest. In an industrial and urban society, work will often act as a dominant strategic position from which a language will spread over the whole range of other roles; the family, in contrast, often marks the dominant strategic position of agricultural societies. In the four theoretical cases in Tables 1 to 4, the precedence of roles was not taken into account, and for simplicity's sake only marks of 0, 40 and 80 were given.

9 Among the many studies of bilingualism according to the social role, see two classic examples: Rubin (1968) and Fishman et al (1968).

TABLE 1
Example of perfect bilingualism
(marks out of 100)

	Family	Work
English	80	80
French	80	80

TABLE 2
Example of bilingualism by juxtaposition
(marks out of 100)

	Family	Work
English	0	80
French	80	0

TABLE 3
Example of unidominant bilingualism by superposition
(marks out of 100)

	Family	Work
English	40	40
French	80	80

TABLE 4
Example of alternating bilingualism by superposition
(marks out of 100)

	Family	Work
English	40	80
French	80	40

Let us re-examine some of these examples and introduce a factor of precedence between work and family. For example, let us re-examine Table 4 – with alternating bilingualism by superposition – and introduce modifications into it, as in Table 5. If work is more important than the family, as in case 5(b), English will be in a very favourable position; but if the family is more important than work, as in 5(c), French will be in the better position.

TABLE 5
Variations of precedence on the model of an alternating bilingualism by superposition
(marks out of 100)

	(a) Family = work		(b) Family < work		(c) Family > work		(d) Family < work		(e) Family > work	
English	40	80	40	80	40	80	40	10	40	10
French	80	40	80	40	80	40	80	5	80	5

The studies of Fishman et al (1971) in Puerto Rican circles in New York showed that the relative importance attached to the family and to work – and hence to the precedence of the two roles – was a major factor in the survival or decline of the immigrant's language. Finally, and quite obviously, the degree of knowledge of a language also affects the relationship of force between superposed languages. If we had case 5(d) instead of 5(b), work could well be always superior to the family, but its effect would nevertheless be very weak, if the language of the dominant role itself were very weak. Inside the factory, 'word' language is often sufficient to understand the foreman or answer him. In the office, it will normally be necessary to have the language of the sentence, or even the language of conversation. To put it another way, in the study of the assimilative pressure of one language on the other in a bilingual, it is necessary to take into account not only the precedence of roles but also the linguistic pressure of one role on another, which can be measured by the degree of knowledge and the frequency of use. The roles move forward, as it were, along a path that stretches from ignorance and mutism to the heights of knowledge and an ever-ready tongue. Some roles have little linguistic impact, even though they rank among the highest in terms of importance, for they are too poor in linguistic content and too infrequently practised – the religious role in some cases, sport or work in others. Taciturn peasant societies are better able to resist the assimilative pressure of other languages than are the garrulous societies of the cities, for among the former a language is often thought rather than spoken. The dominance of English as the working language of the factory employee is less dangerous to the survival of French in Montreal than is the dominance of English as the working language of the office-worker.

Languages operate as though they were species of animal, and people who speak them are like territories with restricted resources. The ideal for a language is to control the whole territory. Failing this ideal, a language will benefit from winning dominant strategic positions for itself, the value of which depends typically on the role (social quality), knowledge (linguistic quality), and frequency of use (quantity) of the language.

Figure 3 illustrates the hypothetical case of the 'occupation' of an individual by two different languages – English and French. The two-dimensional representation of the individual's roles, and the territorial metaphor, by which I sought to define a person in terms of the languages that 'occupy' him or her, (in the military and geographical sense of the word), lead us to transform Figure 3 into a three-dimensional representation of an inclined plane, as shown in Figure 4. Figure 4 is to be read from the top downward and runs from a dominant role or group at the top left down to secondary roles or groups at the bottom right: languages, like rivers, flow naturally from top to bottom and do not reverse their flow. To reduce, block, divert, or overturn this tendency would require a complicated system of principles and practices to act as dams and locks.

In fact, the 'occupation' of an individual by several languages is much more complex than the simple model shown in Figures 3 and 4, which presuppose bilingualism by juxtaposition. Now, in bilingualism by superposition (the general case), we would need to add a measurement of proximity between the dominant and the subordinate languages for each of the roles in

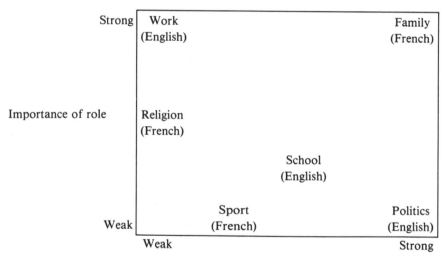

Degree of knowledge and frequency of use

FIGURE 3

Dominant language according to social role, the importance of this role, and the linguistic production associated with it – hypothetical case. The degree of knowledge and the frequency of use are not necessarily closely linked to one another. In this hypothetical case they are assumed to be so, in order to keep the graph simple.

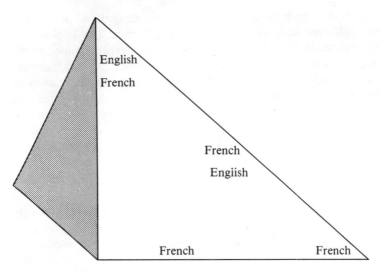

FIGURE 4
Spatial representation of the linguistic positions shown in Figure 3

Figures 3 and 4. The subordinate language would then appear either as a loser, with decreasing influence, or as an interior enemy, more or less able to reverse the existing precedence and pass from the role of subject to that of master. To illustrate these phenomena, let us return to Figure 3 and consider the three variations shown in Table 6.

In case 6(a), the subordinate language is too weak to endanger the dominant language. In case 6(b), a strategic position – work – can easily fall to the other language. In case 6(c), which approaches perfect bilingualism, the dominant language may easily become subordinate. What are we to understand from this? Is the dominant language, to which we gave 80 marks, going to fall suddenly to 60, or 40, or 20? No – such a loss of linguistic memory or ability would be pathological. A language that is no longer dominant will indeed atrophy – but not overnight. Every francophone who ceases to use French as an everyday language will notice after a certain time that he or she no longer knows how to use prepositions and is forgetting spelling; does one say 'demander à' or 'demander de,' and is it 'abilité' or 'habilité'? To some people, it is not important whether one says or writes the one or the other; the importance one attaches to the quality of language varies according to roles and social contexts.[10] Some who notice this loss of

10 Lamy (1976b) notes, for example, that intereferences did not seem to upset the subjects he interviewed in Montreal.

TABLE 6
Variations on the model of subordinate bilingualism
(marks out of 100)

	(a)		(b)		(c)	
	Family	Work	Family	Work	Family	Work
English	20	20	20	79	79	79
French	80	80	80	80	80	80

ability, even if it is minimal, will avoid using a language in which they no longer feel secure, in which they feel forgetful and thus disadvantaged not only in relation to others but also in relation to their former selves. Thus only a slight change of balance between the first language and the second – in Table 6 the step from the 79-mark level to 80 marks, or vice versa – may be the final little touch that sets off a long evolution leading first to the reduction of frequency of use and later to at least the partial forgetting of the formerly dominant language. To explain the importance of the distance between first and second languages, I will introduce two factors hitherto in the background: the order of precedence of languages in the social context . in which one lives, and the evolution over time of the ranking of these languages at both the individual and the family levels.

At the Quebec Liberal Party Congress in March 1980, a delegate of Hungarian origin described with some emotion and enthusiasm the advantage of trilingualism; his children, he said, spoke Hungarian, French, and English – and spoke all three of them equally well. The delegate's perception of equality was doubtless the result of pride and paternal blindness, for he went on to say: 'My children speak Hungarian at home, and French at school; and they'll need English in their jobs.' Now let us suppose that these three languages were in fact in a state of almost perfect equilibrium, of the type shown in Table 6(c). In order to compare the paths of the three languages, and to measure their chances of survival, we can construct a model similar to those used in computer-programming, with a series of choices (of residence, of spouse, of profession), and give each choice a value that assesses the likelihood of progress, weakening, or disappearance of the language with respect to the choices made.

In Quebec and North America – liberal societies with a wide population mix – the chances of Hungarian surviving more than one generation are slight. For it to survive, there would have to be a most unlikely combination of circumstances. How many Hungarians marry other Hungarians and work in Hungarian? (This set of circumstances is more likely for a Chinese than for a Hungarian in North America.) Thus, because of the lack of territorial and social density of the Hungarian language in Quebec and North America, the Hungarian spoken by the Hungarian immigrant into Quebec will probably disappear in less than a hundred years, and it will start declining as soon as the immigrant sets foot in Quebec.

As for this same Hungarian's French and English, they both have a good chance of holding their own, but the closer one gets to the position shown in Table 6(c), the more precarious becomes the position of French. Indeed, an excellent knowledge of English increases the immigrant's chance of meeting and marrying an anglophone partner and of making a career in the federal public service – and thus of going to Ottawa, where the chances of being assimilated into the anglophones by work and marriage are greater than in Quebec. However, a mediocre knowledge of English would make it more probable that his choice of university, residence, and career will ensure that French becomes his dominant language. In so far as English is, in North America, a lingua franca that the political, economic, and academic élite cannot do without, upward social mobility is associated with the acquisition and perfection of that language. Thus the higher one rises in the hierarchy of Quebec, the more one risks putting one's French into a precarious position, from which it may collapse into oblivion within one or two generations. It is hardly surprising, then, that so many Quebec separatists have such a good command of English. From the peak of bilingualism that they have attained, they can see more clearly than a unilingual of the same ethnic background the hazards and temptations that might well lead them or their descendants to go over to the English side. Hence the relation between the temptation to become assimilated into the socially dominant language and the desire to protect oneself by strong political structures.

Let us return to Table 6 and note that in the North American and Quebec milieu the two situations (a) and (b) are very different. In case 6(a), English is supported and driven upward by the continental context, while in case 6(b) this same context drives French downward. In 6(a), the subordinate language, however weak, awaits its turn to become the dominant language; in 6(b), French is probably on the downward path. To reverse the latter, one must be able to control the social context in Quebec and isolate it from the rest of North America; this is what every Quebec government has sought to do, more or less energetically, and with more or less success. In a bilingual society, the stronger the domination of the master language, the greater the danger of assimilation of the minority tongues by means of social upgrading. Thus the more closely Quebec becomes integrated into the North American economy, and into North American politics and culture, the more separatist it becomes; increasing the temptation also increases the reflexes of rejection. A comparative study of young Québécois from Quebec City, which is in a unilingual French zone, and from the city of Hull, which is in a bilingual zone (Georgeault 1981), showed that contacts with the English language were much more frequent in Hull than in Quebec (26 per cent of the Quebec subjects preferred an English program on TV, whereas in Hull the figure was 41 per cent); but more in Quebec (75 per cent) had favourable opinion of anglophones than in Hull (59 per cent).

The size of the minority group is not necessarily the cause of growing hostility on the part of the dominant group (Kalin and Berry 1982); but Georgeault's study shows that assimilation and rejection may go hand in hand. Indeed, verbal rejection may facilitate factual assimilation. Be that as it may, the two languages of a bilingual society have very different powers of recuperation. They will thus have different strategies. The dominant language – the one that flows downward from the peak toward the base – wishes the social plane (the inclined plane of Figure 4) to be free of barriers, floodgates, or embankments. The subordinate language's desires are quite the contrary – it wishes the flow of the dominant language to be dammed and diverted. The dominant language preaches liberty and equality; the subordinate language talks of borders, security, exclusivity, privileges. In the absence of natural embankments, artificial barriers will be erected by means of laws and institutions. The closer Quebec approaches the North American norm in its culture, the more it resorts to legislative constraint to protect itself against English – which keeps flowing downward from its heights, eroding the defensive barriers of French, infiltrating and threatening to level everything, in its own interests.

These metaphors and explanations might seem simplistic, if the evidence they express were not so frequently ignored. The constitutional debates of the early 1980s, in Quebec and in Canada as a whole, clearly showed the difficulty of comprehension that existed between those whose thinking was 'inclined plane' and those whose thinking was 'horizontal plane.' Both the federal and the Quebec Liberals seemed to see a 'flat-plane' linguistic Canada, rather like a politico-geographical map, while the Parti québécois thought more of mountains and avalanches – being at the base made it afraid of the heights.

In short, the theoretical 80:20 ratio of force between the dominant and the subordinate languages differs significantly in meaning, according to whether the lower mark measures the condition of a language of the heights, or a language in a pocket half-way down the slope, or a language in the hollow of the valley, with no protective embankment. A 'summit' language, infiltrating into a minority 'pocket,' can survive despite its permanent state of inferiority, thanks to the infiltrations coming from the heights above; this is the case with English in Quebec. But a 'mid-slope' language which becomes the subordinate language in a pocket where it was formerly dominant is a language on the way to disappearing; this is the case with Romansch in Switzerland and with many minority languages in Asia, Africa, and the Soviet Union.

Societies with bilingualism by juxtaposition and by superposition

To pursue these typological distinctions, let us note a certain similarity between the distribution of languages at the level of individual roles and that of languages at the territorial level. There is bilingualism by geographical superposition when two languages are intermingled throughout a territory; and there is individual bilingualism by superposition when two languages cover the whole gamut of roles in one single person. Conversely, in the case of bilingualism by juxtaposition, each role or each region has its own language. Territories lend themselves to linguistic segregation better than roles do. It is as though the inclined plane, which served as a model to explain the relationship of strength between the dominant and the subordinate languages, were at a steeper and sharper angle at the level of the individual than at the level of the group. A bilingual's languages pass relatively easily from one role to another, unless – which is rare – these roles do not have the same vocabulary. However, the languages of a bilingual state find it much harder to pass from one territory to another. A bilingual's languages tend to intermingle, to superpose themselves on one another (at least in the short term, for in the long term the dominant language often ousts the other); but individuals tend to group themselves territorially according to their language of preference, which is generally (though not always) their dominant language. Societies and states called bilingual are thus nearly always states in which a certain territorial linguistic segregation is observed at the levels of the street, the village, the town, or the region. Minority languages on the way to disappearing have scattered ghettoes, often of very insignificant geographical dimensions – a block of houses, a quarter, a village, one or two caravans. In contrast, languages of full civilization (languages that cover the gamut of the community's linguistic needs) often have concentrated geographical aggregations over vast territories – and this is so both for dominant languages such as Russian in the Soviet Union or Portuguese in Brazil, and for subordinate languages such as Ukrainian in the Soviet Union or Tigranya in Ethiopia. In a multilingual state, it is usually not difficult to recognize a particular territory associated with each language. Bilingual states are thus generally those in which bilingualism is geographically juxtaposed, rather than superposed. There are exceptions; for example Malaysia, where, since Singapore's separation from the rest of the peninsula, the territorial segregation of Chinese and Malay is no longer as striking as it was in former days. Chinese remains an urban language; but in none of the major towns of Malaysia does it have the importance that it has in Singapore. This lack of concentration of Chinese in Malyasia made it easier to establish Malay as the sole national language.

Bilingualism and biculturalism: 'step-ladder' and assimilative languages

In future chapters we shall have occasion to use typologies other than those we have just examined. We shall distinguish various types of language: vernacular from vehicular, written from non-written, codified (or standardized) from those that are neither (Kloss 1969; Héraud 1978), first from second and from translation (Roland Breton 1976), and universal from regional, national, or local languages (Roland Breton 1976; Mazrui 1976). We shall also distinguish various types of bilingualism: élite bilingualism vs. mass bilingualism (Paulston 1980), bilingualism in a stabilized ethnic hierarchy vs. bilingualism in a mobile hierarchy (Tajfel 1974; Taylor et al 1977), and bilingualism in a situation of territorial separation vs. bilingualism in a situation of professional segregation (Hechter 1978; Allardt 1979). Finally we shall distinguish linguistic minorities in a hostile environment from those in an assimilative environment (Laponce 1960; Schermerhorn 1970).

Here I would add only one other classification to those already considered – Fishman's, (1980), which correlates bilingualism and biculturalism. Biculturalism may exist without bilingualism, since there are other cultural cleavages besides the linguistic; but can there be bilingualism without biculturalism? If we examine the matter from too close a viewpoint, it would seem that the answer must be no, since learning a second language also involves recognizing a second culture and also usually coming to close quarters with that culture. According to Lamy's figures (1979), 85 per cent of unilingual Canadians feel closer to their linguistic ethnos (English or French) than to the other. For imperfect bilinguals, this proportion drops to 80 per cent; and for conversational bilinguals, or at least those close to it, the proportion is only 43 per cent.[11] Communication leads to better

---

11 But Lamy points out that factors other than knowledge of a second language must be used to interpret ethno-lingualism correctly – notably the factors of 'ethnic hierarchy' and 'geographical environment' (unicultural or bicultural). He notes that his three groups of French Canadians – unilinguals, passable bilinguals, and balanced bilinguals – were more ethnocentrist than the corresponding anglophone groups. For the importance of the geographical context in transfers of identity, see Merton (1968, 348), Diebold (1968), and Soffietti (1955).

mutual knowledge; and better mutual knowledge is not so much drawing closer to one another as seeing oneself as one is – less different from others than one had thought. But whatever the closeness of cultures that every bilingualism creates, a differentiation should be made between the bilingual who lives in a bicultural context and the bilingual who lives in a unilingual context. [12] English-French bilingualism of an engineer in Paris does not have the same social importance as that of his or her equivalent in Montreal. Even if he or she has an excellent command of English, the Parisian is in no danger of cultural destabilization. Ethnic bonds are not at risk – English is merely a professional instrument of the same order as Fortran, Pascal, or any other computer-language; it is a 'step-ladder' language that permits one to see further or ascend higher; personality is not affected by it. For the hypothetical Montrealer, however, a knowledge of English may well determine marriage, friendships, and career; knowledge of the second language may profoundly affect perception of others and self, unless there are conscious efforts to assert ethnicity in order to display a refusal to be assimilated. Let us therefore distinguish, as does Fishman, bilingualism that involves culture and ethnicity from instrumental bilingualism, which does not involve them or does so very slightly. This allows us to separate the bilingualism of the dominant group from that of the subordinate group – the former is often less likely to affect the speaker's identity than is the latter.

Language and identity

We find it hard to distinguish one fish from another of the same species, or one bird from another with the same plumage; but when it comes to human beings, our power of discrimination is quite remarkable. We are sensitive to very small differences, mere details. When we look at a playground in which the children are as numerous as birds in a tree, we do not get the impression of an undifferentiated mob; they do not resemble each other. Despite this quite remarkable power of differentiation, when we come to define our social identity we use only relatively few criteria, which differ according to the context; the family has its own criteria, the school has others, and the · profession has yet others. Let us consider the problem of social identity at the level of major political groupings such as the state and the nation. What

---

12 The importance of the context, whether geographical or social, is in the equation used by Loman (1972) for the analysis of any expression, oral or written: $M = f(S + L + I + C + E + R)$, where M = the message, S = the sense, L = the language, I = the intention, C = the context, E = the emitter, and R = the receiver.

are the factors at the heart of these groupings that we use habitually to distinguish our group affiliations? What are the major stable criteria that enable us to define ourselves in social terms? There are hardly even ten in more or less universal use: biological or social origin (family, clan, tribe, ethnos, nation), place of residence (town, region, state), profession, race, sex, age, religion, language, and political ideology (at least in industrial societies).

According to individuals and according to cultures, these different criteria play a variable role. To facilitate analysis of these variations, let us distinguish the generalized self from the specific identity.[13] The generalized self – the essential being, or the soul, for example – cannot be reduced to any of the basic elements of personality. The essential being is more than the group of factors that express and embody it, whence the idea of a generalized self that expresses itself, in part, through specific identities.

Language of self and of identity

I assume that between the generalized self and the specific identity there exists a central-peripheral type of relation. If the centre is strong, the peripheries are weak; and when the centre is weak, some of the peripheries become strong. According to this model, a strong generalized self is normally accompanied by weak specific identities. The strong inner self is but little influenced by its particular embodiments. A change of profession, religion, citizenship – even a change of sex – will not be considered as fundamentally affecting the self. However, if the generalized self is weak, there will be a tendency to shelter this weakness in well-defined specific identities which act as protective cages hindering diffusion, depression, and disintegration of a vulnerable personality. It is well known that the minority is more conscious of being the minority – and thus different – than the dominant group is conscious of being dominant. The minority is afraid that its identity may be challenged, for the dominant group sets the norm. The left-handed individual is more concious of being left-handed than the right-handed individual is of being right-handed; the poor are more conscious of being poor than the rich are of being rich, at least in societies in which it is

13 On the notion of identity, in particular that of ego identity, see among others Arieti (1967) and Erikson (1974). Among the studies of ethnic identity, see Berghe (1981) and Tajfel (1974). On linguistic identity in particular, see J.A. Ross (1979), Pool (1974; 1979), Deutsch (1953), and Fishman (1966). See also the reports of psychoanalysts that show that some mentally ill bilinguals have different personalities in each of their languages (Edgerton 1971; Marcos 1976a, b).

normal and desirable to be rich, for the reverse would hold good in societies in which it is normal and desirable to be poor.

When language is the cleavage, or at least one of the cleavages, that separates the subordinate group from the dominant, the minority will be particularly conscious of the importance of its language when it defines the specific aspects of its minority status and sets the limits of its field of action. The minority that is conscious of its minority status and accepts this status will thus often have a fairly weak generalized self, but a linguistic identity that can only be the stronger thereby.

The importance attached to the specific identity is a frequent source of misunderstanding between dominant group and linguistic minority. The former does not understand that the latter attaches so much importance to its language – often, of course, because it thinks that this minority language is worth less, but also (and irrespective of the opinion it holds of languages other than its own) because it identifies only very feebly with its own language. If one's language is dominant, one does not think about it any more than one thinks about one's health, provided that this is good. Now the minority, provided it is conscious of its minority status, is from this very fact in poor linguistic health; and this poor health contributes to the malign condition of its specific identity, this peripheral identity that it attaches to its different way of speaking.

The force of the linguistic factor as a definer of specific identity is linked to the relations that exist between language and the other criteria of this peripheral identity – for example, religion and profession. Study of a minority language thus implies that we are aware of the relations not only between generalized self and specific identities, but also between different peripheral identities.

Are there any privileged and foreseeable relationships between language and the other criteria of identity listed in Table 7? Clearly, there are. In contemporary societies, language is often associated with the tribe or the state, sometimes with age, and almost never with sex. The order of frequency of the bonds between language and the other criteria of identity varies, of course, with the societies involved; but on the whole it is probably close to that shown in Table 7.

I do not know of any example of association of sex and language in modern societies, though such association sometimes appears in primitive societies in which the women belong to tribes with different languages, and in which the men sometimes learn, in addition to the common language, a secret language that sets them apart from the women – as among the Arawaks of the Antilles (Roland Breton 1976, 33). In modern immigrational societies such as Canada and the United States, association between age and language is more frequent; in North America, Yiddish and Ukrain-

TABLE 7
Assumed frequency of bonds between language
and other criteria of identity

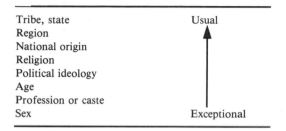

Tribe, state	Usual
Region	
National origin	
Religion	
Political ideology	
Age	
Profession or caste	
Sex	Exceptional

ian are increasingly, parental languages, if not grandparental. Growing languages are associated with particular age-groups, as are languages in decline. Hebrew was at one time the language of the aged; but in later days it became the language of the young.

Profession sometimes has a lasting association with language as a result of ethnic minorities spreading through the social tissue along specific professional channels. In Canada in the 1900s, Chinese filtered into the dominant group not only along the railways but also via small businesses such as groceries and drycleaners. The language of Indian businessmen in Kenya and Tanzania is identified with wholesale; and the term *Hutterite German* spells *farmer*.

The bond between language and political ideology is much more common than the correlation between language and profession, or even between language and age, at least for the most territorial of the great contemporary ideologies, namely nationalism, which is often used as a definer of specific identity.

Correlation between race and language is common, for there are many societies in which individuals are conscious of both their race and their language. This association is particularly strong in former colonial areas in which the colonizer stood out and continues to stand out more by language and race than by language and religion.

The association between language and religion, which is normal among primitive peoples, still remains common in modern societies, even though language is not always a good indicator of religion (see chapter 4). To know that an individual's language is German does not tell us whether he is Catholic or Protestant; but it is probable that the German who uses language as a definer of his specific identity also uses religion as an additional definer.

Finally, our progression from the exceptional to the usual leads us to consider the privileged bond between language on the one hand and national origin, state, and tribe on the other hand. This nationalistic bond is written into history, as it is into geography; for even when they are widely spread, languages have origins that are easy to pinpoint in physical space. The relationships French-France, English-England, Spanish-Spain are so obvious that one often forgets their importance. The privileged bond between language and territory (past or present) gives us one of the stable reference points by which we locate our identity in the universal order. It is thus not suprising that language should be on a par with nation as a definer of ethnicity.

Language not only allows us to assert our sociability, it also links us to a territory. It give us two of the three elements that make up a state. It normally gives us a nation and a territory, past or present; and when it does not give us the third element of the state as a fait accompli, it often leads us naturally to the search for this missing link, which is self-government.

Let us return to the theory of the bond between the generalized self and the specific linguistic identity, illustrated diagrammatically in Table 8. Cases lie along one or other of the diagonals according to the particular bonds between the language and the other criteria of specific identity. If the language is linked to race, for example, and the race is a minority one, the force of the specific identity will be strengthened thereby. But if the minority language is linked to a dominant race, it will be the generalized self that is strengthened, in so far as the feeling of being in the minority is weakened and the generalized self becomes more able to pass from one linguistic group to another without change of personality. The language of the dominant group will be, for the minority, a 'language of the heart' rather than instrumental, synonymic (convergent) rather than co-ordinated, or in other words probably a second language learned in infancy and used thereafter. The association of a weak generalized self with a weak specific identity describes the case of a disintegrating minority, which has lost its wish to survive but remains in a minority position as long as the dominant group has not finished assimilating it, or refuses to do so. Such a minority becomes lost in a universe, with no reference points to which it can associate either its self or its specific identity. The language of such a minority will become an outcast; others will think nothing but evil of it, and the minority itself will share their opinion.

The categories of Table 8 suggest those of Table 9, which are ambiguous, to be sure, for they use individual categories to define group attitudes and politics of a linguistic minority. In terms of political personalities, active separatism was illustrated by René Lévesque, and accommodating bilin-

TABLE 8
Theoretical bonds between the generalized self and the specific linguistic identity

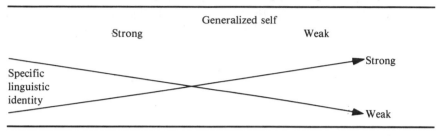

	Generalized self	
	Strong	Weak
Specific linguistic identity		Strong
		Weak

TABLE 9
Typology of minority attitudes, by deduction from Table 8

		Generalized self	
		Strong	Weak
Linguistic identity	Strong	Active separatism	Narcissistic separatism, alternately passive and aggressive
	Weak	Accommodating bilingualism	Assimilation into the dominant group

gualism by Pierre Trudeau. Separatism of the narcissistic type, with its alternations of passive contemplation and sudden aggressiveness, displays an attitude characteristic of many minority groups, and in particular of an ambivalent Quebec proud but lacking in self-assurance (Laponce 1982).

Second language as a threat to self-identity

Let us re-examine the distinction between language as instrument of communication and language as instrument of social affiliation. Why does one learn a language other than one's mother-tongue? Is the prime purpose communication or affiliation? Lambert, Gardner, Olton, and Tunstall (1968) showed, from an analysis of attitude and behaviour in francophone students at McGill University, that it is appropriate to distinguish subjects whose learning of English is purely instrumental from those who learn it for the purpose of integration into a socially and economically superior group. This distinction led the authors to distinguish additive bilingualism from subtractive bilingualism – the latter depriving the subject of a part of his or her identity.

Let us systematize these observations by comparing the intentions under-lying the acquisition of a second language and the subject's perception of the effect of this acquisition. Both intention and effect can be either instru-mental or integrative. When the intention is intrumental, and the effect purely instrumental, then the linguistic identity of the subject is not brought into question. The fact that former chancellor Helmut Schmidt speaks very good English has, I assume, no effect on his German identity. In the German context, the acquisition of English could not have any integrative effect by subtraction. However, the Flemish politician of thirty or forty years ago who spoke French willingly and well risked in some cases losing part of his Flemish identity not only in the eyes of his electors but also per-haps in his own eyes. In this second case, an intention that at the start might have been purely instrumental may have had disintegrative effects. Then one can notice also a certain resistance to the acquisition of the second lan-guage in some subjects who are afraid of losing their basic linguistic iden-tity. One needs this language as an instrument of communication, so one learns it; but one fears that acquiring it may set one apart, distinguish one from the ethnic group that gives one a social identity. This leads to certain compromise situations such as learning the language but speaking it less well than one might – for example, with an accent that gives the required psychological distance (Giles 1977, a, b). One may also counterbalance one's acquisition of the foreign language by reinforcing one's specific linguistic identity.

To sum up, let us imagine a meeting between two bilinguals of the same sex, males for example, each capable of expressing himself in the other's language; and let us imagine that each has a preferred language that differs from the other's. Which will be the language of communication, and what will be the effect on each of the speakers, first of using his first language, and then of using his second? We can measure these effects in terms of cost of communication and of cost of identity. To give an illustration, let us imagine two meetings between French and English bilinguals – one in France between a Frenchman and an American, the other in Quebec between an anglophone Canadian and a Québécois. Let us consider first a conversation of the 'passive bilingualism' type, in which each speaker uses his preferred language. First, the cost of communication can be measured instrumentally, in terms of speed and accuracy of communication. This cost will be shared if each speaker has an equal knowledge of the other's lan-guage; if there is not equality of language, the cost will be borne by the one who is less fluent in the other's language. Whether it be equally or unequally shared, the cost of communication will in any event be higher than if the communication had been between speakers of the same language. Every linguistic communication is a construction built from materials – words, images, ideas that are being exchanged. In every conversation or communication there is mimesis. Now this mimesis, this batting the ball to and fro, is more difficult – if not impossible – when the two sides are not playing with the same symbols or instruments. 'Passive bilingual' communications do not have the precision, the 'bounce,' or the life of unilingual conversations. They always tend to be more or less awkward; they are dissociative and tangential, as though the communication were not quite bridging the gap – somewhat like those nightmares in which imaginary sheets of glass stop one from ever completing a handshake. However, in passive bilingualism the cost of communication need not be shared equally, even if knowledge of the languages being used is equal. The cost of passive bilingualism is linked to the effects of the second language, whether these are additive or subtractive. If the second language is a step-ladder language, by which one becomes 'bigger' than the unilinguals of one's own ethnos, then not to use it keeps one at one's normal level. An example of purely instrumental passive bilingualism is a conversation in Paris between a Frenchman and an American. In Montreal, in such a conversation between an anglophone and a Québécois, the mere fact of each participant's having confined himself to his own language – to his own position of ethnic identity – will be considered a linguistic victory by whichever participant would have the most to lose by using the other's language.

Now let us imagine the commonest case in oral communication – conversation in one language only. Let us suppose that the exchange is in English. For a Frenchman in Paris, English is probably a step-ladder language; thus any effect that the use of English has on his identity will be positive. In Montreal, the conversation is likely to belittle the francophone's identity if English is being used. Conversely, if the conversation takes place in French, relation will be reversed. If the American uses French in Paris, he feels himself more American, since he has moved up his linguistic step-ladder; in Montreal, the anglophone is likely to feel himself handicapped. Depending on the form of communication (written or oral), the location, and the social rank of the speakers, the relationships of strength and of social status, and thus the linguistic effects, will vary considerably. The geographical context must also be taken into account. In so far as a language has geographical limits defined by mental maps, the speaker will have a fairly clear idea of 'home' and 'away' – and hence of the difference between a visit and an invasion. At home, good manners demand that one try to speak the visitor's language, while honour requires one to reject the language of an invader. The more geographically concentrated a language, the more other languages will be treated as 'visitors,' and the less will foreign languages used 'at home' risk being resented as a diminution of identity (Laponce 1980). Conversely, the more languages are mixed at the territorial level, the more will bilingualism imply diminution of identity, at least among people who reject assimilation. Paradoxically, English would have a better chance of being well received in an independent Quebec than in the province of Quebec; English would then be considered more a step-ladder than an invader, and less as identity-diminishing than as facilitating communication.

To sum up and draw conclusions from the examples we have adduced, let us formulate two hypotheses:

1 The weaker the generalized self (and, conversely, the stronger the specific self rooted in language), the greater the need for territorial boundaries that protect linguistic security.

2 The less linguistic cleavages are linked to other social cleavages, the more the linguistic minority will feel the need for territorial borders to assure the protection of its specific identity.

3

Language, territory, and hierarchy

Let us imagine that an ethnic group, all the members of which spoke and wrote the same language, was suddenly split apart by physical frontiers and impermeable political systems. Would there be any differentiation between the languages of these autarkies? Which would diverge more quickly – speech or writing? How long would it be before the communities formed by these new frontiers ceased to understand each other?

Before the invention of the phonograph record and magnetic tape, mankind had only very approximate methods of fixing the sounds of languages into some sort of collective memory, accessible to all. If we do at last know how the Romans pronounced Latin, the reproduction of their way of speaking was difficult (Allen 1978).

A children's game shows how quickly sounds are changed. Players form a circle, in which a starting-point is arbitrarily chosen. The starting player rapidly recites some phrase or other, first into the ear of the right-hand neighbour, then into that of the neighbour on the left. In turn, each of the 'sound receivers' transmits the phrase to the next child and so on, till the sounds meet opposite their starting-point. Then the two versions of the original phrase are compared; the difference between them gives rise to much amusement.

Of course, this game has no experimental value, since the participants' main interest is that there be as much divergence as possible in both the sound and the meaning of the words. But the game remains a game only because it is difficult to reproduce exactly the sounds one hears. This difficulty, physiological in nature, explains how languages of a common origin become mutually incomprehensible as a result of reciprocal isolation and how, conversely, languages in frequent contact tend to coalesce into a single tongue.

The Moroccan who smiles when hearing Arabic from Yemen or from Comoro and the Pole who is amused by the unexpected turn of phrase of the Slovak or the Czech are both laughing at differences attributable to phenomena of communication neatly illustrated by the children's sound game. If there are 700 different languages in Papua–New Guinea, this is so almost certainly because the ethnic groups of the island have been isolated from one another for a long time. If Haitian Creole, which the hasty tourist might consider only a form of bad French, is an original language, it is because it seeks the median path between several languages. Language is a privileged measure of communication.

Genealogical trees that systematize the evolution and differentiation of languages recall those that trace the evolution of animal species. For example, on the 'family tree' of Latin, we see some languages fragmenting, some adapting, some wearing out and disappearing or surviving in descendants that are no longer mutually understandable. The frontier that separates the spoken language in Figure 5 is sometimes a product of class – e.g. that separating Demotic and Katharevousa in Greece, or even (though to a lesser degree) Bokmal and Nynorsk in Norway; but typically the tree of historical evolution is easily translated geographically. The diversity of languages shows itself in physical geography and can be explained by the phenomena of communication. Americans and English Canadians who telephone each other often from one end of the continent to the other, and who listen to the same radio and TV programs, speak the same language, and increasingly with the same accent. The few Indian hunters and fishermen on the north coast of this same continent – at least those among them who have not yet abandoned their language for that of the dominant group – often cannot understand each other at a few kilometres' distance from the villages where they live, and the castes of a North Indian village studied by Gumperz (1958), separated socially and segregated territorially develop distinct dialects of the same language.

The inventory of languages: high- and low-density zones

How many languages are written or spoken in the world? If we follow the path of the sun and count every spoken and written word everywhere beneath its steadily moving zenith, we shall note thousands of different languages and even more dialects.[1] This linguistic round-up would reveal strik-

1 Muller (1964) estimates the number of languages spoken today throughout the world at 2,500. Ferguson (1964) puts the total between 5,000 and 7,000; Burney (1966) places it between 2,500 and 3,500; Barrett (1982) sets it at 7,010; and Roland Breton (1976) thinks that while there are at least 12,000 ethno-linguistic groups, there are only about

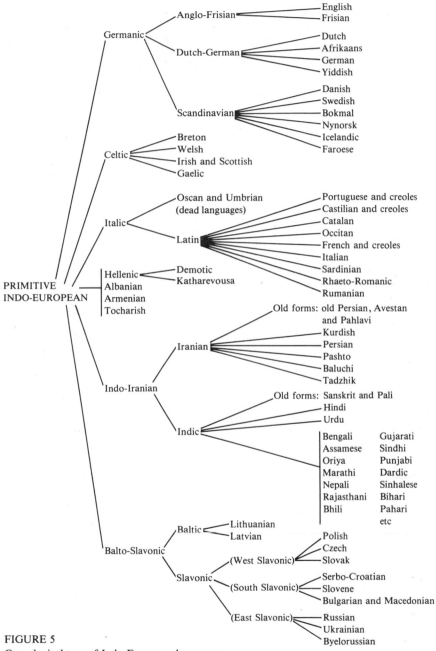

FIGURE 5
Genealogical tree of Indo-European languages

ing contrasts. There are vast stretches where for hundreds and hundreds of kilometres, and for millions upon millions of words, the language remains the same – except for a few odd little islands here and there. Between New York and Los Angeles, our linguistic census would doubtless include at least one example of all the major languages of civilization (French, German, Arabic, Chinese, Japanese, Russian, Hindi, etc.) and of hundreds of other little tongues such as Icelandic. However, were we to ignore these isolated cases and retain only those languages with a density of usage of 25 per cent – even 10 per cent – all we might find across the 5,000-kilometre stretch of the continent would be a continuous series of English-speaking areas, with a few Spanish enclaves at points of entry and exit. In contrast, a voyage of a few dozen kilometres in certain Pacific islands would give us a large number of different languages.

In this connection it is revealing to compare North America and New Guinea. At different moments in their history, both were lands of refuge: New Guinea for groups from Malaysia, Melanesia, and Polynesia; North America for groups coming mainly from Europe. On the welcoming American continent, the dozens of principal languages at entry have been reduced to three – English, French, and Spanish; while in New Guinea, the languages at entry have split up and multiplied.

To illustrate the principle that weak intensity of communication leads to great variety of languages, let us take the case of the island of Yapen (off New Guinea), for which J.C. Anceaux (1961) drew the linguistic map for the 1950s. On this island, some 150 kilometres long, live 20,000 people divided into 14 different linguistic groups. The Yavas, probably descendants of the original inhabitants, occupy the centre of the island. They speak a Papuan language quite different from the other languages which were introduced into the island at indeterminate dates. Some of the 13 other languages are mutually understandable but sufficiently different (according to Anceaux) to be classed as distinct languages rather than as dialectal variations. In certain villages with close economic relations, Anceaux noted the presence of two languages in the same village (a dominant language and a clearly minority language), but normally each language occupied territories exclusively its own, as shown in Figure 6.

There is one notable exception to this territorial monolingualism – the region of Serui, the principal point of contact with the exterior. In this

3,000 distinct languages. Kloss, quoted by Weinstein (1983, 101), estimates that 2,000 languages have at least a rudimentary form of written literature. The enumeration of languages runs into difficulties similar to those encountered by biologists when they classify animal or vegetable species. On the subject of these difficulties, see Gumperz (1967), Naroll (1971), and Berry (1979).

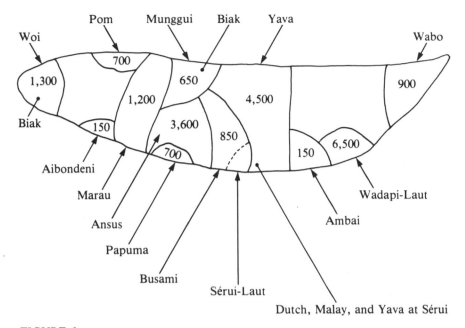

FIGURE 6
Linguistic map of Yapen, from data collected by Anceaux in 1958 – languages, approximate frontiers, and numbers of speakers (from Anceaux 1961)
Aibondeni, Busami, and Yava are Papuasian languages. The other languages are Austranesian or Malo-Polynesian. To illustrate the differences among these latter, here is how 'head' is said in some of them: durere (Wabo), dukami (Ansus), munkamia (Ambai), munkavinic (Sérui-Laut), rinkami (Woi), dunkami (Papuma), numukamei (Wadapi-Laut), riunkami (Marau), rehina (Pom), dukampori (Munggui), and rwu (Biak).

region many indigenous languages are found, but at that time the local economy, politics, and to a lesser degree religion were dominated by two foreign languages: Dutch and Malay. A linguistic bond had been established over the island as a whole through three common languages based outside the island: a regional language, Biak, that had put down somewhat tenuous local roots and served as a lingua franca in the northern part of the island, and two foreign languages – Dutch and Malay – that came from further away and served as means of communication, especially in the south.

At the time of Anceaux's study, there were thus some 15 languages on the island of Yapen, all limited to village use; a local lingua franca, Biak; a regional language, Malay; and an international language, Dutch (since replaced by English). Yapen gives us an approximation of what Europe was like during the Middle Ages – different languages of insignificant stature used in specific territories, linked together by a few common languages, the languages of business, religion, and government.

Two contradictory movements can be seen in Yapen and could doubtless also have been observed in eleventh-century France. Local languages are diverging; Anceaux notes that certain languages he described as dialects are in some isolated villages in process of becoming true languages quite distinct from the mother-tongue, while certain exterior languages, of the colonial type, have a centrifugal effect. Will one single language replace local languages in Yapen, as French has replaced Langue d'Oc dialects? This seems probable. Political and economic factors will decide the issue – the same that have decided that Dutch, though prominent two generations ago, should not take root in the region. The establishment of a mine or a factory attracting labour from all over the island or a religious or political authority imposing its own language in the schools or churches would be enough to bring about the rapid destruction of little linguistic 'pockets' that could survive only in isolation.

Let us forecast the state of affairs in Yapen in one or two hundred years' time, using as an example the west coast of Canada, a region particularly rich in aboriginal Indian cultures. The Canadian census of 1980 identifies 194 Indian communities in British Columbia; among these, 21 of the larger communities have between 500 and 2,000 inhabitants each.[2] In those communities nearest to large urban centres, the indigenous language has practically disappeared; only a few fragments remain – a few songs, a few words – museum-pieces, as it were. When the community is isolated, the language holds its ground better but is often in process of disappearing none the less. One of the rare systematic surveys on the use of Indian languages shows that among the Tahltans in the northern part of the province, even though they are far from any large town, of the 790 persons deemed by the official census to be Tahltan-speakers, only 50 were able to use that language easily.[3] In some communities – the Shunshags, for example – the situation is

2 Of the 53 Indian languages spoken in Canada, only 3 – Cree, Ojibway, and Inuktitut – are spoken by more than 5,000 people; 8 have fewer than 10 speakers (Foster 1982). Of the 30 Indian languages spoken on the territory of what is now British Columbia, Haig-Brown estimates that only 3 are systematically still transmitted to young children (Haig-Brown 1983). In Vanuatu, the penetration of English and French not being on the same scale as in Canada, 100 indigenous languages remain very much alive. Lindstrom (1983) estimates that since the eighteenth century only about 5 per cent of Vanuatu's native languages have died.

3 According to personal observations by Professor Shaw of the Linguistics Department of the University of British Columbia

worse; in others, as for example the Chilcotins, it is better. But even in this latter case, where the Indian tongue is more robust, the linguistic situation is precarious.

Efforts made in the late 1970s to maintain the language by teaching Chilcotin in the reservation school did not reduce the establishment of English. Instruction in the Indian tongue was aimed more at strengthening the cultural identity of the child by means of a 'flag' language than at giving him a linguistic system of universal communication. Paradoxically, strengthening of the Indian ethnos during the 1970s and 1980s, in so far as this ethnos transcends tribal structures and asserts itself over a multilingual whole, takes place through the medium of English, the only common tongue in which the Indians can achieve unison in their opposition to the English-Canadian community.

This collapse of the Indian language has taken several decades. Boaz was fortunate enough to find an informant who spoke English as well as he spoke Qwagul; those who followed him had difficulty in finding informants who spoke Qwagul as well as they spoke English.[4] The social, religious, economic, and political weight of English – a language that a hundred years ago was a foreign and a minority tongue, but has become indigenous and dominant – is such that the lesser languages with which it is in contact can resist it only by isolating themselves or by refusing to join the twentieth century. A lesser language in proximity with a greater can often be maintained only at the price of economic development; and economic development can often be achieved only at the price of the language.

The powerful machinery of assimilation that is crushing Indian languages into oblivion is also eliminating non-English languages from abroad. This phenomenon is well illustrated by the results of a survey carried out by York University's Survey Research Centre (O'Bryan, no date) in the early 1970s. In large urban centres, among those whose mother-tongue was other than French or English, 70 per cent considered themselves able to speak their mother-tongue fluently. But only 11 per cent of second-generation respondents spoke their ancestral tongue; and after the third generation the language of origin was annihilated, since only 1 per cent were able to speak it. Within the same ethnic groups, daily use of the language of origin (whether spoken well or poorly, fluently or in fragments) dropped from 74 per cent to 18 per cent, and then to 3 per cent in three generations. There are of course marked differences among these groups; Chinese and Ukrainians resist assimilation better than Dutch and Germans; but for all minority languages the drop between the first and the third generation is considerable.

4 Reid (1981), whose study of the Qwaguls goes back to the 1970s, reports difficulties of this nature.

TABLE 10
Use of a minority language in major Canadian cities by non-Anglophones and non-Francophones, according to social context

---

A Respondents who say they use exclusively the minority language (percentage):

with intimate friends	20
with a priest, clergyman, or rabbi	16
with a grocer	14
with school or work mates	10

B Respondents who say they use exclusively either French or English (percentage):

with a priest, clergyman, or rabbi	50
with a doctor or a grocer	53
with intimate friends	66
with school or work mates	78

SOURCE: Secondary analysis of data collected around 1970 by O'Brian (n.d.)

The mechanism of assimilation is clearly illustrated by statistics obtained from the same surveys. The minority language (Table 10) is more easily sustained in private life than in the public sphere. It maintains itself by endogamy (which works to the advantage of Indian languages and Chinese, in comparison with European languages in which ethnic groups are more willing to intermingle) and dwindles at contact with the surrounding social scene, especially at school and at work.

Breton in France and Welsh in Great Britain are further examples of the rapid and truly catastrophic decline of a language when a society changes from agricultural to urban and its system of communication shifts from local to regional and national. Until the Second World War, Breton was holding its own despite the strong Francizing pressure of school and government and Breton acquiescence in learning French. The local language survived through the family and the church, thanks to the relative isolation of the region. After the war, the clergy stopped preaching in Breton, and French became spoken more and more in the home. The autonomist Breton movements of the years 1960–80 were ineffective and tardy countermeasures against the increasingly close integration of Brittany with the rest of France as a result of urbanization, industrialization, mass tourism, easy communication, and large-scale interminglings of population. A survey of the Trégor region by Wolfgang Dressler and Ruth Wodak-Leodolter (1977b) indicates that 93 per cent of those over 70 could understand Breton, but for those under 20 the proportion was only 40 per cent (Figure 7). In 1985 only 300 children were enrolled in Breton-language private schools and only 200 in public bilingual programs (Cans 1985). The recording of conver-

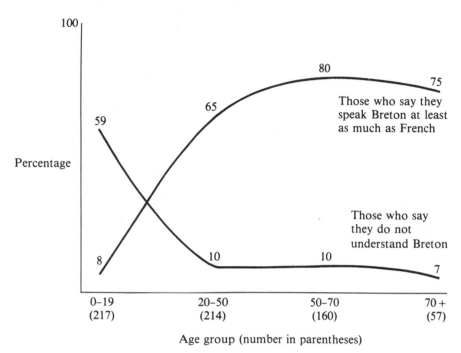

FIGURE 7
Incidence of Breton in Trégor by age group (from Dressler and Wodak-Leodolter 1977b)

sations between clients and sales personnel in another linguistic periphery, in the Alsace, in the city of Strasbourg, provides similar statistics: among those under 45, French was used in 87 per cent of the cases, compared to 47 per cent for the older clients (Gardner-Chloros 1985).

In Wales, Welsh declined at a rate similar to that of Breton in Brittany.[5] In 1851, more than 80 per cent of the inhabitants claimed that they could speak Welsh; by 1971, the proportion had fallen to 21 per cent. As in France, the dominant language, starting from a powerful cultural, economic, and cultural centre, spreads out victoriously across its periphery. It

5 Though the downward curves of Welsh and Breton look similar, they start from different peaks. Welsh, with half a million people who claim they understand it, has maintained partial tuition at university. Samplings in the late 1970s and early 1980s indicated a small increase in the percentage of Welsh speakers (Williamson 1982). But these samples may measure sentimental rather than practical positions, for public discussions on the use of Welsh have been more frequent and more spirited during the past decade than before.

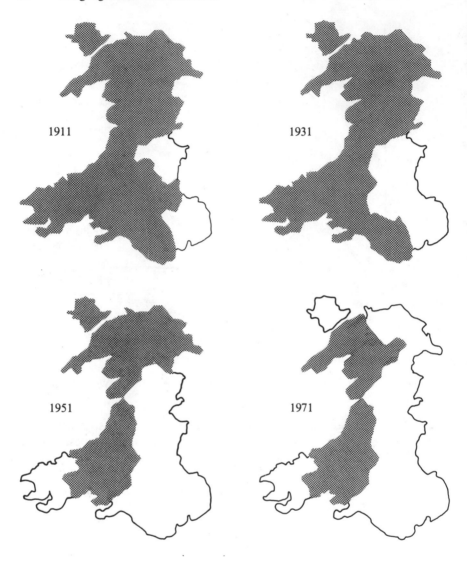

FIGURE 8

Evolution of Welsh in Wales

Dark areas: counties in which more than 30 per cent of the population claimed to speak Welsh, according to census data and statistics quoted by Betts (1976). See also E.G. Lewis (1981) and the *Sunday Times* of 7 September 1980. A map based on territorial units smaller than the county would show that at points of contact Welsh is seriously penetrated and fragmented by English (Ambrose and Williams 1981).

gains a foothold first in urban centres, then wins over the countryside, and before long all that is left is a few islands where the language, diminished by the constraints of a restricted area and role, survives as a folk-lore language – often thanks to the help of the ethnic group that has contributed to its destruction and that is now enjoying the pleasure of generosity after that of victory.

The geographical retreat of Welsh during the past century clearly shows the effect of pressure from the east – the pressure of England on Wales. It clearly shows also the effect of the cultural diffusion of the big cities; the assimilative pressure runs from north to south in the case of Liverpool, and from south to north in the case of Cardiff (Figure 8). Figure 8 illustrates also the role of the terrain; the lowlands of Radnor were the first to be over-run by English.[6]

When a subordinate language is no longer regarded by the dominant group as a danger, an obstacle, or even simply as an embarrassment and receives 'first-aid' measures from the government, the subordinate group itself may take over the task of the dominant group and destroy its own language by refusing to be shut away in a linguistic ghetto. Norman Denison (1977) has called this phenomenon 'linguistic suicide.' When a community decides that the cost of retaining its language it not satisfactorily counter-balanced by social and psychological gains, the language disappears – as the Celtic of Yorkshire has done to all intents and purposes, being no longer used except for tallying sheep (Denison 1977).

The life of languages: resources and hierarchies

According to the author of *The Doomsday Book of Animals* (Day 1981), vertebrate species are disappearing at the rate of about one a year. We have no such yardstick for the disappearance of languages. Muller (1964) has identified some 250 dead languages. Within a radius of a few hundred kilometres from my study, even as I write these lines, a dozen or so Indian languages are breaking down, their vocabulary and structure in total disarray; only a few dozen elders can speak them fluently, and there is at least one case known of a language spoken by one single person.

To produce statistics comparable to those of Day's *Doomsday* animals, it would be necessary to treat dialects as distinct species. Despite the meticu-

6 Among the works that deal with Wales, see particularly: Sharp (1973), Pill (1974), Hechter (1975), Betts (1976), Birch (1977), G. Williams (1978), C.H. Williams (1979; 1981b), Rawkins (1980), and Agnew (1981a, b). In Ireland, as in Wales, the assimilative march of English has taken place from east to west. See R.D. Edwards's *An Atlas of Irish History* (1973).

lous work of Kloss and McConnell (1974–81) and of other contemporary sociolinguists, we have no complete catalogue of languages and dialects. How many dialects die each year? How many languages? We do not know. It seems likely that at least one language dies. How many are born in the same period? Cailleux's estimate in 1953, based on the major linguistic groups (for example, Chinese or German), with dialectal variations excluded, was that from pre-history to the present day for each language that disappeared two new ones were born. He gave each language an average life of 2,000 to 2,500 years; but these controverted statistical approximations, even if they measure the diversification of languages and speech modes over the centuries, describe an era in which languages were transmitted almost exclusively by word of mouth (as in the children's sound game), and their era precedes what is commonly called, after Valéry, 'le monde fini.' In this completed world in which the written word and easy, speedy means of communication are becoming more and more important, the tendency may have been reversed and today probably more languages are dying than are being born.

The comparison between languages and animals should not, however, be carried too far.[7] What determines whether an animal species will survive or perish is its adaptation to the environment. An equilibrium is generally established between animals of different species that results in rival species supporting each other. If every fly larva came to maturity, and if every fly died of old age, the earth would be covered in flies within a few months. In the sphere of languages, however, there is nothing qua language to prevent one single language becoming the exclusive language throughout the planet. If in certain contexts – in Switzerland, for example – languages appear to be in a state of equilibrium that recalls the equilibrium between animal species, it is for quite other reasons.

If certain languages succeed and others disappear, the reasons have almost nothing to do with the relations that the language, qua symbolic system, maintains with the physical or cultural milieu that it must express. It is perhaps easier to reduce analphabetism with the aid of the Latin alphabet than with Japanese ideograms; and it is certainly much easier to type in English than in Chinese. The technical environment – the equivalent of the physical environment for an animal – can thus give the advantage to one language as opposed to another and bring pressure to bear on a poorly functioning system to adapt to new conditions. But such factors, inherent in the language, do not explain the evolution of a language in contact with other

7 See Seliger (1977) for an application of an ethological typology to the coexistence or conflict of languages. Berghe (1981) notes that relationships between ethnic groups are rarely symbiotic; they are normally hierarchic or parasitic.

languages, nor does the semantic quality of a language at a given moment in its history, for this merely reflects factors that are not strictly linguistic.

Twentieth-century Arabic lends itself poorly to the teaching of science – so poorly, indeed, that science is taught either in French or in English in Arab universities. However, if Arabic is not suited to modern scientific thought, the explanation is religious, not linguistic. It would be possible to modernize Arabic as Hebrew was modified after the creation of the state of Israel, and as Demotic Greek was modified in the 1970s to make it suitable for technical communication within the European Community.[8] Any language – at varying cost – can be developed and enriched to render it capable of expressing in translation any concept originally formulated in any other language (Hagège 1985). In the sphere of language, the function creates the organ, provided that the community that speaks the language is willing to adapt it and has the necessary resources. The explanation of the evolution of languages, of their successes and their failures, is sociological, not linguistic. Let us examine five factors in the process: number, cultural strength, economic strength, wealth, and military strength.[9]

Number of speakers

To establish the number of people who speak a given language can usually be done only approximately, either because languages have ill-defined linguistic boundaries or because the census is badly carried out; it is difficult as well to discover the language of fluency or of preference among multilingual individuals (Ohannessian et al 1975). Is Afrikaans to be considered a variant of Dutch or a separate language? Are Farsi and Dari two variants of Persian or distinct languages? Are we justified in classing certain regional forms of American and English as special aspects of one and the same language, when certain English TV programs must be subtitled when shown on some American TV screens? Should Chinese be considered one single tongue

8 Thousands of Greek technical terms had to be created or standardized at Brussels, the headquarters of the EC, during the years that preceded admission of Greece. During the past generation there has been a remarkable increase in the technical and scientific vocabulary. In October 1983, the terminology-bank in Ottawa contained 1,744,421 terms – 892,344 in French and 852,087 in English.

9 Mackey (1973) suggests a formula with six factors for measuring the strength of a language: demographic (number of speakers); geographical dispersion (establishment in different regions of the world); mobility (tourism); economic; ideological (religions of universal appeal, political ideologies of the same type); and cultural (publishing of books, etc). Of these six factors, I have not dealt here with dispersion, mobility, or ideology. We shall return to dispersion, from the viewpoint of the number of states of the same language, and to political ideology in chapter 4.

since it is written in one single fashion? Or should we say there are as many Chinese languages as there are Chinese dialects unintelligible to other Chinese? Should one – as we will do – count only one Arabic language, when even among themselves Arabs can sometimes understand each other best when they speak English or French? Should we consider Hindi or Urdu, or Serbian and Croatian, as distinct languages because they are written in different scripts, or as single languages because – apart from regional accents – they are spoken in almost identical fashion? And how should we classify bilinguals and multilinguals? Pierre Elliott Trudeau, Brian Mulroney, or Julien Green – should they be counted twice, once in French and once in English? How many citizens of India have been grouped statistically in accordance with their ancestral language, although they have adopted English as their first language? And should we classify as French-speaking those who know French well enough to speak it almost fluently (there are probably more than 70 million in this category), or only those who use it as their first language (about 60 million)? Too often, there are no statistical data to make the distinctions we wish to make. Few censuses separate one's mother-tongue – as does the Canadian census – from both the official language and the language of common usage.

In the absence of definitions and precise statistics, the numbers I propose to attribute to the principal languages of the world can be only approximate. To determine the relative numbers of speakers of these languages, I shall use two different lists – those of Culbert (1977) and Muller (1964). They can both be challenged for their shortcomings – the one for being somewhat out of date, the other for underestimating languages such as French or Hausa; but these two lists have, from our research point of view, the advantage of having been established at different points in time and of using two different criteria of classification: dominant language for Muller, language understood for Culbert (see Table 2; its notes report two other classifications: that of Breton 1981 and that of Barrett 1982). Both Culbert and Muller consider the principal Chinese tongues as distinct languages but treat Arabic as one single language. For ease of comparison I have shown the various Chinese tongues as one single tongue on Table 11. Similarly, Hindi-Urdu, Serbo-Croatian, Farsi-Dari, Czech-Slovak, and Nynorsk-Bokmal are each shown here as one single language, even though I separate them later, when detailed analysis calls for distinction between them.

These joinings and sunderings, to which I am often driven by the statistics available to me, are arguable. For this reason, whenever the data permit, I shall show the component members of the various compound languages. In Table 11, in which Muller's list shows languages with more than 4 million speakers, I have included Culbert's figures, which despite a differ-

TABLE 11
Languages with more than 4 million speakers

	Muller (1964)*			Culbert (1977)†		
	No.	%	Rank	No.	%	Rank
Chinese‡	645	20.1	1	821	19.3	1
English	265	8.2	2	369	8.6	2
Hindi/Urdu§	185	5.7	3	278	7.8	3
Spanish	145	4.4	4	225	5.2	5
Russian	135	4.1	5	246	5.7	4
German	100	3.1	6	120	2.8	9
Japanese	95	2.9	7	113	2.6	10
Arabic#	90	2.7	8	134	3.1	6
Bengali	85	2.6	9	131	3.0	8
Portuguese	85	2.6	10	133	3.1	7
French	65	2.0	11	95	2.2	12
Italian	55	1.7	12	61	1.4	13
Javanese	45	1.3	13	45	1.0	19
Telugu	42	1.3	14	55	1.2	15
Ukrainian	38	1.2	15	42	0.9	20
Korean	37	1.1	16	55	1.2	15
Punjabi	37	1.1	17	58	1.3	14
Tamil	37	1.1	18	55	1.2	15
Marathi	35	1.1	19	53	1.2	18
Polish	33	1.0	20	36	0.8	21
Vietnamese	31	0.9	21	38	0.8	23
Turkish	27	0.8	22	41	0.9	22
Thai	24	0.7	23	32	0.7	24
Gujarati	22	0.6	24	31	0.7	25
Romanian	20	0.6	25	22	0.5	28
Burmese	18	0.5	26	24	0.5	27
Dutch	17	0.5	27	20	0.4	29
Kannada	17	0.5	28	29	0.6	26
Malay-Indonesian	17	0.5	29	101	2.3	11
Malayalam	15	–‖		27	0.6	
Oriya	15	–		24	0.5	
Persian (Farsi/Dari)**	15	–		26	0.6	
Rajasthani	15	–		22	0.5	
Serbo-Croatian††	15	–		19	–	
Pashto	14	–		16	–	
Sundanese	14	–		15	–	
Hungarian	12	–		13	–	
Swahili	11	–		23	0.5	
Visayan‡‡	11	–		19	–	
Czech/Slovak	14	–		16	–	
Greek	10	–		10	–	
Hausa	9	–		19	–	

TABLE 11 (continued)

	Muller (1964)*			Culbert (1977)†		
	No.	%	Rank	No.	%	Rank
Swedish	9	–		10	–	
Nepali	8	–		10	–	
Sinhalese	8	–		11	–	
Amharic	7	–		9	–	
Azerbaijani	7	–		8	–	
Bulgarian	7	–		9	–	
Belorussian	7	–		9	–	
Madurese	7	–		8	–	
Tibetan	7	–		6	–	
Uzbek	7	–		10	–	
Assamese	6	–		13	–	
Berber§§	6	–		9	–	
Fula	6	–		8	–	
Galla	6	–		7	–	
Quechua	6	–		7	–	
Tagalog	6	–		22	0.5	
Khmer	5	–		7	–	
Catalan	5	–		6	–	
Danish	5	–		5	–	
Finnish	5	–		5	–	
Ibo	5	–		11	–	
Kazakh	5	–		6	–	
Kurdish	5	–		7	–	
Malagasy	5	–		8	–	
Rwanda	5	–		7	–	
Tatar	5	–		7	–	
Yoruba	5	–		13	–	

*World's population estimated at 3.225 billion
†World's population estimated at 4.246 billion
‡The main subdivisions of Chinese are as follows: according to Muller, Mandarin 75 per cent, Cantonese 7, Fukienese 7, Wu 8, and Hakka 3; according to Culbert, Mandarin 81 per cent, Cantonese 6, Wu 5, Min 5, and Hakka 2.5.
§Culbert gives 72 per cent to Hindi and 28 per cent to Urdu. If one adds Punjabi to Hindi, as does Roland Breton (1976), Hindi comes ahead of English. Breton gives the following hierarchy (in millions): Chinese 800, Hindi/Urdu/Punjabi 350, English 320, Spanish 210, Russian 150, Arabic 130, Bengali 130, Portuguese 120, Japanese 110, German 105, French 80, Javanese 65, Italian 60, Telugu 55, Korean 53, Marathi 50, Tamil 47, Vietnamese 40, Turkish 40, Ukrainian 39, Polish 38, Gujarati 35, Thai 35. Barrett (1982) gives a slightly different ranking: Chinese 886, English 265, Spanish 227, Hindi/Urdu 206, Arabic 144, Russian 142, Bengali 138, Portuguese 135, Japanese 117, German 90, Punjabi 80, French 67, Javanese 65, Italian 63, Marathi 62, Tamil 58, Korean 58, Telugu 55, Ukrainian 44, Turkish 43, Vietnamese 42, Polish 39, Kannada 37, Gujarati 34, Rajasthani 28, Bihari 27,

ent basis of calculation provide fairly similar results (except in the case of Malay-Indonesian, where Muller's total is doubtless underestimated and Culbert's figure is probably overestimated).

The 69 languages listed in Table 11 represent less than 3 per cent of the 2,500 languages – give or take two or three hundred – which, according to Muller, are currently being spoken in the world; they represent only 44 per cent of the 155 languages listed by Culbert as having a minimum of one million speakers, and only 34 per cent of the 201 languages so listed by Muller. If Barrett (1982) is right in estimating that the number of languages currently spoken is about 7,000, rather than 2,000 +, then the percentages shown above must be reduced almost three times.

If the pyramid of languages in Table 11 is divided into five portions, each containing the same mass of humanity, it will be seen that roughly speaking the first slice belongs to one single language – Chinese. The second consists of ony three or four languages, the third has some nine or ten, and the fourth perhaps a couple of dozen. The fifth slice contains the rest of the language – i.e., some 90 per cent of the whole. From a numerical point of view, the majority of the languages are in extremely poor condition. Given that it requires roughly a million speakers to warrant a university, only some 140 languages qualify. Far less than this number actually have universities at present; but the 140 languages that do qualify represent less than 5 per cent of the total number of languages being spoken. It is among those with large numbers that we find the élite of the armed forces, the economy, and culture; but when we compare these different hierarchies we shall find that

---

Oriya 27, Malayalam 27, Thai 27, Burmese 25, Sundanese 21, Dutch 20, Pashto 19, Romanian 19, Assamese 18, Persian 17, Serbo-Croatian 17, Hausa 14, and Quechua 14, for a total world population of 4.374 billion. In Muller's as in Barrett's, Culbert's, and Breton's lists, eleven languages – Chinese, English, Hindi-Urdu, Spanish, Russian, German, Japanese, Arabic, Bengali, Portuguese, and French – appear among the top 12. Additionally, Muller includes Italian, while Culbert lists Malay, Breton lists Javanese, Barrett lists Punjabi. The overall structure measured by the distribution of percentages is basically the same in the four lists.

#The major dialectical divisions of Arabic are between east and west, and between nomadic and sedentary populations.

‖The sign − indicates that the figure is less than 0.5 per cent. The following languages, not included in the table, have at least 5 million speakers in Culbert's compilation: Malinke (6), Oromo (7), Provençal (5), Somali (5), Twi-fante (5), Uighur (5), Zhuang (9), and Zulu (5).

**Farsi 80 per cent, Dari 20 per cent

††Serbians account for about 65 per cent, and Croats about 35 per cent.

‡‡Culbert distinguishes Cebuano, at 65 per cent, Panay-Hiligaynon, 28 per cent, and Sammar-Leyte 7 per cent.

§§Berber is considered by Muller to be not a separate language but a group of dialects.

mere numbers, unaccompanied by political sovereignty, are not an essential element in the power of a language. There are almost as many languages with more than a million speakers as there are independent states, but – as we shall see in a later chapter – the match between these two statistics is far from perfect.

Table 11 merely shows the order of precedence by numbers among the most widely spoken languages. The smaller languages predominate, since about 60 per cent of them have less than 10 million speakers, and about 75 per cent have less than 20 million. As in the animal and material world, there are few major species in the realm of languages, and many minor ones; but there is one difference, already mentioned but worth repeating: the major animal species *need* minor ones, and so do material objects; but languages rarely need one another. In bilingualism by juxtaposition (diglossia), an individual or a culture may use two different languages to carry out functions that it is desirable to keep distinct. A major language of civilization can be used to tie people into a universal communication system (e.g. Latin or English); while a minor language such as Yiddish will keep outsiders at a distance. But a dominant language in close contact with a minor language tends to exclude, eliminate, and achieve total victory over the minor. A normal state between languages is that of war.

In Culbert's review, as in Muller's, one single language – Chinese – dominates all the rest. This remains true even if we consider each Chinese dialect separately. Mandarin, with more than half a billion speakers, covers more than 15 per cent of the world's population. This tongue could well reach the billion mark fairly soon, not only by natural demographic expansion, but also by assimilation of other Chinese dialects that already use similar ideographs. Four other languages – English, Hindi/Urdu, Spanish, and Russian – trail far behind Chinese, with from 4 per cent to 9 per cent of the total. The five most widely spoken languages represent every continent, even Africa (provided that we consider English to be a native African language); and each has its strongest geographical base in one of the continents or in distinct regions: English in North America, Spanish in Latin America, Russian in Europe, Hindi/Urdu in tropical Asia, and Chinese in central Asia.

Between the five most widely spoken languages and those that follow them, there is no such clear division as there is between Chinese and all other languages. The line of demarcation between 'major' and 'middle-size' languages is even less clearly marked. Let us take, somewhat arbitrarily, Muller's figure of 40 million and Culbert's of 50 million as the demarcation line. This gives us fourteen 'middle-size' languages: three based in Europe (German, French, and Italian), one in South America (Portuguese), one in the Middle East and North Africa (Arabic), and nine in Asia (Japanese,

Bengali, Javanese, Telugu, Korean, Punjabi, Tamil, Marathi, and Malay/Indonesian). The major tongues – according to the number of speakers – of the second rank are thus concentrated in Asia, where ten of them are found, while Europe has only five, Latin America two, and North America and Africa one apiece. Taking into consideration only concentrations of at least 40 million speakers in a given continent, we find that only English is multicontinental.

Scientific culture

It is impossible to establish a cultural hierarchy of language that does not involve some discriminatory preference; in the absence of a world culture, there can be no one single hierarchy. How is the strength of a culture to be measured – by its myths, its cinema, its books, its scientific publications? The religious strength of a language may be more important for its survival than its literary or scientific strength; but in the absence of data that would enable me to measure such relationships, and at the risk of sinning by modernism in its extremest form, I shall examine the participation of languages in scientific culture. The choice can be defended – at least partly – by the fact that my objective is not literary. When I speak of cultural hierarchy, it is not culture itself that concerns me, but its political consequences. At the world level, conflicts between languages are bound up with struggles among states, and in these struggles the level of scientific culture is an essential element of the hierarchy of nations.

Let us first consider the languages used in at least one of the articles listed in *Chemical Abstracts*, the most systematic service in existence for documentation and indexing. Between 1977 and 1980, these *Abstracts* indexed slightly more than 1.5 million articles in the sphere of chemistry, over 400,000 of them in 1980. English accounts for nearly 65 per cent of the total, Russian covers less than 20 per cent, and no other language reaches 6 per cent (Table 12).

The differences in the order of precedence are impressive. One language has an absolute majority; four languages (English, Russian, Japanese, and German) represent 90 per cent; the first twelve languages account for 98 per cent of the total scientific production; the other forty-two (if we include the eight mentioned in the note to the table) share the remaining 2 per cent. The source of these data tends to favour English, since *Chemical Abstracts*, an American documentation service, is more likely to ignore a repetitive article in a small foreign-language journal than in an English-language one. However, it is unlikely that the bias amounts to much. Unlike history or political science, chemistry is sufficiently well defined, identifiable by its specialized

TABLE 12
Languages of the articles indexed by *Chemical Abstracts* in 1980
(*N* = number of original articles)*

Language	N	%	Language	N	%
English	263,430	64.7	Belorussian	101	–
Russian	72,483	17.8	Slovene	96	–
Japanese	21,180	5.2	Norwegian	88	–
German	16,155	4.0	Greek	86	–
French	8,310	2.0	Vietnamese	78	–
Polish	4,559	1.1	Persian	68	–
Italian	3,126	0.8	Malay-Indonesian	55	–
Chinese	3,118	0.8	Hebrew	47	–
Spanish	2,542	0.6	Afrikaans	43	–
Czech	1,960	0.5	Albanian	40	–
Bulgarian	1,680	0.4	Armenian	23	–
Romanian	1,478	0.4	Thai	17	–
Hungarian	1,159	0.3	Macedonian	12	–
Portuguese	928	0.2	Georgian	14	–
Korean	890	0.2	Hindi	13	–
Serbo-Croatian	886	0.2	Azerbaijani	8	–
Slovak	817	0.2	Latvian	8	–
Ukrainian	588	0.1	Lithuanian	8	–
Dutch	381	0.1	Arabic	7	–
Swedish	307	0.1	Estonian	3	–
Turkish	207	0.1	Esperanto	2	–
Danish	123	–	Swahili	2	–
Finnish	102	–	Punjabi	1	–

*Other languages in which at least one original article was published in the previous twenty years are Gaelic, Icelandic, Interlingua, Kazakh, Mongolian (Khalkha), Sindhi, Turkoman, and Welsh.

Other languages used for summaries or translations are Amharic, Bengali, Burmese, Feroian, Gujarati, Kannada, Kirghiz, Latin, Malayalam, Marathi, Moldavian, Sanskrit, Sinhalese, Tadjik, Tagalog, Tibetan (Dzonkha), and Uzbek.

English has increased its dominance over the years. In 1977 it stood at 61.0 per cent, in 1980 at 64.7, and in 1984 at 69.2. In that last year (1984) the ranking was as follows (in per cent): English 69.2, Russian 15.7, Japanese 4.0, German 3.4, Chinese 2.2, French 1.3, Polish 0.7, Spanish 0.6, Italian 0.4, Bulgarian 0.4, Czech 0.4, Korean 0.3, Hungarian 0.2, Romanian 0.2, Portuguese 0.2, Serbo-Croatian 0.2, Slovak 0.2, Ukrainian 0.1, Dutch 0.1, Swedish 0.1, Turkish 0.1 (information supplied by *Chemical Abstracts*).

TABLE 13
Languages of the articles indexed by *Index Medicus* in 1980 (order of frequency of use)

Language*	%	Language	%
English	72.6	Portuguese	0.3
Russian	6.3	Romanian	0.2
German	4.9	Bulgarian	0.2
French	4.1	Slovak	0.2
Japanese	2.7	Hebrew	0.1
Italian	1.6	Slovene	0.1
Polish	1.4	Finnish	0.1
Spanish	1.1	Greek	0.1
Czech	0.6	Ukrainian	0.05
Swedish	0.4	Chinese	0.04
Danish	0.4	Afrikaans	0.03
Dutch	0.3	Turkish	0.03
Hungarian	0.3	Thai	0.03
Serbo-Croatian†	0.3		

*Other languages that had appeared from time to time but not in 1980: Albanian, Arabic, Azerbaijani, Georgian, Icelandic, Lithuanian, Pashto, Vietnamese, Persian, Armenian, Malay, and Korean
†In Latin script 80 per cent, in cyrillic 20 per cent

publications, and important – not only to chemists but also to the American government – for the *Abstracts* surveys to be as systematic and as universal as we wish.

The differences in position within the chemistry hierarchy in relation to the order of precedence among numbers of speakers are quite remarkable. Chinese is less important than Polish, and only slightly more important than Czech. Although their contribution is very small, quite recent languages such as Afrikaans (the first book in Afrikaans was published in 1886), or recently revitalized ones (for example Hebrew, which during the nineteenth century looked as though it were becoming a dead language restricted to religious functions), rank relatively high, outstripping such widely spoken languages as Arabic and Hindi/Urdu.

Other scientific disciplines would give us different results, but the overall impression would remain the same: one single major language of scientific culture, a few minor languages, and a whole host of quite tiny languages with no real influence. For example, let us look in comparison at the order of precedence in medicine, as shown in the records of the *Index Medicus* for 1980 (Table 13). English dominates medicine as it dominates chemistry; in contrast, Russian is much weaker. However, we see the same languages

TABLE 14
Number of books translated in 1973, by language of original

	Number	%
English	18,350	39.0
French	5,993	12.7
Russian	5,113	10.8
German	4,277	9.0
Spanish	1,368	2.9
Italian	1,136	2.4
Swedish	1,006	2.1
Polish	626	1.3
Other	9,183	19.8

SOURCE: UNESCO, Annuaire statistique, 1976

in the dominant group in each case – English, Russian, German, French, Japanese, Italian, and Polish; and in each case these seven languages cover about 90 per cent of the world research.

It would be interesting to establish the evolution of the languages of science over the past, but we have no systematic data for the period prior to the Second World War. Changes in the cultural hierarchy of languages are frequent and rapid. Latin, which dominated the sciences until the eighteenth century, has practically disappeared from them; Russian and Japanese, which played only a minor role at the beginning of the present century, have equalled or displaced German. Hebrew and Afrikaans now precede Chinese – but if the evolution that began at the end of the 1970s continues, Chinese could reach the level of Japanese, and perhaps even Russian, in one or two generations.

Two apparently contradictory tendencies characterize the present period. More and more languages are being used for the dissemination of scientific culture, but a small number of major languages are playing an ever more important role. Languages other than English, Russian, Japanese, German, and French accounted in 1959 for 11.2 per cent of the works listed by *Chemical Abstracts*; in 1965, they accounted for only 9.1 per cent, in 1977, 8.4 per cent, and in 1980, 8.3 per cent. A similar tendency to concentration is apparent in biology and in physics.

Scientific culture is dominated by European and North American languages; Japanese is an exception. Only one language, English, serves as a lingua franca world-wide; on a planetary scale, it corresponds to what Latin, French, and Italian were in earlier days for Europe and the Mediterranean basin. This dominance, which appears in other areas of the scientific realm, is only partly counteracted by translation, since the best-known tongues are also the most frequently translated,[10] as is shown by the 1973 UNESCO statistics reproduced in Table 14. These statistics do not always show the country of translation – a pity, for it would be of interest to know whether the translation was done in the publishing country or in the importing country. In the Soviet Union, for example, according to UNESCO statistics, 41 per cent of the 5,113 Russian studies translated into other languages were translated and published in the Soviet Union; whereas only 25 per cent of the 626 Polish studies were translated in Poland – a difference explained to a large extent by the multilingual character of the Soviet Union and the unilingual character of Poland.

Translation permits cultural contact while avoiding penetration by a foreign language; but publication within a country in a language other than the country's own has the opposite effect. The percentage of Pakistani scientists who publish in English in Pakistan, or of French scientists who publish in English in France, is a measure of the degree of penetration of Urdu and French by English. The journal *Travaux chimiques des Pays-Bas*, published in Holland under this French title since 1882, contanied 94 articles in 1980–81: 92 in English, 1 in German, and 1 in French. The periodical *Nouveau Journal de chimie*, though published in France, contained in 1981 only articles written in English. A study dealing with the 1970s (Cans 1981) showed that francophone researchers outside France often published in English: in Algeria, in 30 per cent of the cases, in Switzerland 65 per cent, and in Quebec 82 per cent. According to De Chambrun and Reinhardt (1981), the proportion of francophone biochemists who publish in English rose from 56 per cent to 80 per cent between 1975 and 1979.

The penetration of one language by another can be measured also by the number of foreign books in a library, by the number of references in foreign languages in a bibliography, and by the number of scientific papers at international meetings in languages other than that of the host country. According to data presented at the symposium 'The Future of French in Scientific Publications and Communications' held in Montreal in November 1981, half the books in the D'Orsay library – the biggest French scientific library – were in English and only 30 per cent were in French. Of 337 sets of bibliographic data computerized in Europe, 70 per cent used English as the common language, 10 per cent German, and 10 per cent

10 According to Vickery (1968), 850,000 scientific articles were published in 1965, 400,000 of them in English. See also Hutchins et al (1971), Chan (1976), and Bishop and Pukteris (1973). The demands for translation from a foreign language are a measure both of the importance of that language and of the ignorance of those who require the translation.

French. In 1976 English was used in 75 per cent of the papers at symposia of exact and natural sciences held in France under the aegis of the National Council of Scientific Research. In their list of books and articles published in 1977–78 in a foreign language by Polish academics living in Poland, Sulek and Sulek (1978) identify 453 studies, broken down as follows: English 72 per cent, French 8 per cent, German 7 per cent, Russian 5 per cent, and other languages 8 per cent (Bulgarian, Czech, Hungarian, Italian, Japanese, Portuguese, Serbo-Croatian, Spanish, Swedish).

Obviously, this last statistic is a measure of the combined influence of both scientific and political factors. Whatever the set of causes that lead to the use of one foreign language rather than another, these statistics of reciprocal penetration give us precise measurements of a hierarchy that we should, ideally, compare with other cultural hierarchies – religious, or artistic, for example, though for these latter, the data lack precision. If culture is a way for one language to dominate another, the methods of this dominance are varied. English penetrates Bulgarian culture through the exact sciences, if not through the humanities. Arabic spreads in Africa through religion, but not through science.

Economic hierarchy

The statistics at our disposal do not enable us to measure the economic power, wealth, or standard of living of a language from individual data; we have to use collective statistics – typically, state statistics. When the state is unilingual – for example, Austria or Brazil – no difficulty arises; but when the state is multilingual, how does one make precise allocations, in accordance with the language of the individuals, of the statistics obtained for multi-ethnic groups? This is usually impossible. We have a choice between allocating state wealth proportionately to the linguistic groups that make up the state and allocating the whole of the economic wealth of the state to the dominant language. The first solution is justifiable in states such as Finland and Switzerland, but it is inadequate in the case of the Soviet Union, and absurd in the cases of Senegal or South Africa. The second, and simpler, solution has the advantage of being more politic; it favours the dominant group. I have accordingly adopted this second solution for all states that recognize only one official language at the level of their central institutions, thus allocating all the economic power to French in France, and to Russian in the Soviet Union. In the cases of officially multilingual states, we shall make several distinctions. We shall consider as unilingual those in which multilingualism is mainly symbolic and is applicable only at the regional or local levels of government – Ireland and Bolivia, for example. For those that are multilingual in their central institutions (albeit in varying degrees), we shall use two different measurements. The first set of figures (column A in Table 15) shows only the dominant language of the central institutions (Serbo-Croatian in Yugoslavia, German in Switzerland, English in Canada, etc), while the second set (column B) allocates wealth or economic power in proportion to the numerical strengths of the speakers of the different official languages of the state in question.

The classifications I have adopted have consequences that should be explained before their results are analysed. Keeping only official languages, we eliminate subordinate languages which – although important by virtue of their number of speakers or their cultural strength – have no state of their own. For this reason, neither Ukrainian, nor Georgian, nor the majority of the major languages of India is shown in Table 15. Thus we shall often be exaggerating the economic strength of dominant languages, especially of lingua francas such as French, English, or Russian; conversely, at other times the definitions do not reveal a language which, however, plays an important – sometimes even a dominant – role in the administration of the state. This occurs when a state adopts just one of its languages as its official language but in fact continues to use a foreign language – as in Morocco and Malaysia. The former (Bentahila 1983) recognizes only Arabic as its official language, and the latter only Malay – while the central administration continues to operate in the first case partly in French and in the second case partly in English. It thus may seem contradictory to 'give' English – as we have done in column A of Table 15 – all the economic resources of India, while those of Malaysia are allotted to Malay. Obviously one single method of measurement is not enough. However, this difference of treatment between India and Malaysia is justified, even if only as a form of anticipation. The fact that a state such as Malaysia, which continues to use a foreign language in its government, has been able to promote one of its indigenous languages to the status of sole official language suggests that the exterior lingua franca will sooner or later be eliminated. Malaysia is in a better position to do without English than is India; and Algeria is better able than the Ivory Coast to dispense with French.

Too much must not be read into the figures of Table 15; they are based on statistics that are sometimes approximate. According to which sources are used, the gross national product of the Soviet Union may vary by as much as 100 per cent; and the variation may be even greater in Poland, depending on whether the złoty is costed at its official or its black-market rate of exchange. Whether one uses World Bank statistics, as reported in the *Europa Yearbook* (as I have done in Table 15), or the estimates of the CIA and other state intelligence and information services, the margin of error

TABLE 15
Languages ranked by economic power, 1978 (GNP in millions of US dollars)

A*			B†		
Language‡	GNP	%	Language	GNP	%
English	2,938,850	33.9	English	2,739,766	31.6
	(2,699,300)§			(2,640,394)	
Russian	965,520	11.1	Russian	965,520	11.1
Japanese	836,160	9.6	Japanese	836,160	9.6
German	811,960	9.3	German	789,145	8.9
French	565,220	6.5	French	587,325	6.6
	(534,460)			(557,884)	
Chinese	448,550	5.1	Chinese	454,317	5.1
Spanish	400,970	4.6	Spanish	400,970	4.6
	(400,870)			(400,870)	
Arabic	219,590	2.5	Arabic	222,789	2.5
Italian	218,320	2.5	Italian	218,320	2.5
Portuguese	210,340	2.4	Portuguese	210,340	2.4
	(206,730)			(206,730)	
Polish	128,330	1.4	Polish	128,330	1.4
Dutch	118,010	1.3	Dutch	168,441	1.8
	(117,190)		Hindi/Urdu	127,936	1.4
Swedish	84,750	0.9	Swedish	84,750	0.9
Persian	72,700		Persian	70,229	
Czech	71,320		Malay	66,256	
Malay	65,180		Turkish	53,120	
Turkish	53,120		Danish	50,410	
Serbo-Croatian	52,340		Czech	48,490	
Danish	50,410		Serbo-Croatian	41,549	
Afrikaans	40,940		Norwegian	38,500	
Norwegian	38,500		Romanian	38,170	
Romanian	38,170		Hungarian	36,860	
Hungarian	36,860		Greek	31,557	
Finnish	32,380		Korean	30,570	
Greek	31,557		Afrikaans	30,295	
Korean	30,570		Finnish	30,113	
Bulgarian	28,450		Bulgarian	28,450	
Thai	21,790		Slovak	22,830	
Hebrew	15,300		Thai	21,790	
Vietnamese	8,870		Tagalog	19,297	
Bengali	7,630		Hebrew	13,005	
Burmese	4,900		Vietnamese	8,870	
Swahili	3,686		Bengali	7,630	
Amharic	3,640		Slovene	6,334	
Sinhalese	2,720		Swahili	6,107	

TABLE 15 (continued)

A*			B†		
Language‡	GNP	%	Language	GNP	%
Albanian	1,920		Burmese	4,900	
Icelandic	1,880		Macedonian	4,457	
Nepali	1,850		Amharic	3,640	
Khalkha	1,470		Pashto	2,471	
Khmer	570		Albanian	1,920	
Somali	470		Sinhalese	1,900	
Lao	300		Icelandic	1,880	
Dzonkha	120		Malagasy	1,804	
Divehi	20		Nepali	1,580	
			Khalkha	1,470	
TOTAL	8,665,933		Tamil	1,159	
			Rundi	610	
			Khmer	570	
			Somali	470	
			Maltese	365	
			Sesotho	356	
			Lao	300	
			Dzonkha	120	
			Samoan	47	
			Kiribati	38	
			Divehi	20	

SOURCE: The Europa Yearbook 1981 (the GNP is that for 1978).
*Measure A allocates the GNP of officially multilingual states to the language that dominates in the state's central institutions (French in Belgium and German in Switzerland, for example).
†Measure B allocates the GNP of the same states in proportion to the number of speakers of each of the ethnic groups whose language is official. Languages that are not officially and effectively used in the state's central institutions (Catalan in Spain, Malayalam in India) are thus, by our definition, excluded from being attributed any of the GNP. The following languages, typically 'national' rather than official, whose use, at the level of the state's central institutions, is either symbolic or limited, have not been included in measure B: Aymara, Bichlamar, Chichewa, Comorean, Gaelic, Guarani, Papua Pidgin, Quechua, Ruanda, Tonga, and Tswana.
‡The following states and principalities have not been counted: Namibia, Venda, Ciskei, Vatican, Monaco, San Marino, Liechtenstein. Additionally, for lack of available statistics on their GNP, Nauru, Surinam, and Swaziland have not been included. The GNP of Papua-New Guinea has been attributed to English and that of Luxembourg to French.
§The figures in parentheses were obtained after exclusion of the GNP of the states where the languages are a lingua franca without indigeneous roots (India in the case of English for example).

remains wide. None the less, Table 15 gives a revealing overall view: the wealth of the world is controlled by only a few languages. Just 12 of them – English, Russian, Japanese, German, French, Chinese, Spanish, Arabic, Italian, Portuguese, Polish, and Dutch – share 90 per cent among them- selves.[11] Fifty years ago, Arabic would not have appeared in the leading group; a hundred years ago, Japanese would have been missing; and of the 12 current major economic languages, only Chinese existed two thousand years ago. The two major languages that dominated the Mediterranean ten centuries ago have retained almost no economic power: Latin has managed to hang on in the Roman Catholic church; and modern Greek, which has replaced classical Greek, has slipped to the economic level of Finnish and Bulgarian.

Nine of these twelve major languages are of European origin, and by the seventeenth century they were already powerful. However, their 'survival strategies' have been very different. German and Italian have not changed their territorial bases; French has moved only slightly, since its economic base remains European; while English, Spanish, and Portuguese have changed continents. Without Brazil, Portuguese would be a minor lan- guage, on the same level as Tagalog and Thai.

In these days, when the confines of the world seem set – unless they are altered either by extra-planetary colonization or by nuclear holocaust – the

11 According to Adler (1966), who bases his figures on each country's volume of imports, 50 per cent of the world's businessmen use English as their first language, and for 70 per cent it is either their first or their second language. Adler relies on data furnished by the London Board of Trade and on personal impressions. Again according to him, the percentage who do not know English, or know it only poorly, varies between 5 per cent in North America and 43 per cent in Europe. As a guide, I reproduce below some tenta- tive statistics, not easily verified:

First and/or second language of business, by continent, in percentage

	Africa	North America	South America	Asia	Europe	Oceania	World
English	55	89	1	43	36	98	48
Chinese	–	–	–	21	–	–	3
French	37	1	–	5	20	2	14
Russian	–	–	–	–	9	–	5
Spanish	–	15	74	–	2	–	7
German	–	–	–	–	29	–	16
Arabic	26	–	–	2	–	–	3
Portuguese	3	–	25	–	1	–	2
Italian	3	–	–	–	7	–	4

In each column the maximum total is 200.

survival and spreading of a language by means of mass migration no longer seems the available option it was a hundred years ago.

Standard of living

When we move from the order of precedence according to the gross national product (GNP) to that according to the national product per capita, the picture changes considerably, since individual economic wealth is not tied to the number of speakers of a language and since colonial or imperial expansion lowers the average income per head. Let us consider the statistics of Table 16, which translates the figures of Table 15 column A into per capita averages for official languages. Northwest Europe is the most prosperous area in the world, and this prosperity is unaffected by the size of the state – Germany and Luxembourg are equally favoured. Further, statistics grouped by languages rather than by their states tell us that the prosperity we know not to be tied to the number of inhabitants is not tied either to the language spoken in the state. A language as minor as Icelandic, in which the small number of speakers debars any cultural influence other than locally, a language so weak that it cannot aspire to the level of university education save in a few restricted disciplines, has been able from its isolated island to carve out a highly prosperous economic niche for itself.

The differences in the averages for French and English in any of the measurements used in Table 15 are remarkable. These averages vary appreciably according to whether the GNP is attributed only to the dominant language of the state or is shared proportionally among the ethnic groups whose languages are official, or, finally, whether or not account is taken only of indigenous languages, to the exclusion of imported lingua francas. Certain languages know only wealth – the Scandinavian tongues and German, in particular; the majority of other languages know only poverty. Only two languages, French and English, run the whole gamut, from the richest and most highly industrialized states to the poorest and the most primitive. French is the official government language of Luxembourg, where the GNP per capita ($10,410) is as high as that of Sweden; it is also the language of Haiti, where the figure is only $260. The most prosperous base of English is the United States ($9,700), but English is also the language of Dominica ($440), and the language of government in India ($180). Only Arabic has comparable variations, since it is the language both of Kuwait ($14,890) and of Sudan ($320). Following the independence of Brunei, Malay is in a similar position, since GNP per capita runs from $10,640 in Brunei, through $1,090 for Malaysia, to $360 in Indonesia.

The GNP gives us a measurement of influence, or at least of potential influence; the per capita average gives us a measurement of a language's experience with either wealth or poverty, or both. Conflicting experiences may explain, in part, the tensions that occur in some inter-state alliances. Language favours political coalitions such as the Commonwealth, the French Community, or the Arab League; but differences of status can be more deeply resented within one single linguistic community than among different communities. Frenchmen and Englishmen find it easier, thanks to their language, to form coalitions and world-wide markets than do Russians or Germans; but paradoxically France, England, and the United States are more prone than Germany or the Soviet Union to cause envy and resentment among underprivileged speakers of their language. Where this condition exists, it tends to encourage the replacement of an international lingua franca – such as French, English, or Spanish – by an indigenous language, which would assist withdrawal from a hierarchy in which one's position is disadvantageous.

Military strength

Languages sometimes encroach upon one another so slowly that those involved scarcely notice it; a shop closes, a neighbour moves away, a mother-tongue becomes a second language for a few people here and there – until one day Welsh or Provençal is in danger of disappearing. At other times, however, the process results from highly visible events or public actions – wars or treaties that change the geographic distribution of languages in contact. If Italy had kept or acquired Nice and Corsica, if Germany had kept Alsace, if Napoleon had not sold Louisiana, if Spain had

TABLE 16
Languages, ranked by wealth, 1978 (GNP per capita)

A*			B		
Swedish	10,210		Swedish	10,210	
Danish	9,920		Danish	9,920	
Norwegian	9,510		Norwegian	9,510	
German	8,831		German	8,597	
Dutch	8,217	(8,379)	Dutch	8,462	(8,546)
Icelandic	8,320		Icelandic	8,320	
Japanese	7,330		Japanese	7,330	
Finnish	6,820		Finnish	6,820	
Czech	4,720		English	5,676	(8,011)
Italian	3,840		Czech	4,720	
Hebrew	4,120		Slovak	4,720	
Russian	3,700		Hebrew	4,120	

TABLE 16 (continued)

A*		B	
Polish	3,600	Italian	3,940
Hungarian	3,450	French	3,713 (7,923)
French	3,303 (7,824)	Russian	3,700
Greek	3,207	Polish	3,660
Bulgarian	3,200	Hungarian	3,450
Serbo-Croatian	2,390	Greek	3,207
Romanian	1,750	Bulgarian	3,200
Spanish	1,593	Serbo-Croatian	2,390
Arabic	1,498	Slovene	2,390
Afrikaans	1,480	Macedonian	2,390
English	1,478 (8,033)	Maltese	2,160
Portuguese	1,472 (1,651)	Persian	1,766
Persian	1,444	Romanian	1,750
Turkish	1,225	Spanish	1,633
Khalkha	940	Afrikaans	1,566
Albanian	740	Arabic	1,496
Thai	490	Portuguese	1,472 (1,651)
Chinese	460	Turkish	1,225
Malay	441	Korean	1,026
Swahili	222	Khalkha	940
Sinhalese	190	Albanian	740
Vietnamese	170	Tagalog	510
Burmese	150	Thai	490
Divehi	150	Chinese	465
Somali	130	Malay	446
Nepali	120	Tamil	383
Amharic	120	Samoan	350
Dzonkha	100	Sesotho	280
Bengali	90	Swahili	260
Lao	90	Malagasy	250
Khmer	70	Pashto	240
		Singhalese	190
		Hindi/Urdu	186
		Vietnamese	170
		Divehi	150
		Burmese	150
		Somali	130
		Amharic	120
		Nepali	120
		Dzonkha	100
		Lao	90
		Bengali	90
		Khmer	90

*For an explanation of the measures see Table 15.

not lost Flanders, if Montcalm had not been beaten at Quebec, if St Lucia had remained French, if Martinique had remained English, the linguistic map of the theatres in which France, England, Italy, Germany, and Spain waged their wars would be very different today. The military strength of languages – or more accurately the military strength of the states that these languages 'use' for their defence or growth – is thus an essential element of the linguistic hierarchy.

We shall use two measurements of military strength: the number of soldiers, and the military budget, both as recorded by the London Institute of Strategic Studies in 1981. [12] As before, we shall use two different methods of calculation for each of these two measurements. In the first method, military strength is attributed to one single language – the dominant language at the level of the central institutions; in the second method, the strength is distributed proportionally among the official languages. A deliberate consequence of these two methods is that languages that have no official status at central state level do not appear in our list.

Since the first explosion of an atomic bomb in 1945, only four languages have acquired the means and the weapons for waging atomic warfare: English, Russian, French, and Chinese. In addition, Hindi and perhaps Hebrew and Afrikaans too have the capacity to produce atomic bombs and probably some limited launching capacity. Spanish, Portuguese, Arabic, and Urdu should shortly acquire the same second-rank capabilities. The atomic revolution thus gives quite small states – and very minor languages – possibilities of military action out of all proportion to the size of their populations. This is a completely new element in the history of war between languages and increases the importance of the state as a vehicle of culture. This possibility, now available to small cultures, of defending themselves by nuclear power when they would be unable to do so by sheer numbers is not without some serious risks. Nuclear war makes it more likely that minor languages closely concentrated geographically will be destroyed, if not completely eliminated.

Our measurements of military strength (number of soldiers and military budget) tend to magnify the effects of short-term trends. As an example, take Switzerland, a peaceful state not threatened by its neighbours. It has only 3,000 soldiers (though it can mobilize 600,000 within 48 hours) and adds but little to the military strength of German; in contrast, the two Koreas, mobilized against each other, add considerably to the military strength of Korean. Actual military strength corresponds only roughly to a military potential for which the GNP gives us another approximation. How-

12 See also Sivard (1980).

ever, desirable though it may be to reduce the effect of occasional events on the military hierarchy of languages, in the absence of a satisfactory and lasting method of securing this reduction, I prefer to let the reader evaluate their probable effect on the measurements of Tables 17 and 18. These list languages in order of the strength of their states in 1979–80 – i.e. after the invasion of Kampuchea by Vietnam, and of Afghanistan by the Soviet Union, and just as the régime of the Shah of Iran was collapsing. Our list reveals that certain languages of little economic or cultural importance have a military strength greater than what simple demography would lead one to expect. More soldiers spoke Vietnamese than Spanish; and Turkish disposed of more bayonets than Portuguese. Of the twelve major languages with large armies, only seven were European; and of the twelve that topped the list by the size of their military budgets, three were Asiatic (Chinese, Japanese, and Vietnamese), a fourth covered North Africa and the Middle East (Arabic), while the other eight were those of the large empire-building warrior states of Europe. Further, Vietnamese figures among the top twelve languages in the order of precedence given in Table 18B, which lists military budgets; on the regional level in southeast Asia, Vietnamese plays an imperialistic role comparable to that played by German and French in earlier days and over a wider area – for in those days vacuums of power covered whole continents. [13]

Evaluation of hierarchies

Let us review our different hierarchical measurements through the twelve leading languages in each of the categories we have established. One single language, German, appears in each of these categories (Table 19); it figures among the major languages by demography, culture, economic power, indi-

13 The deployment of the military strength of a language on the territory of other languages gives us one measurement of the penetration of weaker languages by dominant languages. Taking into account only military establishments of some importance that have been in existence for some length of time – those that the International Institute for Strategic Studies (1982) lists under the heading 'Deployment Abroad' – among the major languages only English, Hindi/Urdu, Russian, and French (except in Chad after the Libyan intervention, and in one other minor exception because of the presence of Tanzanian troops in the Seychelles) were not penetrated by the armed forces of other languages at the beginning of the 1980s. On this reckoning English has penetrated German, Greek, Italian, Turkish, Korean, Spanish, Japanese, Malay, Chinese, Tagalog, Dutch, and Icelandic; Russian has penetrated German, Polish, Hungarian, Czech, Slovak, Pashto, Persian, Vietnamese, and Bulgarian; French has penetrated German and Arabic; Dutch has penetrated German; Turkish has penetrated Greek; Vietnamese has penetrated Loa and Khmer; Spanish has penetrated Portuguese and Amharic.

vidual wealth, and military strength. If we abstract the two measurements that list languages in order according to the average GNP per capita, defining prosperity rather than power, only seven languages appear in at least one of the two measurements we used for each of the four major factors: demographic, scientific, economic, and military. These are English, Spanish, Russian, German, French, and Italian. This does not mean that each of these seven languages has the advantage over those that follow in terms of global power, because I know of no formula that allows one to give specific weightings to military strength, economic power, and cultural power. The object of comparing hierarchies as different as the number of soldiers and the number of articles on medicine or chemistry is simply to show the weak spot in certain languages that lack either numbers, or scientific creativity, or economic power, or military strength. The weakness of French (relative weakness) lies in the number of it speakers; that of Arabic in scientific culture; that of Portuguese in scientific culture and military strength; that of Vietnamese in the corpus of factors other than military strength. But there, too, an overall look tells us that these relative strengths or weaknesses should be analysed within their own particular geographical context. Within its area, Vietnamese is far more powerful in comparison with the languages against which it is exerting pressure than is German in comparison with the languages around it.

TABLE 17
The military hierarchy among languages, by number of soldiers, 1979–80

A*	Number	%	B	Number	%
Chinese	4,888,200	21.0	Chinese	4,919,700	21.1
English	4,601,000	19.7	Russian	3,658,000	15.7
	(2,499,200)		English	2,950,300	12.7
Russian	3,658,000	15.7		(2,477,900)	
Arabic	1,476,900	6.3	Hindi/Urdu	1,565,500	6.7
Vietnamese	1,029,000	4.4	Arabic	1,496,100	6.4
Spanish	1,026,700	4.3	Vietnamese	1,029,000	4.4
German	709,700	3.0	Spanish	1,026,700	4.3
French	691,200	2.9	German	708,700	3.0
	(585,000)		French	646,000	2.7
Turkish	567,000	2.4		(562,100)	
Portuguese	397,900	1.7	Turkish	576,000	2.4
	(332,000)		Portuguese	397,900	1.7
Italian	366,000	1.6		(332,000)	
Polish	317,500	1.4	Italian	366,300	1.5

TABLE 17 (continued)

A*	Number	%	B	Number	%
Malay	310,700	1.3	Polish	317,500	1.4
Persian	280,000	1.2	Malay	316,500	1.4
Serbo-Croatian	264,000	1.1	Persian	252,200	1.1
Japanese	241,000		Japanese	241,000	
Romanian	184,500		Thai	230,800	
Dutch	114,900		Amharic	229,500	
Thai	230,800		Serbo-Croatian	209,000	
Amharic	229,500		Greek	185,400	
Czech	195,000		Romanian	184,500	
Greek	185,400		Burmese	173,500	
Burmese	173,500		Hebrew	169,600	
Hebrew	169,600		Dutch	161,400	
Bulgarian	149,000		Bulgarian	149,000	
Korean	127,800		Czech	132,600	
Hungarian	93,000		Korean	127,800	
Afrikaans	86,000		Hungarian	93,000	
Bengali	72,000		Tagalog	82,000	
Swedish	66,100		Bengali	72,000	
Somali	61,500		Swedish	68,900	
Lao	55,700		Slovak	62,000	
Swahili	49,000		Somali	61,000	
Albanian	41,000		Swahili	56,000	
Khmer	40,000		Lao	55,000	
Finnish	39,900		Afrikaans	52,000	
Norwegian	37,000		Albanian	41,000	
Danish	35,000		Khmer	40,000	
Khalkha	28,100		Norwegian	37,000	
Nepali	22,000		Finnish	37,000	
			Danish	35,000	
TOTAL	23,310,200		Slovene	32,000	
			Pashto	28,000	
			Khalkha	28,000	
			Macedonian	22,500	
			Nepali	22,000	
			Sinhalese	15,000	
			Malagasy	11,000	
			Tamil	6,200	
			Sesotho	4,000	
			Maltese	400	

SOURCE: International Institute for Strategic Studies (1982)
*The explanation of A and B is given in Table 15. For lack of data, the following languages are not included: Dzonkha, Divehi, Icelandic, Tonga, Siswati, Samoa, Nauru, and Kiribati.

Generally speaking, the more speakers a language has, and the higher its position in the economic, cultural, and military hierarchies, the better able it will be to resist the assimilative pressures of other languages and to assimilate weaker languages itself. However, despite its lack of numbers or military strength, a small language can maintain its position and even blossom forth, even when it is in contact with languages further up the hierarchy; examples here are Slovak and Afrikaans. For this to occur, however, the small language must have control either of a government (Afrikaans) or of a linguistic border (Slovak). If there were no obstacle to the geographical mobility of languages, and if in addition there were no endogamy-inducing ethnic cleavages between languages, small languages could not withstand the assimilative pressure of more powerful ones for long.

Let us suppose, for example, that the 200 languages with more than a million speakers (according to Muller's list) were to intermingle in random fashion. Let us suppose that each individual were to choose his or her mate at random from a world list of all the unwed of marriageable age. For simplicity's sake, let us further suppose that celibacy were not permitted, that each couple were to have two children, and that these children were to adopt the language of the parent who belonged to the more numerous linguistic group. In the second generation – the one springing from these chance-organized marriages – nine languages would gain speakers: Mandarin, English, Hindi/Urdu, Spanish, Russian, German, Japanese, Arabic, and Portuguese. In the next generation, only Mandarin, English, and Hindi/Urdu would have more speakers than they had originally started out with. In the eighth generation, no more than ten people would be speaking Russian; and in the tenth generation, the whole world would be speaking Mandarin.

TABLE 18
The military hierarchy among languages, by military state expenditures
(in millions of U.S. dollars, 1979–80)

A*			B		
	Number	%		Number	%
English	185,817	32.2	English	177,422	30.7
	(176,225)			(175,860)	
Russian	152,000	26.4	Russian	152,000	26.4
Chinese	58,650	10.1	Chinese	59,595	10.3
Arabic	35,334	6.1	Arabic	36,129	5.3
German	28,065	4.9	German	27,525	4.8
French	24,755	4.2	French	24,036	4.2
	(24,028)			(23,483)	
Spanish	12,221	2.1	Spanish	12,221	2.1

TABLE 18 (continued)

A*	Number	%	B	Number	%
Japanese	8,960	1.5	Japanese	8,960	1.5
Vietnamese	8,500	1.5	Vietnamese	8,500	1.5
Italian	6,580	1.1	Dutch	7,334	1.3
Dutch	5,240	0.9	Italian	6,760	1.2
Hebrew	5,200	0.9	Hindi/Urdu	5,492	0.9
Korean	4,760	0.8	Korean	4,760	0.8
Polish	4,670	0.8	Polish	4,670	0.8
Persian	4,267	0.7	Hebrew	4,420	0.7
Malay	3,711		Persian	4,227	
Serbo-Croatian	3,600		Malay	3,887	
Swedish	3,590		Swedish	3,636	
Czech	3,520		Serbo-Croatian	2,854	
Portuguese	2,788		Portuguese	2,788	
Turkish	2,590		Turkish	2,590	
Afrikaans	2,560		Czech	2,393	
Greek	1,806		Greek	1,806	
Norwegian	1,570		Afrikaans	1,536	
Romanian	1,350		Norwegian	1,570	
Bulgarian	1,140		Romanian	1,470	
Hungarian	1,090		Danish	1,350	
Finnish	656		Bulgarian	1,140	
Amharic	385		Slovak	1,127	
Swahili	287		Hungarian	1,106	
Burmese	198		Finnish	610	
Albanian	170		Tagalog	557	
Khalkha	127		Slovene	435	
Bengali	115		Swahili	387	
Thai	109		Amharic	385	
Somali	95		Macedonian	306	
Lao	38		Burmese	198	
Nepali	19		Albanian	170	
			Khalkha	127	
TOTAL	576,549		Bengali	115	
			Thai	109	
			Tamil	108	
			Somali	95	
			Malagasy	89	
			Pashto	47	
			Lao	38	
			Sinhalese	25	
			Nepali	19	
			Maltese	5	

*For the source and measures see Tables 15 and 17.

TABLE 19
The twelve top-ranking languages in the demographic, scientific, economic, and military domains

			Economy			
	Population		Scientific culture		Gross national product‡	
Rank	Muller	Culbert	CA*	IM†	A	B
1	Chinese	Chinese	English	English	English	English
2	English	English	Russian	German	Russian	Russian
3	Hindi/Urdu	Hindi/Urdu	Japanese	Russian	Japanese	Japanese
4	Spanish	Russian	German	French	German	German
5	Russian	Spanish	French	Japanese	French	French
6	German	Arabic	Polish	Polish	Chinese	Chinese
7	Japanese	Portuguese	Italian	Italian	Spanish	Spanish
8	Arabic	Bengali	Chinese	Spanish	Arabic	Arabic
9	Bengali	German	Spanish	Czech	Italian	Italian
10	Portuguese	Japanese	Czech	Serbo-Croatian	Portuguese	Portuguese
11	French	Malay	Bulgarian	Swedish	Polish	Dutch
12	Italian	French	Romanian	Danish	Dutch	Polish

*CA = *Chemical Abstracts.*
†IM = *Index Medicus.*
‡For an explanation of A and B see Table 15.

A similar hypothesis applied to the 33 languages (other than indigenous Indian tongues) that figured in the 1970 Canadian census gives the simulated results shown in Table 20; every language but English would disappear in 5 generations – i.e. within about 150 years. If the children of the random marriages were not to choose the language of the most numerous group in every case, as was required in our first hypothesis, but were so to choose in only 60 per cent of the cases, it would then take not 5 but 77 generations to obtain the same result in Canada; however, by the 20th generation there would be no greater number of francophones than there are now speakers of Indian and Inuit languages (about 130,000). In the case of Muller's 200 languages, a hypothesis of 60 per cent choice would require 100 generations for Mandarin to become universal; but by the 30th generation its closest rival – English – would be reduced to some 15 million speakers (Table 21).

Things do not happen like that; they move more quickly or more slowly, according to the degree of exogamy in the groups concerned, the assimilative power of the superior language, and the place of the weaker language in

Economy (continued)		Defence			
GNP per head‡		Number of soldiers		Military budget	
A	B	A	B	A	B
Swedish	Swedish	Chinese	Chinese	English	English
Danish	Danish	English	Russian	Russian	Russian
Norwegian	Norwegian	Russian	English	Chinese	Chinese
German	German	Arabic	Hindi/Urdu	Arabic	Arabic
Dutch	Dutch	Vietnamese	Arabic	German	German
Icelandic	Icelandic	Spanish	Vietnamese	French	French
Japanese	Japanese	German	Spanish	Spanish	Spanish
Finnish	Finnish	French	German	Japanese	Japanese
Czech	English	Turkish	French	Vietnamese	Vietnamese
Italian	Czech	Portuguese	Turkish	Italian	Dutch
Hebrew	Slovak	Italian	Portuguese	Hebrew	Italian
Polish	Hebrew	Polish	Italian	Korean	Hindi/Urdu

the hierarchy.[14] It took only a few generations for French to overcome the obstacles of Breton, Provençal, and Alsatian; in contrast, Slovak has prospered vis-à-vis Czech. However, the information to be drawn from our theoretical simulation remains no less valuable. Contact and communication between languages favour the strongest language, the one with numbers and power. When numbers and power are not united in the same language, there may well be situations of equilibrium between languages in contact – as for example in Finland, between Swedish and Finnish, or in Switzerland, between German and French. However, such situations of equilibrium are rare, and often temporary. Generally speaking, the language that controls the political power eliminates its rivals; and to do this, the preferred instrument is the state. A language without a state does not necessarily lack an immediate future – Armenian, Slovak, Georgian, and many other small languages attest to that; but it has a very uncertain long-term future.

14 On this subject, see a simulation of a different kind – that of Pool (1978), which is based on hypothetical costs of acquisition and benefits from use of a given language, in multilingual situations.

TABLE 20
Simulating the disappearance of languages in Canada*

	Number of speakers at each generation				
	First	Second	Third	Fourth	Fifth
English	14,446,235	19,140,188	21,160,947	21,396,816	21,399,475
French	5,546,025	2,166,749	238,128	2,659	
Italian	425,235	47,476	305		
German	213,350	17,453	59		
Ukrainian	144,760	9,420	20		
Greek	86,830	4,710	7		
Chinese	77,890	3,626	4		
Portuguese	74,765	2,947	2		
Polish	70,960	2,314	1		
Hungarian	50,670	1,364			
Dutch	36,170	827			
Serbo-Croatian	29,285	580			
Yiddish	26,330	453			
Hindi/Urdu	23,110	344			
Finnish	18,280	237			
Spanish	17,710	200			
Arabic	15,260	149			
Czech	15,090	126			
Russian	12,590	89			
Japanese	10,500	62			
Estonian	10,110	50			
Lithuanian	9,985	40			
Slovak	9,465	30			
Latvian	9,250	21			
Danish	4,690	8			
Romanian	4,455	5			
Flemish	3,190	3			
Swedish	2,210	1			
Norwegian	2,160	1			
Welsh	1,175				
Icelandic	995				
Slovene	375				
Gaelic	370				

*Assuming the twin hypotheses that marriages are made randomly from a national list and that the children (two per marriage) adopt the language of the parent from the larger language group

TABLE 21
Simulating the disappearance of languages world-wide*

	Generations				
	1st	10th	30th	40th	60th
Mandarin	515,000,000	1,622,436,950	2,949,244,353	2,978,595,421	2,982,134,064
English	265,000,000	401,419,237	15,165,493	1,659,664	19,178
Hindi/Urdu	185,000,000	199,223,832	5,213,324	566,174	6,536
Spanish	145,000,000	124,564,091	2,735,680	296,213	3,419
Russian	135,000,000	97,023,541	1,903,098	205,705	2,373
German	100,000,000	62,330,601	1,130,228	122,027	1,408
Japanese	95,000,000	52,898,378	907,587	97,914	1,130
Arabic	90,000,000	45,198,820	740,448	79,833	921
Bengali	85,000,000	37,184,040	576,468	62,109	716
Portuguese	85,000,000	37,184,040	576,468	62,109	716
French	65,000,000	25,166,072	372,809	40,144	463
Italian	55,000,000	19,029,881	271,738	29,248	337
Javanese	55,000,000	19,029,881	271,738	29,248	337
Telugu	55,000,000	19,029,881	271,738	29,248	337
Ukrainian	50,000,000	15,593,624	215,588	23,195	267
Korean	45,000,000	13,426,376	183,273	19,715	227
Punjabi	42,000,000	12,039,931	162,526	17,481	202
Tamil	38,000,000	10,504,523	140,412	15,101	174
Marathi	37,000,000	9,573,951	125,816	13,529	156
Polish	37,000,000	9,573,951	125,816	13,529	156
Vietnamese	37,000,000	9,573,951	125,816	13,529	156
Turkish	35,000,000	8,491,895	109,815	11,806	136
Thai	33,000,000	7,775,218	99,846	10,733	124
Gujarati	31,000,000	7,106,853	90,682	9,748	112
Romanian	27,000,000	6,039,420	76,629	8,236	95

*Assuming that marriages are determined randomly from a world list and that the children (two per marriage) choose, in 60 per cent of the cases, the language of the parent whose language group is the more numerous. The simulation has for its starting-point the 200 languages with more than 1 million speakers in Muller's enumeration. The table records the evolution of the 25 most numerous.

4

Multilingual states and multi-ethnic languages

Should a state that is multilingual regret that fact or congratulate itself? Can a unilingual state better integrate its economy, mobilize its political system, develop and diffuse its culture? Conversely, is it better for a language to be concentrated in one single state, to express one single political ideology, to have only one type of economic system? Or should it, for survival and diffusion, diversify its options? I ask these questions in the same way that one asks whether the two-party system is better than the multiparty or the single-party system. In both cases, it is unreasonable to give an answer without knowing which state is involved, or its objectives, its internal hierarchies, its attitudes, and, above all, the degree of reciprocal tolerance among its various social forces. Switzerland's multilingualism is probably a factor of political tolerance; the multilingualism of the Soviet Union is just as probably quite the opposite – a cause of intolerance. The multilingualism of Canada, Belgium, or Singapore does not seem to result in economic retardation; but Nigeria's is, very likely, one of the factors responsible for the shambles of its economy.

Even if we were to compare every state in the world and found a positive statistical relation between multilingualism and underdevelopment, how could we control the effect of historical, demographic, economic, and social factors? It would be a useless exercise.[1] Let us then proceed in simple descriptive fashion, in order to establish a typology, and allow ourselves to

1 For a quantitative study of the relation between the degree of linguistic partitioning of a nation and its level of economic development, see Pool (1972), who notes that countries that are very split up linguistically are always underdeveloped, while developed countries have a fairly high degree of linguistic homogeneity. If factors other than the linguistic are brought into play, then few states can be classed as ethnically homogeneous – only 9 per cent in 1971, according to Connor's 1978 classifications.

make occasional suppositions that seem appropriate. Let us take as our unit of contextual analysis first the state, and then the language.

Unilingual and multilingual states

Strictly speaking, there is no such thing as a unilingual state. Nations as homogeneous as Poland and Japan have citizens whose dominant language is not that of the majority and people who do not understand the national language. However, from our point of view, it matters little whether a state is 100 per cent or only 95 per cent unilingual.

In some states, linguistic statistics are trustworthy; but in most of them, they are not. No other country offers data as useful as those from the Canadian census, which distinguishes 'mother-tongue still understood,' 'official language or language known,' and 'language usually spoken at home.' Some states, such as Belgium and Pakistan, that could obtain similar data are unwilling, for political reasons, to assess their linguistic equilibrium;[2] other countries do not have the administrative machinery to take relatively precise linguistic measurements. Further, according to how a minority is defined – by the dominant language, language of ethnic identity, language learned, or language understood – considerable variations occur even when the statistics are completely trustworthy; for example, for Gaelic in Ireland, the figures vary from 2 per cent to 30 per cent.

I must thus have recourse to a certain amount of approximation as I proceed. The category 'habitual tongue' of Table 22 is unusual. The most frequently used definition classifies individuals according to their mother-tongue. However, this definition does not permit meaningful comparison between 'immigration' and 'stable population' countries. Only 87 per cent of Americans and only 90 per cent of anglophone Canadians have English as their mother-tongue; yet more than 90 per cent of Americans and more than 90 percent of anglophone Canadians use English in their daily lives and in their relation with public authorities. For countries little affected by immigration, I have assumed that the data on the mother-tongue give an approximate measure of the language in current use; but for 'immigration' countries, I have taken statistics (where they exist) on the language in current use, and where they do not exist, I have extrapolated from statistics and studies dealing specifically with the state in question. The basic data are those adduced by Muller (1964), Katzner (1975), Banks and Overstreet (1981), Voegelin (1977), Barrett (1982), and Kloss and McConnell (1974–81). The grid of Table 22 is broad enough to reduce to very few the

2 The latest Belgian linguistic census dates from 1947.

TABLE 22
States whose central government is officially unilingual,* classified according to the percentage of the citizens who use habitually the official language, in public (the estimates are approximate)

	Language*	Type 1 (90–100%)	Type 2 (50–90%)	Type 3 (less than 50%)
Albania	Albanian	x		
Algeria	Arabic		x	
Angola	Portuguese			x
Argentina	Spanish	x		
Australia	English	x		
Austria	German	x		
Bahamas	English	x		
Bahrain	Arabic	x		
Bangladesh	Bengali	x		
Barbados	English	x		
Belize	English			x
Benin	French			x
Bhutan	Dzonkha (Tibetan)		x	
Bolivia	Spanish			x
Botswana	English			x
Burkina-Fasso	French			x
Brazil	Portuguese	x		
Brunei	Malay	x		
Bulgaria	Bulgarian	x		
Burma	Burmese		x	
Cape Verde Islands	Portuguese			x
Central African Republic	French			x
Chad	French			x
Chile	Spanish	x		
China (People's Republic)	Mandarin		x	
Colombia	Spanish		x	
Comoro Islands	French			x
Congo	French			x
Costa Rica	Spanish	x		
Cuba	Spanish	x		
Denmark	Danish	x		
Djibouti	French			x
Dominica	English	x		
Dominican Republic	Spanish	x		
Ecuador	Spanish		x	
Egypt	Arabic	x		
El Salvador	Spanish	x		
Equatorial Guinea	Spanish			x
Ethiopa	Amharic			x

TABLE 22 (continued)

	Language*	Type 1 (90–100%)	Type 2 (50–90%)	Type 3 (less than 50%)
Fiji	English		x	
France	French	x		
Gabon	French			x
Gambia	English			x
Germany, West	German	x		
Germany, East	German	x		
Ghana	English			x
Greece	Greek	x		
Grenada	English	x		
Guatemala	Spanish		x	
Guinea	French			x
Guinea-Bissau	Portuguese			x
Guyana	English		x	
Haiti	French			x
Honduras	Spanish	x		
Hungary	Hungarian	x		
Iceland	Icelandic	x		
Indonesia	Malay			x
Iran	Persian		x	
Iraq	Arabic		x	
Italy	Italian	x		
Ivory Coast	French			x
Jamaica	English	x		
Japan	Japanese	x		
Jordan	Arabic	x		
Kampuchea	Khmer		x	
Korea, North	Korean	x		
Korea, South	Korean	x		
Kuwait	Arabic	x		
Laos	Lao		x	
Lebanon	Arabic	x		
Liberia	English			x
Libya	Arabic	x		
Liechtenstein	German	x		
Malawi	English			x
Malaysia	Malay		x	
Maldives	Divehi	x		
Mali	French			x
Mauritius	English			x
Mexico	Spanish		x	
Monaco	French	x		
Mongolia	Khalkha (Mongolian)		x	
Morocco	Arabic		x	
Mozambique	Portuguese			x

TABLE 22 (continued)

	Language*	Type 1 (90–100%)	Type 2 (50–90%)	Type 3 (less than 50%)
Nauru	English			x
Nepal	Nepali		x	
Netherlands	Dutch	x		
New Zealand	English	x		
Nicaragua	Spanish	x		
Niger	French			x
Nigeria	English			x
Oman	Arabic	x		
Panama	Spanish	x		
Papua–New Guinea	English			x
Paraguay	Spanish			x
Peru	Spanish		x	
Poland	Polish	x		
Portugal	Portuguese	x		
Qatar	Arabic	x		
Romania	Romanian		x	
Rwanda	French			x
St Kitts and Nevis	English	x		
St Lucia	English	x		
St Vincent and Grenadines	English	x		
San Marino	Italian	x		
São Tomé and Principe	Portuguese			x
Saudi Arabia	Arabic	x		
Senegal	French			x
Sierra Leone	English			x
Solomon Islands	English			x
Somalia	Somali	x		
Spain	Castilian		x	
Sudan	Arabic		x	
Surinam	Dutch			x
Sweden	Swedish	x		
Syria	Arabic		x	
Taiwan	Mandarin			x
Tanzania	Swahili			x
Thailand	Thai		x	
Togo	French			x
Tonga	English			x
Trinidad and Tobago	English		x	
Tunisia	Arabic	x		
Turkey	Turkish	x		
Tuvalu (Ellice Islands)	English			x
Uganda	English			x

TABLE 22 (continued)

	Language*	Type 1 (90–100%)	Type 2 (50–90%)	Type 3 (less than 50%)
USSR	Russian		x	
United Arab Emirates	Arabic	x		
United Kingdom	English	x		
United States†	English	x		
Uruguay	Spanish	x		
Venezuela	Spanish	x		
Vietnam	Vietnamese		x	
Yemen, Arab Republic	Arabic	x		
Yemen, People's Democratic Republic	Arabic	x		
Zaire	French			x
Zambia	English			x
Zimbabwe	English			x

*In nearly all cases I have followed the classification of the Canadian Commission for Official Languages (Berdoulay et al 1980). The exceptions are the following: unlike the commission, I have considered Comoro, Djibouti, Rwanda, and Botswana as unilingual. Inversely, I considered Kiribati as multilingual because of the use made of Kiribati in its parliament and executive. Further, taking into consideration its 1984 language law, Luxembourg is treated as multilingual although the situation has not changed markedly since 1984, the date at which, in the French edition of this book, I had put Luxembourg in the 'officially unilingual' category. Botswana, Papua–New Guinea, Paraguay, Rwanda, and Tonga, classified here as unilingual, could arguably have been put, like Kiribati, in the multilingual category.

The estimates of speakers of the official languages are based on the works of Barrett (1982), Banks (1981), Kloss and McConnell (1947–81), Voegelin (1977), Katzner (1975), and Muller (1964).
†If one includes illegal resident aliens, the United States should be moved to the second column.

number of tangential cases. These few cases (Romania, Colombia, and Bulgaria) lie around either 90 per cent or 50 per cent, and if they were moved into the adjacent category, the typology suggested by our classification would not be noticeably altered.

States officially or effectively unilingual in their central institutions are of three different types.[3] The first type – the linguistically unified state (90–100 per cent in Table 22) – is most frequently found in Europe and

3 A state may declare a language official, even if it is used only in symbolic fashion. Peru can proclaim an indigenous language, Quechua, as an official language, even though it uses Quechua in its government less than Senegal uses Wolof – though Wolof has only

America. The second type (50–90 per cent), of which there are only a few examples, whether in Europe (Spain and the Soviet Union), South America (Paraguay and Peru), Africa (Somalia and Sudan), or Asia (Thailand and Kampuchea), represents situations of incomplete dominance by an indigenous language. In such states, though multilingual, the dominant language alone is recognized and used as the official language of the central government; subordinate languages are often located on the peripheries, and the dominant language plays the role of lingua franca throughout the whole state. These states are, in the 1980s, at the level where many states of type 1 were in the nineteenth century. France and Mexico were type 2 a hundred years ago; in 2080, if their evolution resembles that of France, Peru and perhaps even the Soviet Union could be in the linguistic category of type 1.

The third category (less than 50 per cent in Table 22) combines two different types which a more diversified classification would no doubt have enabled us to distinguish. The bigger sub-category is provided by the African states whose official language is not indigenous but international – French or English – and is used for the governing of a state in which no other language has either the numbers, or the prestige, or – often – sufficient semantic quality to allow it to become a language of government. In some cases, an indigenous language (Wolof in Senegal, Ruanda in Rwanda, Susu in Equatorial Guinea, for example) is sufficiently distinguishable from other local languages that it may one day become the national language and replace French. But in most cases in black West Africa there does not appear to be any indigenous language capable of taking exclusive control of the state and using this control to impose itself by the force of law; it is hard to see how the state could dispense with a lingua franca that is all the more acceptable because it is foreign.

The second and smaller sub-category of type 3 consists of Luxembourg before 1984, Haiti, Taiwan, Ethiopia, and Indonesia. Although officially unilingual between 1948 and 1984, Luxembourg was and continues to be trilingual, with French as the language of law and administration, German one of the languages of the press and of business, and Luxemburgian the language of everyday life. Luxembourg is a small state, the site of international institutions, an enclave between powerful neighbours who were frequently at war for long periods. Luxembourg's army cannot protect it

---

the status of a national language. Linguistic fractionalism is not the same in the two countries; to proclaim Wolof an official language would offend many ethnic groups who do not wish to be relegated to the second rank.

My classification of bilingual states with few exceptions follows that of the Canadian commissioner for official languages (see note to Table 22).

against its neighbours and the country lacks mountains to isolate it like Andorra; but like Andorra it is a curious accident of European history – a state that owes its survival to its smallness. Its indigenous language was too sparsely distributed and too feeble to impose itself in politics or commerce, but the very fact that it has survived in the family and colloquial speech illustrates clearly the protective effect of a border on a minority language. The language conflicts in Luxembourg are less among groups than within the individual, who is drawn in different directions by his triglossia, which impels him to use Luxemburgian at home and among friends, French or German in business correspondence, and French in government and cemetery (Hoffmann 1979; Jakob 1981).

In Haiti, where the official language is international-type French, the tongue of the former colonizers has become indigenous, though it split between the Creole of the people and a classical type of French (Stewart 1962). The fact that there are only two principal languages, both with numerous common bonds, favours linguistic unification which would, how-ever, require rapprochement of the classes and the social strata that would appear most unlikely under present conditions. Depending on whether this hypothetical rapprochement comes about from below or from above, as a result of prosperity or of revolution, the chance of one or the other language achieving a clear-cut victory would vary considerably. Classical French has its quality and its universality working for it, while Creole has the numbers.

Taiwan presents another classic case of domination of one language by another as a result of state control. The official language, Mandarin, has been imposed by the ruling political class – the Nationalists, who fled main-land China after their defeat and sought refuge on the island, where they took control at the end of the 1940s. More than 80 per cent of the Taiwanese speak Fukienese, but the language of government is Mandarin. However, the political control exercised by the former mainlanders does not fully explain how Mandarin may soon reduce considerably the areas of use of the indigenous language. Mandarin benefits from the fact that it is the lingua franca for all the various Chinese tongues.

In Ethiopia, the official language, Amharic, is spoken fluently by a third of the population; but unlike other languages with as many speakers (Galla in particular) Amharic is the language of the country's political centre.

Finally, Indonesia offers the example of an official language that is the mother-tongue of only a small minority of the population. Less than 10 per cent of Indonesians learn Malay as their first language, but three-quarters of them learn it at school. Indonesia shows how quickly a national language can supplant a former colonial language. In the space of a generation, a

TABLE 23
States officially multilingual in the operation of their central government*

State	Official languages			
Afghanistan	Dari	Pashto		
Belgium	French	Dutch		
Brunei	Malay	English		
Burundi	French	Rundi (Kirundi)		
Cameroon	French	English		
Canada	English	French		
Cyprus	Greek	Turkish		
Czechoslovakia	Czech	Slovak		
Finland	Finnish	Swedish		
India	English	Hindi		
Ireland	English	Gaelic		
Israel	Hebrew	Arabic		
Kenya	English	Swahili		
Kiribati	Kiribati	English		
Lesotho	English	Sesotho		
Luxembourg	French	Luxemburgian	German	
Madagascar	French	Malagasy		
Malta	Maltese	English		
Mauritania	French	Arabic		
Norway	Bokmal	Nynorsk		
Pakistan	English	Urdu		
Philippines	English	Pilipino (Tagalog)		
Seychelles	French	English		
Singapore	English	Mandarin	Malay	Tamil
South Africa	Afrikaans	English		
Sri Lanka	Sinhalese	English	Tamil	
Switzerland	German	French		
Swaziland	Siswati	English		
Vanuatu	French	English		
Vatican	Italian	Latin		
Western Samoa	English	Samoan		
Yugoslavia	Serbo-Croatian	Slovene	Macedonian	

*Here, as in Table 22, I have, unless otherwise stated (see the note to Table 22), followed the Berdoulay classification.

Since the partition of the island, Cyprus has ceased to be in fact bilingual but remains so in theory. The bilingualism of Ireland and the Philippines is also (see the text) mostly symbolic. Some states, in addition to their official languages, give 'national' status to other languages, for example Ruanda in Rwanda, Bichlamar in Vanuatu, Romansch in Switzerland, Guarani in Paraguay, and Motu and Pidgin in Papua–New Guinea. A case could thus be made for removing Cyprus from the table and adding Botswana, Rwanda, Paraguay, and Papua–New Guinea to it.

lingua franca of foreign origin – Dutch – has been replaced by one that is indigenous to the region – Malay. The fact that the foreign language was Dutch rather than English – as was the case in Malaysia or in the Philippines – no doubt contributed to the speed of the substitution (Beer 1977; Perez and Santiago, undated).

To sum up, type 2 states and some type 3 states (Taiwan, Haiti, Indonesia, and Ethiopia) are in the same situation that France was in two centuries ago. An indigenous, minority language is on the way to reducing and ultimately eliminating the other indigenous tongues in competition with it through control of the state and, through it, the administrative machinery and the school system. The remaining states of type 3, the majority, have, like late medieval France, and England, a foreign tongue without popular roots. An African evolution similar to the European would require that the foreign lingua franca be replaced by an indigenous language brought into power by a victorious ethnic group. This is beginning to happen in East Africa, where Swahili is winning at the expense of English. In Central and West Africa, because of linguistic multiplicity and fragmentation, few indigenous languages can hope to impose themselves (Calvet 1979), except perhaps in Senegal and Mali. In contrast to what took place in fragmented medieval Europe, when communication was slow and difficult, the foreign languages of administration – French and English – may become indigenous in the twenty-first century, as happened in the Caribbean in the last century.

The distinctions we have just made, although they started off as strictly political, since they took only the official language into account, have led us to classifications akin to those suggested by Fishman et al (1975) and Houis (1976). Fishman distinguishes four kinds of state: unilingual, bilingual (with no highly developed language), bilingual (with one tongue a so-called language of civilization), and bilingual (with more than one such language). Houis speaks of four types: unilingual, multilingual (in which one language has been dominant for some considerable time), multilingual (with the dominant language of recent origin), and finally states with no dominant language. In these two typologies, as in ours, we shall recognize the contrast (already noted) between young and old states, between young and old civilizations, and between states whose powers are growing and states on the decline. These distinctions are even more clearly apparent in the study of officially bilingual states.

A more refined analytical grid would have enabled us to distinguish administrative systems that are unilingual both in writing and speech and others that are unilingual in writing but bilingual or multilingual in speech. Woulof is often spoken in Senegalese government and administrative circles, Sango in those of the Central African Republic, Bangui in those of Mali, and Pidgin increasingly in the parliament of Papua–New Guinea.

Classifying the 32 multilingual states listed in Table 23 according to the number of official languages in central institutions shows that 84 per cent are bilingual, 13 per cent trilingual, and only 3 per cent quadrilingual. Only two (Cameroon and Vanuatu) have two foreign official languages; twelve (Brunei, India, Kenya, Lesotho, Madagascar, Mauritania, Pakistan, Philippines, Samoa, Singapore, Sri Lanka, Swaziland) have indigenous and foreign official languages; and in the rest – some 60 per cent – the official languages are indigenous. In this last category we find, almost exclusively, European states or states with European culture; Afghanistan is the one exception. In contrast, the first two categories contain no states claiming a popular culture that is European.

This classification into three categories is clearly somewhat artificial. There are probably as many, if not more, Asian Indians as there are Irish for whom English is their mother-tongue; and perhaps as many Filipinos who learn English as their mother-tongue as there are Italian Swiss. I call English a foreign language in India and the Philippines because only a small percentage of Indians claim English as a mother-tongue and in the Philippines it is a language of relatively recent implantation only just beginning to take root.

Relatively few multilingual states have the same official languages. French and English share four states (Cameroon, Canada, Seychelles, and Vanuatu), while Hindi/Urdu and English share India and Pakistan. English is an official language in 19 multilingual states, French in 10, and German and Tamil in 2; the other languages appear as official in only one single multilingual state (unless Afrikaans and Dutch are regarded as one language, in which case this language would appear in two states). Most of the languages of the officially multilingual countries listed in Table 23 are thus either local or regional languages. As a rule, however, at least one of the official languages extends beyond the geographical area of the state in which it is used. In fact, among the 32 multilingual states in Table 23, in only Czechoslovakia and Norway does bilingualism encompass two languages that do not extend beyond the borders of the state.

The rarity of linguistic autarky is explained by historical reasons apparent from a simple reading of Table 23. The officially multilingual state is often a former colony whose independence is fairly recent. The language of the colonizer is then faced either with other colonial languages (Cameroon, Canada, South Africa, Vanuatu) or – more often – with indigenous languages.[4] When a multilingual state is not a former colony, then it is invari-

4 Fishman et al (1975) note that the status of 'former British colony' is the best indication of use of English by a state other than Britain.

ably a small state on the borders of one or more large countries. It is not pure chance that none of the great military powers of today's world is officially bilingual. Modern states geared for war, imperial states, protect their rear even when they are extending their power outward; the assimilation of peripheral minorities is logical for a power that wishes to present a monolithic front to the outside world. The Soviet Union is acting no differently from nineteenth-century France, except that it needs more time to assimilate its minorities, for it faces strong resistance from its subordinate ethnic groups.

Some states glory in their multilingualism, which they see as a sign, if not a guarantee, of tolerance. When Renan defined a nation by its will to live together rather than by its possession of a common language, he was thinking specifically of Switzerland. If bilingualism is a gift of history, it is a gift that history reserves for small, weak states. Austria-Hungary, which became multilingual in its administration only a few decades before it disappeared under the onslaughts of Europe's national wars (also wars of languages), did not survive its ambitions for power; but Switzerland and Belgium, more introverted, maintained their multi-ethnic unity.

The multilingual states of Table 23 are not all multilingual to the same degree; some are so in symbolic fashion only, others are more or less truly so. Let us screen these states to come up with the different categories shown in Table 24. The language of postage stamps, bank notes, and passports provides a first measure of symbolic bilingualism. Surprisingly, some officially multilingual states have unilingual stamps: French in Burundi and Luxembourg, English in Singapore, for example. Bank notes and coinage are unilingual in Norway and Swaziland, while passports are unilingual (English) in Papua–New Guinea, Singapore, and Swaziland. A few of the 32 states listed in Table 23 have for various reasons not proclaimed their multilingualism through the medium of monetary or postal communication, or of travel beyond their frontiers, but that number is diminishing. Norwegian stamps and Luxembourgian bank notes used to be monolingual; they are now bilingual.

Tests of effective use of official languages for political communication, either oral or written, give varying results depending on whether they cover the promulgation of laws, parliamentary debates, conversation at meetings of the executive, or the use of the working language within the central administration.

Luxembourg's laws are written exclusively in French. Kiribati, the Philippines, and Singapore pass their laws solely in English – partly to retain the semantic bond with pre-independence jurisprudence, but also because the national languages lack words or are not yet sufficiently stan-

TABLE 24
Use of official languages in central institutions

Very unbalanced*	Unbalanced	Nearly evenly unbalanced
Afghanistan?	Brunei?	Belgium
Burundi	Canada	
Cameroun	Czechoslovakia	
Cyprus†	Kiribati	
Finland	Lesotho	
India	Madagascar	
Ireland	Switzerland	
Israel	Vatican	
Kenya	Western Samoa	
Luxembourg	Yugoslavia	
Malta		
Mauritania		
Norway		
Pakistan		
Philippines		
Seychelles		
Singapore		
South Africa		
Sri Lanka		
Swaziland		
Vanuatu		

*One could justifiably add to the 'very unbalanced' category the countries where a local language is used in parliamentary debates but not in written communication, notably Botswana, Comoro, Papua-New Guinea, and Rwanda.
†Following the partition of the island into a Greek and a Turkish zone, each sector has become unilingual.
?Indicates a lack of recent information.

dardized to permit of acceptably accurate translation. In Singapore, translation into Mandarin, Tamil, and Malay would be costly for a largely symbolic operation.

In most of the states in Table 23, members can use in parliament the official language of their choice. There are only four major exceptions. Lesotho's parliament uses only Lesotho (which is then translated into English); Luxembourg's, Luxembourgian and French (German is not used in parliament); Malta's, Maltese; and that of the Philippines, English. In Ireland, debates are more than 95 per cent in English (although facilities exist for immediate translation). It is remarkable that so many bilingual states should so often be bilingual in their parliamentary assemblies. It is a different story within executives and cabinets; these bodies are meant not for speeches and delayed consideration, but for conversation and quick decisions. Since the Nationalists came into power in South Africa, their cabinet has operated in Afrikaans; Cameroon's uses French, Finland's Finnish, Yugoslavia's Serbo-Croatian, Switzerland's German, and Malta's Maltese. Conversely, the cabinets of India, Ireland, Kiribati, Kenya, Pakistan, the Philippines, and Singapore all operate in English.

For an executive to be able to function in two different languages, either the two languages must be mutually comprehensible, so that translation may be dispensed with (as in Norway and Czechoslovakia) or known to all (as in Burundi, Lesotho, Luxembourg, Malta, and Western Samoa). Alternatively, if the two languages are not known by every participating member, there must be a system of translation. Few bilingual states make use of immediate translation at cabinet meetings. Belgium does it systematically; Canada has done so intermittently. In the rest of the cases – notably Cameroon, Finland, India, Ireland, Israel, Kiribati, Mauritania, Pakistan, the Philippines, Singapore, South Africa, Switzerland, and Yugoslavia – one of the languages is dominant. The same is true within the public service, where one of the official languages ranks as the working language (see Appendix). Of all the non-diglossal bilingual states, only Belgium approaches equilibrium, though even there, when ministers are deprived of their interpreters, French resumes its dominant role.

If we could bring Table 24 to life, and give it historical depth, we would see how some minority languages – however official they may be – cannot advance beyond symbolic bilingualism, while others advance from postage-stamps to passports over the years until they appear in the text of laws, then in parliamentary or ministerial debates, and finally in schools and universities (see Table 25). Often, over the past hundred years, these successive victories have corresponded to the 'conquests' of cities by countrysides; this was the case with Finnish in Helsinki, and French in Montreal.[5]

There are two types of officially multilingual states – those with indigenous official languages (Canada and Switzerland, for example) and those with a foreign official language that serves as a lingua franca (see Table 26). The latter category subdivides into states in which the foreign language is competing with an indigenous tongue spoken by a majority of the population, as in Malta and Swaziland, and states in which the indigenous languages are so numerous and fragmented that the foreign tongue is the only linguistic cement acceptable both at the political centre and among the ethnic peripheries, as in India and most of black Africa. When one of several official languages is foreign, that language is either French or

5 On this subject, see the relations of cost of mobilization and assimilation as defined by Deutsch (1953).

TABLE 25
Key dates in progress of Netherlandish in Belgium since 1830

1883	Bilingual education in the secondary schools of Flanders
1884	Bilingual stamps
1886	First speech in Netherlandish in parliament
1898	Official language
1898	Laws published in Netherlandish
1921	Language of public administration, the principle of territoriality is established.
1930	Ghent gives university instruction in Netherlandish.
1935	Language of the courts of law
1938	Language of the army
1962	Exclusive language of public administration and schools in Flanders (Brussels being the major exception)
1967	The constitution of 1830 is officially translated into Netherlandish.
1968	The European Court of Justice rejects a complaint against the principle of territorial unilingualism.

English, except in the Vatican; in the two extreme cases where all the official languages are foreign, French and English share power. The colonial rivalries of France and England lie at the origin of four multilingual states – Cameroon, Canada, Seychelles, and Vanuatu. In Canada, English and French – both imposed by conquest – have become indigenous; it is too early to say whether a similar implantation will occur in the other three states.

In the countries in the second column of Table 26, the demographic factor shows two probable types of evolution. When the indigenous language is spoken either as the mother-tongue or as the lingua franca of 50 per cent or more of the population, the indigenous language may eventually supplant the foreign one. When the indigenous official language is spoken by less than 50 per cent of the population – as in Burundi, India, and Lesotho – the foreign language has a better chance either of becoming indigenous or of maintaining its position in government, precisely because it is foreign and thereby avoids the problems of dominance and precedence among local languages. Swaziland, officially bilingual, is not very different from officially unilingual states such as Morocco and Algeria. The élites of the latter two states are unable to dispense completely with French as the language of government; but replacement of the foreign language by the indigenous in the administrations of North Africa seems merely a question of time. The same holds for Tanzania, where Swahili is constantly gaining ground. In the Tanzanian parliament, as in cabinet meetings, English is rarely used, except for technical discussion and the drafting of laws. Although laws are drafted in English, local courts operate almost exclusively in Swahili; intermediate-

TABLE 26
Indigenous or foreign official languages

Approximate percentage of the state's population that uses habitually the more numerous of the official languages	All the official languages indigenous	One at least of the official languages foreign	All the official languages foreign
90–100	Finland Ireland Luxembourg (Paraguay)†	Brunei* Samoa Swaziland Madagascar Malta Vatican? (Tonga)	
75–90	Cyprus‡ Norway Yugoslavia§ Israel	Pakistan Mauritania Kiribati? (Rwanda)	
50–75	Afghanistan Belgium Canada Czechoslovakia Switzerland South Africa#	Singapore‖ Philippines Sri Lanka (Botswana)	
25–50	Vanuatu	Burundi India Kenya	
Under 25		Lesotho (Papua–New Guinea)?	Cameroon Seychelles

*Counting only the citizens, thus excluding most of the Chinese community
†The states in parentheses are those that were not listed as multilingual in Table 23 but could have been under different criteria.
‡Before the de facto partition of the island
§Counting Serbian and Croatian as a single language
‖The balance is shifting to English away from Mandarin. Singapore should thus possibly be ranked in the category immediately above.
#Counting whites only
?Indicates a very tentative classification.

level courts use both languages, while English retains its exclusivity at the highest level, the state's Court of Appeal.

The progressive rise of Swahili in Tanzania, like that of Malay in Malaysia, is the mark of a seemingly irreversible evolution. Technical reasons explain why English maintains its position in legislation and regulation while losing ground in the political sphere: neither Swahili nor Malay is yet well equipped for the precise expression of modern technology. In a legislative system in which judicial precedent plays an essential role, change of language poses problems. However, in Swaziland, as in Malaya and Morocco, the indigenous language is so strong that the foreign language seems unlikely to maintain itself for long in the strongholds to which it is now confined.

In the other countries in the second column of Table 26 that do not top the 50 per cent figure, the foreign language has the advantage. In the Philippines, as in India and Singapore, English has remained or become the prime language of government. For Chinese to compete seriously with English in Singapore, 75 per cent of Singapore's Chinese would have to speak the same language, for despite a policy (now practically abandoned) of promoting Mandarin, the living Chinese languages are still the regional dialects, the most important of which, Hokkien, accounts for no more than 40 per cent of the total. In the competition between the two lingua francas English has the advantage, the schools having abandoned their attempt to make Mandarin a language of instruction. In the 1960s Mandarin primary schools had as many students as their English counterparts. In 1980 enrolment in the former had dropped to 10 per cent of the school population. It dropped further to 5 per cent in 1983 when the government decreed that starting in 1987 the language of instruction, in all primary schools, would be English. In the Philippines, a policy of systematic diffusion of Pilipino could possibly reverse the advantage of English, especially if democratization of the political system were to replace the anglicized élite by rulers for whom English was not a familiar language. As for India, it is hard to see how, even in the long term, Hindi could replace English without creating violent centrifugal tensions among the numerous minority indigenous languages on the geographical peripheries of the federation (Khokle 1986, Racine 1986).

In contrast with the last two columns of Table 26, the first column does not list any cases – other than Vanuatu – where the most often used official language is that of less than 50 per cent of the population. It does, however, list three cases (if we ignore for the moment the states whose names appear in parentheses) where the preferred language is that of more than 90 per cent of the inhabitants – Ireland, Finland, and Luxembourg. The first is in fact a unilingual state, Gaelic being little more than a 'flag' language; the second is on the way to becoming unilingual; the third is an unusual case of triglossia. Cyprus is no longer bilingual except in theory; and Israel is not really bilingual except at the level of local administration and Arab affairs.

The list of states that are factually as well as legally bilingual, and in which the official language is also indigenous, is thus reduced to nine: six European states (Belgium, Czechoslovakia, Finland, Luxembourg, Switzerland, and Yugoslavia) and three non-European – one in North America (Canada), another in Africa (South Africa), and the third in Asia (Afghanistan). To these nine, one may have to add Brunei for which I lack, at the time of writing, post-independence (1984) data. These states are all either small, long-standing buffers between great powers (Afghanistan, Belgium, Switzerland, and Yugoslavia); or the remains of former colonies or shattered empires (Canada, Finland, South Africa and Yugoslavia).

If we add Botswana, Papua–New Guinea, Paraguay, Rwanda, and Tonga (bracketed on Table 26) to the list of bilingual states, the overall pattern is not modified, but a contrast is enhanced, in the top left-hand corner of the table, between diglossic and non-diglossic multilingual states. In the former (Paraguay and Luxembourg) role differentiation in the use of the languages helps maintain the less politically powerful ones at a high level of use and knowledge, while in the latter (Finland and Ireland), in the absence of role 'reserves' or strong territorial protection, the minority languages are in an increasingly weak position.

Uni-state and multi-state languages

The measures of the power of a language set out in the preceding chapter take no account of the fact that although most languages are concentrated within a single state, others are found in several countries, sometimes dispersed over several continents. Let us pick up our analysis where we left off and distinguish three types of language: non-state, single-state, and multi-state. Applied to ethnic criteria, the same typology will allow us to speak of uni- or multi-racial languages, uni- or multi-religious languages, and uni- or multi-ideological languages.

State and sub-state languages

The comprehensive breakdown in Table 28 shows that 63 languages had at least one state in 1982; a less comprehensive breakdown – excluding Ireland's Gaelic, the Tswana of Botswana, the Guarani of Paraguay, the Tongan of Tonga, the Tamil of Singapore and Sri Lanka, the Kirundi of Burundi, and the Motu and Pidgin of Papua, and treating Nynorsk as a

TABLE 27
Sub-state languages, by number of speakers*

Over 20 million	5–20 million	2–5 million
Cantonese	Kannada	Armenian
Wu	Malayalam	Mandingo
Fukienese	Oriya	Sindhi
Javanese	Rajasthani	Sesotho
Telugu	Sundanese	Twi-Fante
Ukrainian	Visayan	Uighur
Punjabi	Hausa	Yiddish
Marathi	Azerbaidjani	Zulu
Gujarati	Belorussian	Ilocano
Hakka	Madurese	Lithuanian
	Tibetan (Dzonkha)	Lolo
	Uzbek	Luba
	Assamese	Miao
	Berber	Mossi
	Fula	Santali
	Galla	Balinese
	Catalan	Batak
	French Creole	Bikol
	Ibo	Bugi
	Kazakh	Fang-bulu
	Tatar	Ganda
	Yoruba	Kanuri
	Quechua	Kashmiri
		Makua
		Mbundu
		Rundi
		Shan
		Shona
		Xhosa
		Tswana
		Chichewa

*Based on Muller's classification (see Table 11)

simple dialectal variant of Bokmal – would reduce the toal to 60. Whether we take 63 or 60 as the total, this shows a large increase in a single generation, for in 1939 there were only 35 languages that were official languages of at least one state. But even if we take the more comprehensive total, the number of official languages still falls far short of the total number of independent states. The number of 'state-owning' languages would grow appreciably if countries such as India, Iran, Nigeria, Pakistan, or the Soviet

TABLE 28
'State-owning' languages, by number of states*

One-state languages		Multi-state languages	
Shared control	Exclusive control	Shared control	Exclusive control
Afrikaans	Albanian	Arabic (2)	Arabic (18)
Czech	Amharic	Dutch (1)	Dutch (2)
Dari	Bengali	English (18)	English (25)
Finnish	Burmese	French (9)	French (19)
Gaelic	Bulgarian	German (2)	German (3)
Guarani*	Danish	Greek (1)	Greek (1)
Hebrew‡	Divehi	Hindi/Urdu (2)	Italian (1)
Kiribati	Dzonkha	Italian (2)	Korean (2)
Latin	Farsi	Malay (2)	Malay (3)
Luxemburgian	Hungarian	Mandarin (1)	Mandarin (2)
Macedonian	Icelandic	Swedish (1)	Portuguese (7)
Malagasy	Japanese	Swahili (1)	Spanish (21)
Maltese	Khmer	Tamil (2)	Swedish (1)
Motu (Papua)†	Khalka	Turkish (1)	Swahili (1)
Pashto	Lao		Turkish (1)
Pidgin (Papua)†	Nepalese		
Pilipino†	Norwegian§		
Ruanda†	Polish		
Rundi†	Romanian		
Samoan	Russian		
Serbo-Croatian	Somali		
Sinhalese	Thai		
Siswati	Vietnamese		
Slovak			
Slovene			
Sotho			
Tongan†			
Tswana†			

*Excluding Monaco, San Marino, and Liechtenstein
†Languages of states not included in the list of multilingual states (see Table 23 and the note to Table 22)
‡Hebrew and Arabic theoretically share the government of Israel. The practice could justify putting Hebrew in the column of exclusive control.
§To be put in the column of shared control if Nynorsk and Bokmal are counted separately.

Union, were dismembered; but in the absence of war or revolution it seems improbable that the number of 'state-owning' languages will grow by more than a few units between now and the end of the century. For languages, even more than for states, the 'closed world' is beginning – one generation after Paul Valéry announced the arrival of this new era. Languages that do not have a state are poorly situated for the coming phase of the conflict of languages, which will be intensified by universal and rapid means of communication that mobilize vast masses of population into multilingual cultural, economic, and political groups. Whether these linguistic battles take place within the bosom of a state, within the framework of a region, at the level of a continent, or even globally, the languages best able to maintain themselves are those that have as their champion the state, which controls national policies and international negotiations.

In this 'closed world,' conflicts of language take place at three main levels: state, region, and world. It is at state level that tendencies to unilingualism are most noticeable; it is there that the dominant languages, the language of power, can best use the instruments of co-operation, communication, and coercion which it exercises through control of a government in the interests of linguistic homogeneity. In a region (sometimes of continental dimensions), the conflict takes place less between the dominant languages of the individuals concerned than between their second and foreign languages; it is often a battle between lingua francas that facilitate communication between neighbours. In western Europe, especially within institutions such as the European Community, the competition lies between English and French; in the Moslem Mediterranean, between English and Arabic; in black West Africa, English and French; in southeast Africa, English and Swahili; in southern Asia, either English and Malay or English and Mandarin, depending on the region; and in so-called Communist Europe, English and Russian. It is only in the Americas that the dominant regional language is no longer a bone of contention; it is English in North America and – less clearly so – Spanish in Latin America.[6] Competition among regional lingua francas is typically a contest between two languages, one of which is nearly always English – the only truly universal lingua franca, which thus assumes the role played by Latin in communication among élites and in scientific communication in Christian Europe in the Middle Ages. It is at state or world level, rather than at the regional, that the dominance of one single language is seen most clearly. In geographical terms, we can thus measure the power of a language according to whether it is the language of a state, or sub-state, and – if it is the language of a state – according to whether its power of communication extends over one state alone, over a region, over one or more continents, or even over the whole world.

6 Spanish 'owns' the biggest number of states, but economic and political power is passing to Portuguese. The dominance of Spanish as a regional language is thus less well established than that of English in North America.

Most of the sub-state languages of Table 27 (for simplicity's sake I have shown only those languages with at least 2 million speakers, from Muller's listing) are Asian or African. Languages without states, defenceless languages, they are also languages without cultural power other than locally. The foremost among them in scientific culture is Ukrainian; but it accounts for no more than 0.1 per cent of the articles listed by *Chemical Abstracts* for 1980 (see p. 72 above); and all these sub-state languages together account for less than 2 per cent of the total number of articles on chemistry in that year. In the group with 2–5 million speakers, only Armenian and Lithuanian appear in *Chemical Abstracts* for 1980, the former with 23 articles, the latter with only 8.

Among sub-state languages (Table 27), as among state languages with shared control (Table 28), a distinction should be drawn between those which, in the bosom of the state, control the central institutions, and those which, at best, control only local government (Kiribati, for example, as compared with Gaelic). Among the latter we should distinguish also those with effective control of a given territory and its local government and those that share power, even at the local level. We shall return to that distinction during the course of this chapter. The languages least able to survive are those without control of the government of either a state or a territory. The minority languages of Indonesia can no longer protect themselves by linguistic federalism, as can some minority languages of India. The abolition of federalism by Indonesia in 1950 favoured the rapid implantation of Bahasa-Indonesia, while in India the reform of federal structures during the 1950s (Roland Breton 1964) made for better correlation between provincial and linguistic boundaries and helped to check the spread of Hindi and English.

The degree of control and the extent of territory needed by a sub-state language vary according to economic development and the number of speakers of that particular language; it varies also as a function of the pressure to which the ethnic group is subjected. The pressure of English on Malayalam is less strong, less subject to rejection, than a similar pressure from Hindi. Against a foreign language the ethnic minority can defend itself better by diglossia; it can more easily isolate the language into special areas – those of administration or business, for example.

On this point, it is of interest to compare India, the Soviet Union, and the Philippines – states where the indigenous dominant language is used by only a slight majority of the population. In India Hindi is subordinate to English in the central administration and does not penetrate, or penetrates only slightly, the governmental structures of the linguistic peripheries; these facts favour the survival of minority languages. In the Philippines, Tagalog or Pilipino is similarly subordinated to English in the central government, but the minority languages are not protected by linguistic federalism. A vigorous policy of development and implantation of Pilipino could thus, as in Malaysia, impose a single indigenous language within the administration and eventually within society; the different languages of the state are of the same family and have no strong implanted written cultural traditions. In the Soviet Union, as in India, minority languages are protected by linguistic federalism, but in the Soviet Union an indigenous language, the sole language of the central state, exerts pressure on them; and since bilingualism is a one-way street (Russian implants itself in the peripheral republics, but the peripheral languages cannot implant themselves in Russia) the minority languages are in the long run in a precarious situation. Of these three states – India, the Soviet Union, and the Philippines – only in India do the sub-state languages have a good chance to maintain and even to develop themselves, at least as long as English remains the dominant language of the central state.

Languages according to the number of 'their' states

Uni-state languages that do not have exclusive control of a single state, that must share their function as official language with another or with several other languages, are typically 'small' languages, both by number of their speakers and by their economic, cultural, or military power. The most important are Serbo-Croatian with about 15 million speakers, Czech with 9 million, Pashto with 8 million, and Tagalog (Pilipino) with about 6 million; the other languages do not top the 5-million mark. Of the uni-state languages with shared control in Table 28, only Hebrew, Serbo-Croatian, Czech, and Slovak appear in at least one of the 12 hierarchies on p. 90 above. Typically, official languages that have only one state which they must share lack speakers, soldiers, and – to a lesser degree – cultural power.

Multi-state languages, with a few rare exceptions, are 'big' languages, either by number of speakers or military, economic, or cultural power. Only 2 of these 17 languages do not have exclusive control of at least one state – Hindi/Urdu and Tamil (which have only recently been promoted to the rank of official languages). Multi-statism is characteristic of the languages of explorers, of empire – languages in which conquest has been hailed, and sung, and wept. English has more than 40 states; French nearly 30; Spanish a little more than 20; but only four languages have more than 5 – English, French, Spanish, and Portuguese; while 11 of the 17 multi-state languages have more than 2.

There are three major exceptions to the rule of the bond between multi-statism and the power of the language: Russian, Japanese, and Polish. These three are powerful (especially the first two) by number of speakers, scientific production, and number of soldiers but do not control more than one state. The contrast is particularly striking when one compares the two languages – English and Russian – that dominate the world by their military power. One of them exercises sole control over 25 states spread over all the continents; the other controls only one single state, though it spreads over vast stretches of territory in two continents. English is a language of exoticism and far-off foreign lands; Russian is also a language of exoticism, but it is a stronghold language too. English has diversified its state options, Russian has concentrated them. English has pratically eliminated the minor languages competing with it in the territories of the two great states that are the source of its power – the United States and England; in contrast, Russian is locked in a multilingual fortress. As for Japanese, it is the perfect example of unity ensconced in its own castle.

Is it strength or weakness for a state not to be bound to other states by a common language? Is it strength or weakness for a language to be uni-state? At any given time the answer can only be specific. Language orients thought, provides common reference-points, and thus facilitates the formation of coalitions among states and cultures. But community of language also facilitates the infiltration of one culture or one state by another and can thus cause conflicts that can only weaken some of the countries that share a common language. The attempts to assemble Germany into one single state increased the power of that language in the nineteenth century but weakened it in the twentieth. Brought together into one single entity, German-speaking states would undoubtedly increase the power of that language; French, however, would grow less obviously, even if France spread out to include French Switzerland and Walloon Belgium. French has a better chance of maintaining itself as an international language if it remains the official language of a number of states. If it were only the French delegates who spoke French in the European committees at Brussels, and in the international organizations in Luxembourg, Strasbourg, Geneva, Rome, Paris, and New York – and even if the number of French citizens were half as large again – French would fall, in international political communication, to much the same level as German and Italian.

But if multi-statism is an advantage to a language, this advantage is even greater if the language is the sole official language and the dominant mother-tongue of the state. In relation to English, French is in a position of relative weakness that is somewhat underestimated by the number of states assigned to it in Table 28. This weakness comes from the fact that it is the exclusive official language and dominant mother-tongue of one state only –

France; in the 28 other countries in which it is an official language, it is the mother-tongue of only a minority of the population; and in the three major industrialized states, other than France, in which it is an official language (Canada, Belgium, and Switzerland) it shares power with a numerically more powerful language. Quebec's independence would have given French what the other great colonial languages – English, Spanish, and Portuguese – have obtained: at least one independent unilingual state on each of the two continents, Europe and America.

Certain languages shared by several states – as with German and Korean – lose power by being divided. But are their chances of survival and influence increased by their having diversified cultural and political options? Would Arabic be more powerful if the twenty Arab states formed but one? An ideal strategy, which would satisfy the contradictory demands of military strength on the one hand and culture on the other, would call for contiguous states speaking the same language to unite in order to increase their military strength and thus their influence in relation to neighbouring languages. But it would also call for these great unilingual states to be dispersed over several continents, so as to favour cultural variations and increase the chances of survival in the event of war. Only English approaches this ideal solution.

If control of several states is reserved without exception for the great languages, it would not seem, from the second column of Table 28, that uni-statism is tied either to number of speakers or to military strength. In this column we find Danish and Norwegian, each with less than 4 million speakers; but we find also Russian and Japanese, each with more than 100 million. We find there languages that appear under the heading of military powers (Russian, Japanese, Polish) and others, like Dzonkha and Icelandic, which have only a few hundred soldiers. Some of these languages are of prime importance in chemistry and medicine, Russian and Japanese in particular; others, like Khmer and Amharic, do not figure therein in any way. Exclusive control of a state would thus appear to be within the grasp of any language – provided, of course, that history and geography are suitable. It is easier for insular Icelandic to achieve independence than it is for the Frisian of Holland, though these two languages are similar as regards number of speakers. Slovene is just as geographically concentrated as is Albanian or Somali, and its cultural power is greater; but the relationships of regional and world strength allow it little hope – in the absence of war – of achieving independence, even if its speakers wished it.

Is it accidental that all the major languages in which democratic pluralism expresses itself appear in one or other of the two 'Exclusive control' columns of Table 28? Is it easier for a linguistically homogenous state to develop pluralist political institutions? This suggestion is usually refuted by quoting the following examples: Switzerland, Finland, Belgium, and Canada. These four states are in fact democratic *and* multilingual; but are they democratic because of, or despite, their multilingualism? Is it irrespective of the relationship between the number of languages and the political system that these four small or middle powers are caught up in a geographical and political context in which the great unilingual states set the tone? To be sure, the answer does not lie in factors that are exclusively internal or exclusively external. However, I am inclined to think that multilingualism is more frequently an obstacle to political tolerance than a cause of institutional pluralism, and that the intervening variable is the perceived legitimacy of the state. This is suggested by the correlations we obtain by linking the factor official language to the factor linguistic homogeneity. In the Soviet Union, as in Ethiopia, democratic pluralism would split the state apart along its linguistic fault-lines: Russian and Amharic cannot allow the democratization of the state they control without risking the loss of a territorial area reserved – since they are the dominant languages – for their eventual expansion. A multilingual state is not necessarily authoritarian or totalitarian; but a multilingual authoritarian state will have more difficulty in accepting democratization than will a unilingual authoritarian state, if, as is normally the case, the languages involved are those of ethnic groups with unequal powers.

On this point, it will be interesting to watch the evolution of the Iberian peninsula. Transition to democracy should be easier – if one disregards other factors – in Portugal than in Spain. And if, despite the difficulties, Spain joins Switzerland and Belgium among the multilingual democratic states, it will do it at a time when it has ceased projecting its power outward; we shall then see a previous observation confirmed – that in the present era multilingualism is easier to accept for small inward-looking states than for great powers on the rise.

Uni- and multi-ethnic languages

Danish is, in Europe, a uni-ethnic language; it is the language of one single state, one single people, one single religion, one single culture; it is the language of a single one of the great political ideologies – capitalist-type democratic pluralism; it is a language without noticeable divisions as to either level or style of life; it is a homogeneous language spread throughout a small area hardly penetrated at all by foreign immigration (in the 1960 census, only 2 per cent of the inhabitants were not born in Denmark, and the German-speaking minority also amounted to less than 2 per cent of the total). It is a language identified almost exclusively with a single state, for the other languages with which Danish is in contact in the heart of Denmark are of insignificant size, and Danish emigrants – in particular those to Canada and the United States – strive to become rapidly assimilated. In contrast, English is the typical example of a multi-racial, multi-religious, multi-cultural, and multi-ideological language. Most languages lie between these two extremes.

Language and race

The notion of race varies according to the times and according to the culture. Linnaeus divided the human species into six races: Savages, Americans, Europeans, Asiatics, Africans, and Monsters. The first was theoretical, since no one had identified it, and the last was essentially pathological in nature. Thus Linnaeus's list was not very different from the classification of the Bible, which depicted Noah's three sons – Shem, Ham, and Japhet – as ancestors of the yellow, black, and white races respectively. Blumenbach, some years after Linnaeus, distinguished five main races, all of different colouring: white, yellow, black, red (American Indian), and brown (Malaysian).[7]

Since the eighteenth century, the classifications have grown in number, and with them the criteria of differentiation (blood group, shape of nose or skull, type of hair, etc). *Encyclopaedia Britannica* of 1968 mentions hundreds of local races, which it groups into nine major 'geographical' races: American Indian, Polynesian, Micronesian, Papuan-Melanesian, Australian, Asiatic, Indian, European, and African. *La Grande Encyclopédie Larousse* of 1976 adopts Henri Valois's classification of 1967: Australoid, white-skinned, black-skinned, and yellow-skinned, which – except for the relatively few Australoids of Australia and Ceylon – follows the former

---

7 For a historical record of the idea of race see, among others, *La Grande Encyclopédie Larousse* (1976). See also Dunn et al (1975). A variant of Blumenthal's typology is used in an article dated 29 July 1982 in the Catholic newspaper *La Croix*; this divides the world Christian community according to skin colour as follows: white 48 per cent, black 19 per cent, brown 12 per cent, swarthy (*bazané*) 11 per cent, yellow 7 per cent, and red 3 per cent. In his *World Christian Encyclopedia*, Barrett (1982) classifies ethnic groups according to race (Australian Primitive, Cape Primitive, Caucasian, Negroid, and Mongoloid) and according to colour (black, brown, grey, red, bronzed, white, and yellow). Under the latter classification the browns include Dravidians, Papuans, Melanesians, and Latin American Mestizos; the greys correspond to Australoids and Hottentots; the bronzed include the inhabitants of the Middle East and certain South Americans.

division by colour, black, white, and yellow. The *International Encyclopaedia* also uses only three major groups, with many subdivisions: Caucasian, Mongoloid, Negroid.

A good universal sociological classification is virtually impossible, for the categorization that interests us, and distinguishes among ethnic groups, consists of a mixture of subjective and objective data that vary in space and time. For each language, we must be able to determine its norm or norms of classification, and to establish, in accordance with these norms, whether or not the speakers of one single tongue are concentrated within one single race. Next, we must be able to determine how each of the other languages describes, in terms of its own criteria, the race or races of the language under analysis. Now even if we wished to set up this enormous matrix of reciprocal classifications, we would have to abandon the task immediately, for lack of the most elementary data. Most human beings do not have a world perception of race – only a regional perception, often very localized. The textbooks – even if we built up a world-wide collection – would only rarely provide us with the perceptions of the students. For example, some French textbooks teach that the Indian of northern India and the Frenchmen are members of the same white race as compared to the Malayan and the Japanese, who are members of the Asiatic race; I doubt if many Frenchmen consider the Asian Indian as closer to the European than to the Asiatic. That would need checking; perceptual data do not exist.

Classifications of contemporary physical anthropology vary between major groupings into the 3 or 4 categories of the *Encyclopédie Larousse* type, the 9 or 10 categories of the *Encyclopaedia Britannica* type, the 30 or 40 categories of the type used by Dobzhansky (1962), or yet more detailed classifications into several hundred categories. A choice must be made, even though it must be somewhat arbitrary. Let us take the risk and decide to use only the nine major geographical races of Garn (1965) listed in *Encyclopaedia Britannica* – except that I shall separate (as does Dobzhansky) the Asiatics of the north (Mongolia, China, Korea, Japan) from those of the south (from Thailand to the Philippines). In other words, I am envisaging the question from the point of view of English, the dominant world language, and more particularly from the point of view of the English of North America. Of the ten races in our list (American Indian, Polynesian, Micronesian, Papuan-Melanesian, Australian, North Asiatic, South Asiatic, Asian Indian, white European, and black African), only the Australian, because of its small numbers, does not appear in Table 29.

To establish the bond between language and race, we shall take into account only official languages, as before. Let us take the state as the framework for analysis and ask ourselves, for each language, which races

TABLE 29
Uni-racial and multi-racial languages (counting only the races that number at least 10 per cent of the state where the language is official)

	American Indian	Polynesian	Micronesian	Melanesian	North Asian	South Asian	Asian Indian	White European	Black African
Afrikaans								x	x
Albanian								x	
Amharic*									x
Arabic								x	x
Bengali							x		
Bulgarian								x	
Burmese						x			
Czech								x	
Danish								x	
Dari								x	
Dutch						x	x	x	x
Dzonkha					x		x		
English	x	x	x	x	x	x	x	x	x
Farsi								x	
Finnish								x	
French				x				x	x
Gaelic								x	
German								x	
Greek								x	
Hebrew								x	
Hindi/Urdu							x		
Hungarian								x	
Icelandic								x	
Italian								x	
Japanese					x				
Khalkha					x				
Khmer						x			
Kiribati			x						
Korean					x				
Lao						x			
Latin								x	
Luxemburgian								x	
Macedonian								x	
Malagasy									x
Malay					x	x			
Maltese								x	
Mandarin					x	x			
Nepali					x		x		
Norwegian								x	

TABLE 29 (continued)

	American Indian	Polynesian	Micronesian	Melanesian	North Asian	South Asian	Asian Indian	White European	Black African
Pashto								x	
Pilipino						x			
Polish								x	
Portuguese								x	x
Romanian								x	
Russian								x	
Samoan		x							
Serbo-Croatian								x	
Sesotho									x
Sinhalese†							x		
Siswati									x
Slovak								x	
Slovene								x	
Somali									x
Spanish	x							x	x
Swahili									x
Swedish								x	
Tamil†							x		
Thai					x	x			
Turkish								x	
Vietnamese						x			

*The Ethiopian cushitic type differs from the negroid by its mixing of populations coming from Africa and Saudi Arabia. A definition of race less tied to geography could be used to classify Amharic as joining African and European races.
†If the Dravidians are included in the black rather than in the Asian Indian category, Hindi, Sinhalese, and Tamil join the black and the Asian Indian groups.

represent more than 10 per cent of the population of at least one state where this language is official. Results are shown in Table 29. Only 12 languages are multi-racial (13 if we place Tamil – hence Sinhalese since they share Sri Lanka – in the African category, on grounds of pigmentation). Among these few multi-racial languages, only 4 include more than two races (English, Spanish, Dutch and French), and French counts as tri-racial only because of the Melanesians of the small archipelago of the Tuvalus, and Dutch only because of the racially mixed population of Surinam. Through the instrumentality of language and state, French – according to our criteria – really covers only two races, the white and the black. Spanish takes in, in addition, the American Indian race. English is the only language that covers nearly all the races of Table 29. Ironically, the only race that 'escapes' English, because of its numerical weakness, is the American Indian race, the original race of the territory in which English is at its most powerful. The other languages that cover more than one race are bi-racial; most frequently, they cover either the African and the European races, or the North Asiatic and the South Asiatic. Thus, only English appears as a universal 'collector'.

The norm of Table 29, which represents over 75 per cent of the cases, is set by the uni-racial language. If we used local rather than world definitions of race, the statistics would be different. The definition we have used does not allow us to distinguish the two black races of Madagascar, or the three races shown in recent censuses in Brazil – browns, whites, and blacks – or Mexican Ladinos from whites and Indians. A uni-racial classification in Table 29 thus in no way means that speakers in states called uni-racial perceive these states as so being. This is not often the case, but data that enable us to establish the relation between language and race, as perceived within each state, exist only in embryonic form. Nevertheless, despite all their limitations, the patterns of Tables 29 and 30 reveal a high degree of geographical concordance between language and race. Mazrui (1976) notes that the English language contains a symbolism of colours that does not apply in the case of black Africa. This is not surprising and is not peculiar to English, for languages normally do have specific racial colours.

The correspondence between language and race appears even more evident if, instead of taking the state as the intermediate framework for analysis, we use only the main language, and if we class as uni-racial every language in which 90 per cent of the speakers are of the same race. We cannot obtain precise figures, for the census data that provide a correlation between race and language exist in only a few countries. However, thanks to the strong geographical correlation between language and race, the problems of estimation are limited to those of English, Spanish, and French. How many Nigerians, how many Zaireans, how many Indians, or Pakistanis have French or English, if not as their childhood language, then at least as the dominant language of daily life or communication with the public authorities? Estimates vary considerably but indicate that in black Africa and Asia the figure is generally below 10 per cent.

If we limit our enumeration to countries in which English, French, or Spanish is the official language, and if in the case of African and Asian countries for which we lack statistics we consider that 5 per cent of the indigenous population uses the former colonial language as the principal

TABLE 30
Language and race, when the state is the unit of analysis*

	American Indian	Polynesian	Micronesian	Melanesian	North Asian	South Asian	Asian Indian	White European	Black African
American Indian								Spanish	Spanish
Polynesian	▲		English	English	English	English	English	English	English
Micronesian		▲		English	English	English	English	English	English
Melanesian			▲		English	English	English	English French	English French
North Asian				▲		English Malay Mandarin Thai	Dzonkha English Nepali	English	English
South Asian					▲		Dutch English	Dutch English	
Asian Indian						▲		Dutch English	
European							▲		Afrikaans Arabic Dutch English French Portuguese Spanish

*Based on Table 29. The table is to be read as follows. For example: American Indian is linked to white European by Spanish, since Spanish is the official language of at least one state where more than 10 per cent of the population is American Indian and of a state (not necessarily the same state) where more than 10 per cent of the population is white European.

language (probably an overestimate), we obtain the following distributions: English is about 70 per cent white, about 15 per cent black, and at least 10 per cent Asian Indian, with other races (in particular South Asiatic) sharing the remaining 5 per cent.[8] The same method of calculation shows French as being almost 90 per cent white and about 10 per cent black. Spanish would be about 80 per cent white (at least if we include the whites, Ladinos, and Mestizos of the Latin American statistics), 15 per cent Indian, and 5 per cent black. (Europeans and the Ladino/Mestizos share the 80 per cent 'white' Spanish in almost equal proportions.) Finally, Portuguese would be about 70 per cent white, about 25 per cent 'brown' (according to Brazilian data), and 5 per cent black. All other languages (according to the approximate estimates of Muller, Katzner, the *Political Handbook of the World*, the *Encyclopédie Larousse*, and the *Encyclopaedia Britannica*) are 90 per cent uni-racial. The result is that few races are linked to one another by one and the same language, according to our definitions and with regard to our requirement that a race have a strength of at least 10 per cent within the states or among the speakers of the language in question. If language more often than not allows one to foretell the race of the speaker (the converse is not true), it is because both race and language are closely linked to territory.

Is it an advantage or a disadvantage for a language to be multi-racial? Race does not in itself carry any particular values, as do language and religion; however, it is a vehicle of culture and of specific political causes. A language common to several races must thus facilitate contacts, reciprocal enrichment, and political co-operation; but it will also, by virtue of the greater facility of communication, bring into sharper relief the differences in standing and power, and will better reveal negative attitudes between different races, where these exist. At the heart of the political coalitions that unite them, different languages will be better able to indulge in racism – for this will be less obvious if it has to be translated. Other coalitions, in contrast, which came about with the help of a common language (English, for example), will be much more affected by racial discrimination of intra-linguistic type.

Language and religion

There is no obvious and precise definition of religion, any more than there is of race. Should one count only those who worship regularly or should one

---

8 Voegelin's estimates, less favourable than ours on the implantation of English in Africa and in Asia, give almost 80 per cent to the white race and less than 5 per cent to the Asiatics.

include occasional worshippers? Should one count sects, or only the great totalities such as Christianity and Islam? Let us be guided again by the statistics at our disposal and by the fact that our comparison is worldwide rather than at the level of state or region. The categories I shall use do not allow us to distinguish Baptists from Lutherans, or the multiple beliefs covered, in Africa or in America, by the terms *animism* and *traditional religion*. We shall deal with only the following religions: Catholic, Protestant, Coptic, Sunni Moslem, Shia Moslem, Orthodox, Buddhist, Hindu, Taoist, Shinto, Jewish, Shamanist/Animist, and what Barrett (1982) lists as Chinese Folk Religionist.

For each of the official languages, Table 31 gives the religions with which they are associated not at the individual but at the state level. From the statistics gathered by the *World Christian Encyclopedia* (Barrett 1982)[9] I have retained only those religions that represent at least 10 per cent of the religious population of any of the states where a particular language is official, whatever the method (which varies according to the state) used in the statistics to estimate this population. Thus we use as the definition of religion 'the cultural framework of thought' rather than a definition based on the level of practice or belief. For each of the independent states of 1985 let us first test (Table 31) the religions that are left after we exclude those that account for less than 10 per cent of the whole state, and let us assign these religions to the official language or languages of the state in question. As an example, this process shows that in Sri Lanka Hinduism and Buddhism are linked together by English, Tamil, and Sinhalese, although the Hindus are Tamil-speakers, and the Sinhalese are Buddhists. Table 31 ignores the direct bond between languages and religion; the state acts as intermediary.

The table thus exaggerates the multi-religious character of international languages such as French and English, just as Table 29 exaggerated their multi-racial character. However, our main interest is not religious practice but the religious orientation of a language, and we measure this orientation from a political point of view. Within the francophone framework, although Léopold Senghor, the former president of Senegal, is a Catholic, in so far as he led a state with a Moslem majority he gave French a political opening onto Islam – which is not given to that language by the

9 The monumental *World Christian Encyclopaedia* (Barrett 1982), which in the sphere of religions is comparable to Kloss and McConnell's work (1974–81) in the sphere of languages, is the principal source of my religious classifications. Table 31 of the French edition was based not solely on the data given by Barrett, but also on data from *Europa Year Book*, *Political Handbook of the World*, *Statesman's Yearbook*, *Encyclopaedia Britannica*, and *Encyclopédie Larousse*. This change of base does not affect the overall pattern or any of the conclusions.

TABLE 31
Uni-religious and multi-religious languages (counting only the religions that number at least 10 per cent of the state where the language is official)

	Catholic	Protestant	Coptic	Islam (Sunni)	Islam (Shia)	Orthodox	Buddhist	Hindu	Chinese Folk	Shinto	Jewish	Animist*
Afrikaans	x	x										x
Albanian				x		x						
Amharic			x	x								x
Arabic	x	x	x	x	x						x†	x
Bengali				x				x				
Bulgarian				x		x						
Burmese							x					
Czech	x	x										
Danish		x										
Dari				x								
Dutch	x	x		x				x				x
Dzonkha							x	x				
English	x	x		x	x		x	x	x			x
Farsi				x								
Finnish		x										
French	x	x		x								x
Gaelic	x											
German	x	x										
Greek‡				x		x						
Hebrew				x†							x	
Hindi/Urdu				x	x			x				
Hungarian	x	x										
Icelandic		x										
Italian	x	x										
Japanese							x			x		
Khalkha							x					x
Khmer							x					
Kiribati	x	x										
Korean		x					x					x
Lao							x					x
Latin	x											
Luxemburgian	x											
Macedonian	x			x		x						
Malagasy	x	x										x
Malay				x			x		x			
Maltese	x											
Mandarin				x			x		x			
Nepali								x				
Norwegian		x										
Pashto				x								

TABLE 31 (continued)

	Catholic	Protestant	Coptic	Islam (Sunni)	Islam (Shia)	Orthodox	Buddhist	Hindu	Chinese Folk	Shinto	Jewish	Animist*
Pilipino	x											
Polish	x					ᵗ						
Portuguese	x	x		x								x
Romanian						x						
Russian				x		x						
Samoan	x	x										
Serbo-Croatian	x			x		x						
Sesotho	x	x										x
Sinhalese§				x			x	x				
Siswati	x	x										x
Slovak	x	x										
Solvene	x			x		x						
Somali				x								
Spanish	x											
Swahili	x	x		x								x
Swedish		x										
Tamil				x			x	x	x			
Thai							x					
Turkish‡				x		x						
Vietnamese									x			

*This category includes the beliefs that Barrett (1982) classifies under 'animism,' 'shaman-ism,' 'primitive religious,' and 'tribal religious.'
†Inasmuch as Arabic is considered an official language of Israel
‡Cyprus is counted here as a single state, notwithstanding the partition between Turkish and Greek zones. If counted separately, Greek and Turkish become monoreligious.
§Includes Divehi in the Maldives

approximately 800,000 people of North African origin who work in France (less than 10 per cent of the total population, hence not recorded by our measure). Be that as it may, the data in Table 31 give only an approximate orientation, which none the less allows us to establish the desired contrast between uni-religious and multi-religious languages.

In contrast to what we noted about race, the norm is no longer so clearly that of uniqueness. Within the framework of the state (Table 31) only 38 per cent of the languages are uni-religious. Geographically speaking, there is dissociation between body and soul; religion is more mobile than race.

TABLE 32
Language and religion, when the state is the unit of analysis*

	Protestant	Coptic	Sunni	Shia	Orthodox	Buddhist	Hindu	Chinese Folk	Shinto	Jewish	Animist

Catholic	Afrikaans
	Arabic
	Czech
	Dutch
	English
	French
	German
	Hungarian
	Italian
	Kiribati
	Malagasy
	Portuguese
	Samoan
	Siswati
	Slovak
	Sesotho
	Swahili
		Arabic	Arabic
			Dutch
			English
			French
			Macedonian
			Portuguese
			Serbo-
			  Croatian
			Slovene
			Swahili
				Arabic
				English
					Macedonian
					Serbo-
					  Croatian
					Slovene
						English	Dutch
							English
								English		Arabic	Afrikaans
											Arabic
											Dutch
											English
											French
											Korean
											Malagasy
											Portuguese
											Siswati
											Swahili

Protestant ..... ▲			Dutch English French Portuguese Swahili	English		English Korean	Dutch English	English		Arabic	Afrikaans Dutch English French Korean Malagasy Portuguese Sesotho Siswati Swahili

Religion								
Coptic	Amharic Arabic ▲						Arabic	Amharic Arabic
Sunni	Amharic Arabic ▲	Arabic English Hindi/Urdu	Albanian Bulgarian Greek Macedonian Russian Serbo-Croatian Slovene Turkish†	English Malay Mandarin Sinhalese Tamil	Bengali Dutch English Hindi/Urdu Sinhalese Tamil	English Malay Mandarin Tamil	Hebrew Arabic	Amharic Arabic Dutch English French Portuguese Swahili
Shia	▲		English	English	English Hindi-Urdu	English	Arabic	English
Orthodox	▲							
Buddhist	▲			Dzonkha English Sinhalese Tamil	English Malay Mandarin Tamil	Japanese		English Korean Lao
Hindu	▲				English Tamil	English Tamil		English Dutch
Chinese Folk	▲					English		English
Shinto	▲							
Jewish‡	▲						Arabic	

*Based on Table 31

†When Cyprus is counted as a bilingual state

‡Jewish is linked to animist by Arabic, since Arabic is an official language of both Israel and Cameroon. See Table 30 for explanations.

TABLE 33
Languages, by political system

	Democratic pluralist*	Authoritarian	Communist authoritarian
Afrikaans		x	
Albanian			x
Amharic		x	
Arabic		x	
Bengali		x	
Bulgarian			x
Burmese		x	
Czech			x
Danish	x		
Dari			x
Dutch	x		
Dzonkha		x	
English†	85%‡	15%	
Farsi		x	
Finnish	x		
French§	40%	60%	
Gaelic	x		
German	80%		20%
Greek	x		
Hebrew	x		
Hindi/Urdu	90%	10%	
Hungarian			x
Icelandic	x		
Italian	x		
Japanese	x		
Khalkha			x
Khmer			x
Kiribati	x		
Korean		70%	30%
Lao			x
Latin		x	
Luxemburgian	x		
Macedonian			x
Malagasy		x	
Malay‖		x	
Maltese	x		
Mandarin		2%	98%
Nepali		x	
Norwegian	x		
Pashto			x
Pilipino	x		
Polish			x
Portuguese#	90%	10%	

TABLE 33 (continued)

	Democratic pluralist*	Authoritarian	Communist authoritarian
Romanian			x
Russian			x
Samoan		x	
Serbo-Croatian			x
Sesotho		x	
Sinhalese	x		
Siswati		x	
Slovak			x
Slovene			x
Somali		x	
Spanish**	55%	40%	5%
Swahili		x	
Swedish	x		
Tamil††	95%(90%)	5%(10%)	
Thai†††		x	
Turkish		x	
Vietnamese			x

*The percentages, rounded to multiples of 5, are approximate. They are based on the total population of the states whose official language (or dominant official language in the case of bi- or multi-lingual states) is one of the languages listed above.

The following countries have been assigned to the 'pluralist democratic' category: Antigua, Argentina, Australia, Austria, Bahamas, Barbados, Belgium, Belize, Bolivia, Botswana, Brazil, Canada, Colombia, Costa Rica, Cyprus (Greek zone), Denmark, Dominica, Dominican Republic, Ecuador, Fiji, Finland, France, Germany (West), Greece, Grenada, Iceland, India, Ireland, Israel, Italy, Jamaica, Japan, Kiribati, Luxembourg, Malta, Mauritius, Nauru, Netherlands, New Zealand, Norway, Papua-New Guinea, Peru, Philippines, Portugal, St Kitts and Nevis, St Lucia, St Vincent, Solomon Islands, Spain, Sri Lanka, Sweden, Switzerland, Trinidad and Tobago, Tuvalu, United Kingdom, United States, Uruguay, Venezuela.

This list corresponds closely to that of free states published in *Freedom in the World* (1986). The states included in the 'communist authoritarian' category are the following: Afghanistan, Albania, East Germany, Bulgaria, China, North Korea, Cuba, Hungary, Kampuchea, Laos, Mongolia, Poland, Romania, Czechoslovakia, USSR, Vietnam, and Yugoslavia. The so-called marxist regimes of Africa have been included in the category 'authoritarian.'

†If one adds Nigeria and Singapore to the democratic pluralist category the percentage of the first column rises to 90. Without the Philippines it declines to 80.

§If one counts Senegal in the pluralist category, the first column percentage becomes 45 per cent. If we were to base the percentages on the sole speakers of the language instead of the total population of the states classified by their dominant official language, French would obtain a democratic pluralist score superior to 80 per cent.

Perhaps state and language are more welcoming, more open, to religion than to race.

At the 10 per cent cut-off we have chosen, languages that bring together the most religions are either colonization languages, such as English, French, and Arabic, or small languages of former colonies recently emancipated, such as Siswati. Of the 38 multi-religious languages of Table 31, 19 are bi-religious, 12 are tri-religious, and only 7 (English, Arabic, Swahili, Tamil, French, Dutch, and Portuguese) link more than three religions (Table 32). The importance of uni-religionism, and this concentration of multi-religious languages in the bi-religionism category, would become even clearer if we no longer took the state as our basis of calculation but used the individual speaker instead.

Multi-religious languages would then appear to belong to three different types, according to whether they have a clear religious dominance, are in balance around 50 per cent or are clearly minorities. The first category – clear dominance – is illustrated by English: roughly 80 per cent of its speakers are Protestants and 20 per cent Catholics; another illustration is Hindi/Urdu: 80 per cent for Hinduism and 20 per cent for Islam. Balanced bi-religionism is illustrated by Dutch and German, which are half Catholic and half Protestant, while Swahili and Siswati are examples of minority multi-religionism.

When the statistical universe is that of speakers rather than states, the major international lingua francas appear either to be unilingual or to be bi-religious with clear dominance of one single language. Arabic is Sunni Moslem; Spanish, French, and Portuguese are Catholic; and English, the international lingua franca the furthest removed from the uni-religious, is 80 per cent Protestant. However, our figures, which exclude minorities of less than 10 per cent, do not take account of the place of these minorities in the social and cultural hierarchy of the states and languages under review.

‖If Malaysia and Singapore are included in the democratic category, the first column percentage becomes 10 per cent.

#If one puts Brazil in the authoritarian category, the first column percentage becomes 5 per cent.

**The number of Spanish-speaking democratic states has increased markedly since the early 1980s; the 1980 classification used by Russett and Starr (1981) resulted in Spanish scoring as low as 35 per cent in the first column of the French edition of this book.

††If one puts Singapore among democratic states, the first column percentage becomes 100 per cent. Inversely, if one does not include Sri Lanka among pluralist democracies, Tamil scores exclusively in the authoritarian category.

†††If following the election of 1986 we put Thailand in the democratic category, Thai scores 100 per cent in the first column.

The isolation of Judaism and Shia Islam is overestimated. Qualitative figures not at my disposal would take account of factors such as the literary, religious, and scientific production of the religious minorities of each of the languages under study. Judaism is probably disseminated more by English than by Hebrew; and Shiite Islam is disseminated by Arabic.

To sum up, our study of links between religion and language leaves us with this impression: if the state is frequently multi-religious, languages are often less so. Among the major languages only three are truly multi-religious – German, English, and Hindi/Urdu – although the first two link two closely related Christian religions. It is thus not surprising that conflicts of language are so often also conflicts of religion.

Language and ideology

There are many ways of classifying political ideologies: according to the degree of freedom enjoyed by the citizens, the authority of the executive over parliament, the degree of intervention by the state in the economy. From these multiple classifications, all of which lack precise boundaries, I have retained but one: that which distinguishes states according to whether they have free elections or not. Among those that do not have free elections or have only conditional freedom in their elections I shall make a sub-distinction between non-communist authoritarian regimes and communist authoritarian regimes (these last I define by their state control of the economy). [10]

Some of the classifications in Table 33 are subject to criticism. The percentages I have allotted to languages with mixed political systems can give only an approximate order of size, for they are based on the relative proportion of populations in states of the same language but different systems. Thus East Germany gives German about 10 per cent in the 'Communist authoritarianism' column, while West Germany, Switzerland, and Austria account for 90 per cent of the 'Pluralist democratic' column. This results from classifying speakers not according to their personal preferences but according to a regime of which they may well not approve. If the Poles had a choice, they would choose democracy; but their regime puts them into the 'Communist' column.

Table 33 shows again a remarkable tendency to concentration of each language, this time by political system. This must be so for a uni-state lan-

---

10 Among the many classifications of states and political systems in the democracy/totalitarianism continuum, see A.K. Smith (1969) and Maruyama (1965).

guage, for in Table 33 we ignore past experience. For multi-state languages, however, concentration does not take place automatically. Among these languages, only two – German and Spanish – occupy the two extremes of Table 33; these are the only languages that establish a bond at government level between the capitalist democratic and the Communist systems. Besides German and Spanish, only English, Arabic, Korean, French, and Hindi/ Urdu straddle two categories,[11] but these are contiguous, unlike the German and Spanish cases. The geography of languages is superimposed on a geography of political systems. Thus conflicts of language at the world level are often also conflicts of race, religion, and political system.

11 On the lack of identification of English with a single economic and political system, see Fishman et al (1975, 119).

5

Ethno-linguistic separatism: an essay in predictive topography

There are three principal methods of scientific reasoning: those of the word, the formula, and the image – either the realistic image exemplified by the tree, the plateau, the river; or the refined image of the geometric type. We shall use here the last kind, without, however, straying too far from the data of real geography, so that we may pass from topology to topography, and then to predictive theory.[1]

Let us compare the relationships adopted in geographical space by a linguistic minority and by the state controlled by a dominant ethnic group. For this comparison we shall use three symbols: a square symbolizing the central state; a circle symbolizing a linguistic minority; and a dot representing the vital centre of this minority (see Figure 9).

There are many ways of combining, separating, interlocking, and superimposing these symbols; one that comes to mind immediately is shown in model A (Figure 10). This enclosure of the smaller within the larger is satisfying, complete, definitive. Even before we invest it with the meaning inherent in our symbolism, model A tells us that a minority has organized itself around a vital centre and is in turn contained within a dominant group. If we had to express the relationship between our environment, our body, and our heart, we would probably have conceived an identical model; the innermost self curls up and seeks protection within a body set in a wider environment. I do not know of any culture that places the inner self, the soul, the mind, at any extremity of the body, at the end of the fingers – or even *on* rather than *in* the eyes. This is important, for if the same notation expresses the social group as well as the individual body, if we think of our ethnic

1 On the application of different methods of reasoning, including the graphical and the metaphorical, see De Bono (1968; 1981).

FIGURE 9
Linguistic minorities and the state – symbols

group and of our state in the same way we think of our own body, then the research of individual psychology into the notion of the corporeal boundary can light the way for researches in ethnic sociology.[2]

We can return to our basic notation and consider first the circle and the rectangle, without the dot. Since, by definition, the circle must lie within the square, at least two different relationships satisfy this condition, model B and model C. In model B, which we have come to think of as 'normal,' the circle is enclosed on all sides by the square and does not touch any of the sides. In model C, the balance is destroyed; the circle touches one of the sides. Model B probably represents the way in which a dominant group encapsulates within itself a minority it wishes to absorb. For this minority, separatism is not conceivable without a rending, a traumatic explosion. Model C, in contrast, can represent several things: the way in which a dominant group treats a minority to which it is hostile, the way in which many minorities see themselves in relation to the dominant group, and also a very real and present geographical fact.

Linguistic minorities are more often peripheral than are racial or religious minorities; they are located at the frontiers. To list the principal linguistic minorities of the Soviet Union is – with exceptions such as the Tatars of Kazakhstan – to make a tour of the state's political borders; we pass from Latvians to Khirgizes, through Lithuanians, Bielorussians, Moldavians, Ukrainians, and Georgians, to Armenians, Azerbaidjanis, Kazakhs, Turkomans, and Uzbeks. The same holds for the linguistic minorities of Iran: Azerbaidjanis, Kurds, Lurs, Bakhtiars, Arabs, Kashkais, Baluchis, and Turkomans take us from the east to the west of the Caspian Sea over the circuit of the land. It is the same also in Switzerland, Spain, or Yugoslavia; most of the linguistic minorities there are located at the frontiers. Linguistic minorities are rarely encapsulated; Quebec is one of the

---

2 The research of Horowitz (1935) and Himelstein (1964) reveals a tendency to locate the 'self' in the head, the chest, or the heart. Laponce (1975b) describes the tendency to regard the capital of one's state as being at the centre of the world.

A   B   C

FIGURE 10
Linguistic minorities and the state – three models

few. To the extent that Quebec is contiguous with the United States, it is
described by model C, but to the extent that Quebec cuts English Canada in
two, it feels itself encircled; it thus approaches model B. During the disputes
caused by the various separatist projects of the Parti québécois in the late
1970s and early 1980s, it was frequently stressed that Canada extends both
east and west from Quebec and that this was a real obstacle to separatism.[3]
Situation B, – whether it describes the geographic perception or the reality,
and most certainly when it describes both – is not favourable to separatism.
Quebec's motto – 'Je me souviens' – can be read as an invitation to use
history as a means of escape from the shackles of geography; while
Canada's motto – 'From sea to sea' – is a reminder to Quebec of a restric-
tive geographic reality.

The vital centre

I have presented the vital centre in the form of a dot. By 'vital centre,' I
mean the equivalent of the heart or soul, a condensation of the essential elements that distinguish the minority from the dominant group. In Parsonian
terms, the centre is the ideal place for the deployment of the functions of
command, social integration, economic adaptation, and historic continuity;
and according to Christaller (1935), the vital centre is that point in physical
space where are concentrated the major functions – the non-specialized
functions, the vital centres of communication of the ethnos as a whole.
There are of course marked differences in the degree of centrism, depending
on whether the ethnic group is dominant or minority. France is more
centred than Germany, and England more centred than Canada. Monotheistic Christian societies have – more than polytheistic Hindu society –

3 On the conceptions of an ethnic territory – either Canadian or Québécois – in the
  history of French-Canadian nationalism, see among others Bergeron and Pelletier
  (1980), Dion (1980), and Legault (1975).

frameworks of thought that tend to make them see themselves in terms of a centre and peripheries. We perhaps ought therefore to elaborate our model and distinguish monocentrist systems from polycentrist – in particular, economic and political centres from cultural centres that need not be superposed. But however important these distinctions, they would overburden our typology, and we shall dispense with them. We shall place only one centre inside one circle. We shall consider polycentric systems as more or less complex variants of monocentrist systems, which pose problems of the same nature, for the object of the encompassing boundary (the circle) is to protect the vital centre or centres that a minority ethnic group wishes to maintain within its collective self rather than to expose outside.

Even if we use one single centre, many variations are possible. Our choice from among all these theoretical possibilities will be guided by the work of the psychologist Seymour Fisher on the relation between mental health and the perception of bodily boundaries. Fisher and Cleveland (1968) reported that those of their subjects who perceived the external boundaries of their bodies as badly defined, or as easily penetrable from outside, were in poor physical or mental health; they were more fearful and had more need to rely on the decisions of others than was the case with those subjects who saw their bodily frontiers as well defined – firm frontiers, which clearly separated the self from the environment.

Do we consider the social body in the same way that we consider the individual body? Our model A suggests that we do, and the language of politics suggest that also – from the metaphors of Plato, Hobbes, and Shakespeare to Valéry to Giscard d'Estaing's 'Madame la France.'[4] Family, ethnic group, and state – if important to us, if the objects of affection and not mere instruments – will be perceived as extensions or large-scale representations of our individual body (Laponce 1985). Thus Fisher's conclusions probably apply to the social and metaphysical bodies to which we feel we belong. Such an extrapolation is not without risk, but it gives us a reasonable theoretical base on which we can build a typology.

Unfortunately, we have almost complete lack of perceptual data concerning the way in which the minorities that interest us perceive their centres and their boundaries (Laponce 1977). Fisher's observations lead me to expect that minorities whose vital centres are sheltered behind rigid and not easily penetrated frontiers feel more secure and better able to exercise self-regulation. In an opposite situation, the minority would feel insecure, which

---

4 In his unsuccessful bid for re-election as president, Valéry Giscard d'Estaing addressed France as 'Madame' in one of his campaign speeches. On the use of corporeal images in classical political thinking, see Schlanger (1971).

could become a cause of separatism. But paradoxically, the minority is, then, less able to effect this separation, because of the paralysis of will and the difficulty of emancipating oneself from others that characterize an entity with a vital centre poorly protected by too easily penetrable borders. In this 'I do but I don't' situation, where it is difficult to dovetail ends and means, we can indeed recognize minorities such as the Québécois. For a better understanding, let us first use the four models D, E, F, and G (see Figure 11).

Model D represents an extreme case, that of an embryonic ethnic group, for example, the Arabs of Palestine at the beginning of the century, when Jewish immigrants could establish themselves in the area without too much difficulty, for the Arabs had no clear perception that their villages, taken together, formed a whole; they had no feeling of being an ethnic group surrounded by a common border. Further, this ethnic group was not politically centred in space, other than on the family and the village; and the religious centring on Mecca weakened the need to define a Palestinian frontier around Jerusalem. In model D, separatism has no meaning. It represents an ethnic group either emerging or on the way to disappearing, like certain ethnic groups in North America – the Germans in Chicago or the Dutch in British Columbia – or again, in France, the Bretons or the Occitans.

Model E is more frequent; here, the minority ethnic group is centred in space – for example, the Franco-Manitobans in St Boniface; but the boundary is 'as leaky as a sieve,' even if one knows where to find it. The Romansches of Switzerland offer another example of a minority with a broken border; their historic centre, Thur, has long since been thoroughly penetrated by German.

Model F is an oddity perhaps illustrated by the case of the Welsh who no longer look upon Cardiff, conquered by English, as the centre of their ethnicity, but who have no alternative, not even the countries of Gwyneed. It is perhaps also the case of the Acadians, for whom Moncton has become too bilingual, too peripheral. Acadia, while it still has its distinctive boundaries, now lacks a specific centre. Case F represents an extreme, the enlargement of the point until finally it becomes both circle and point simul-

D   E   F   G

FIGURE 11
Linguistic minorities: centre and boundaries – four models

taneously. This is the case of minorities that exist perceptually in little strongholds – the Swedish Finns of the Aaland Islands, for example.

Model G we have already met several times, perhaps because of my personal predisposition – attributable to a strongly monocentrist French Catholic culture. If such a cultural predisposition does exist, it would explain why Québécois find it more difficult than do English Canadians to adjust to the idea of 'Canada,' 'Quebec,' 'Ottawa,' and 'Montreal' being all centres within the same perceptual borders. Protestantism, though totally monotheistic, perhaps makes many English Canadians better able to put up with a federal system in which relations between centre and peripheries remain somewhat nebulous. Having separated from Rome, Protestants are perhaps more ready to accept what Jean Gottmann (1973) calls 'the map of the world according to Alexander,' i.e. a many-centred empire. French Catholic Canadians, by the same hypothesis, would accept more readily the model Plato proposed for his ideal city, in which clear separations kept the outsider well away from a vital centre lying far from its coasts – like a capital city in the centre of an island with empty shores.

To continue our exercise in theoretical topology we can vary the position of the dot while keeping the circle and the square unchanged. From the many possible variants, we shall consider five, (from H to L on Figure 12). As in the earlier cases, these figures are meant to portray in simple fashion either objective geographical relationships or perceptual relationships of the 'mental map' type. Though our models have at least two possible meanings, they are no more imprecise than certain key concepts of political analysis – social class, for example, which usually signifies simultaneously 'objective' class (the one we attribute to the other person) and 'subjective' class (the one in which the other person places himself or herself).

The first of these five new models, H, is particularly discouraging to territorial separatism; the minority's vital centre is not only outside the minority's territory but even outside that of the dominant group, the whole stretch of which separates this centre from its 'natural' frontiers. An

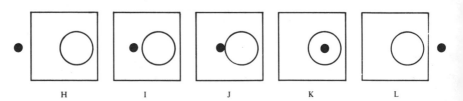

H   I   J   K   L

FIGURE 12
Linguistic minorities and the state – five models

approximation of this model is perhaps offered by the few Jews of the autonomous region of Birobidjan, at least by those among them for whom Jerusalem is the vital centre.

Separatism is not encouraged either by the situation shown in model I, in which the vital centre of the minority, though within the area of the state where this minority is established, comes under the control of the dominant group. An example is Helsinki, for Swedish Finns concentrated along the Swedish frontier but oriented toward a capital that they dominated in the past, though they no longer exercise supreme political and cultural control over it.

Model L is common; it results from the non-coincidence of the state and the ethnic borders. Minority linguistic groups then find themselves on the 'wrong' side of a dividing line. The Romanians in Bukovina, the Albanians in Yugoslavia, the Romands in Switzerland, the Swedes in Finland, and the Germans in Belgium or Italy are relatives of a neighbouring unilingual state from which they are separated by a frontier. In such cases, the vital centre of a minority ethnic group may be situated in a nearby state. Witness Paris, for example, for some Swiss Jurassians (at least in the nineteenth century); Vienna for some Germano-Italians, Tirana for some Yugoslav Albanians, Amsterdam for some Flemings after the creation of the Belgian state in 1830, and, more recently, Paris for some Walloons upset by the idea of becoming a minority group. However, a frontier, if maintained long enough, will often result in an ethnic group's passing from model L to model K. Potential situations of linguistic irridentism frequently crop up in Europe, but irridentists are rare; they are practically non-existent in Switzerland and Finland, and very marginal in Belgium and Italy. About the only places where they have any strength are Yugoslavia and Bukovina, in regions where the 'divisive' borders are comparatively recent.

Models J and K are particularly interesting because of the frequency of the situations they represent and the contrast between them. Model J describes a minority with a territory of its own with clearly defined borders but in a precarious situation, for its vital centre lies at the very boundary that separates it from the dominant group. In K, in contrast, the vital centre is well protected, being well placed in the interior of the ethnic territory. This last model describes, both perceptually and geographically, the cantons of Geneva and Neuchâtel in the Swiss state, while model J describes the case of Belgium, at least for those Dutch and French speakers who consider Brussels not only the capital of their state but also the vital centre of the ethno-linguistic whole to which they belong.

Into which of these two models does francophone Quebec fit? If the city of Quebec, the historical shrine of French Canada and the seat of government, is considered the vital centre of a whole people, then Quebec resembles Geneva and Neuchâtel. If, however, the ethnicity of Quebec is deemed to be centred on Montreal, a large francophone metropolis, the seat of business, and the source of artistic and literary creation, then Montreal – which is only 60 per cent francophone – plays both a central and a frontier role comparable to that of Brussels; it would then be normal for the Québécois ethnic group to seek to shift the language dividing line so that Quebec moves from model J to model K. Quebec's language law of 1977, especially in those provisions that forbid advertising in English, had the effect of francizing if not the population at least the 'frontier' environment. It is a matter of some importance that unilingual French road-signing was extended by law right to the borders with Ontario. This was a symbolic way – and effective, in so far as it affected long-term behaviour – of establishing that the linguistic boundary walls off rather than divides the vital centre of the ethnic group it is desired to protect.

Montreal

The centre/periphery relationship expressed by the representation of the circle and the dot can help us understand Montreal's situation. If Montreal is the circle, the dot represents the mid-town area.

Let us imagine the history of a city from the point of view of its immigrants and their descendants. According to Soja (1971), this history would have three principle phases, to which we will add a fourth (Laponce 1980). In the first phase, immigrants – typically from the countryside or from some small town in the neighbourhood – establish themselves on the periphery of the city, close to work. They feel marginal, poorly integrated into the metropolis, and their marginality is defined not by the centre of the city but in relation to the village or small town left behind. For them, the vital centre, the place where events have more resonance than anywhere else, still lies in the farm, the church, the family in the countryside. In the second phase, some years later, or in the next generation, the bonds to the place of origin have slackened and the new citizens centre themselves on their new city. They clasp the vital centre, though still attaching only minor importance to the big city as a whole. They now locate this vital centre, brought from the countryside, within the framework of their new homes; they live now in an urban environment, geographically restricted, circumscribed by the factory, the church, and the local pub.

In these first two phases, the city is tolerant of ethnic and linguistic diversity. Minorities situated at the peripheries can ignore each other and the dominant group that normally controls the business centre at the heart of the city.

In the third phase – the city's most centrist phase – the peripheries realize that they are peripheries; citizens locate themselves in relation to the city as a whole, and hence in relation to their centre, of which they are very conscious, for it is there that the architecture distinguishes power, creativity, dominance. Now, if it is relatively easy to share multiple peripheries that have but few contacts between them, how can one divide a single centre where one meets? This centre is intolerant of multilingualism, for it is at the centre that communication is most intense; it is also there that linguistic conflicts will be the most bitter.[5] Destabilization of the federal Canadian state by the linguistic laws, and by the attempt at partial separatism in Quebec between 1976 and 1982, could not be reduced to one single geographical factor. But among all the factors to be considered, the geograhical was primary; the battle that sought to free Quebec in the matter of language was largely over control of a few square kilometres that form the business centre of Montreal.

A fourth phase could conveniently be added: that of the city of suburbs. Certain modern cities, such as Los Angeles, pass directly from the second to this fourth phase, in which citizens locate themselves in relation neither to the city's centre (phase 3), nor to their own quarter of the city (phase 2), nor to their old village (phase 1), but in relation to an ethnic group or a non-centralized state. If Los Angeles is a city of suburbs, are these suburbs of Los Angeles or suburbs of the United States? For Montreal, we can envisage a fourth phase in its history in which residents would locate themselves not in relation to the city's centre but in relation to their Canada-wide ethnic group. If the role of the centre were thus devalued not in its economic or political importance but in its psychological aspect, then it would be easier for one of the linguistic groups that were struggling for territory in phase 3 to withdraw from the contest and agree that the centre become unilingual. Between the anglophones and the francophones the former are more likely to pass from phase 3 to phase 4; this would make it easier for French to obtain its objective of many years: conquest of Montreal's centre. Conversely, if the Flemings in Belgium, by virtue of their ever-growing influence in the Belgian political system, were to centre themselves increasingly on Brussels instead of on Flanders, linguistic conflicts would be increased thereby. In phase 3 of the city, the centre, where the entropic movement

5 On the role of the city in mobilization and assimilation of populations coming from the countryside, see Deutsch (1953).

toward unilingualism is accelerated, seems indivisible, or at least divisible only with some considerable difficulty between ethnic groups each of which seek exclusive possession of the whole place.

Canada, Switzerland, and Belgium

In addition to the differences we have just noted concerning the location of the vital centre in relation to its boundaries – differences that separate Geneva and Lausanne from Fribourg, Brussels, and Montreal – it would also be appropriate – in our application of models K and J – to take into account the degree of porosity of the ethnic border, which we represent by a circle.

Switzerland and Belgium provide examples of rigid linguistic boundaries; Canada, Finland, South Africa, and Yugoslavia offer examples of porosity. The linguistic division that separates Flanders from Wallonia is – except for Brussels – a border that separates two unilingual areas and thereby avoids conflicts of precedence and usage between the two official languages. Schools, road-signing, public administration, and usually businesses as well operate in one language only – French in Wallonia, Dutch in Flanders (Brussels being an exception). Similarly, in Switzerland all the cantons except four (Berne, Fribourg, Grisons and Vaud) are unilingual; and in those bilingual cantons straddling the linguistic frontier, languages are grouped geographically, so that the social and political organization may be as unilingual as possible. Villages in the canton of Fribourg are administered either in German or in French, and in the city of Fribourg the schools use one or other of the two languages; the germanophone minority is concentrated in clearly defined quarter of the town.

The linguistic borders of Yugoslavia are porous in theory, and linguistic minorities coming from other republics may gain the right to schools, courts of law, and municipal governments, all of which may eventually deal with them in their own language. Movements of population from one ethnic group to the other, however, are relatively limited; for even if the legal border is open, the social border is not. The profound cleavages between different linguistic and religious ethnic groups, while not precluding the geographical superposition of these groups and the intermixture of their languages, do in fact discourage these events. In Finland and South Africa the intermixture is more pronounced: the language that used to control the political apparatus used also to control the big cities. Immigration of a peasant population speaking a different language has reduced the former dominant language to a minority position; and this new minority language, though a language of international communication much farther-reaching than its rival, now sees its former positions slipping from its grasp, one after the other, especially in Finland. A porous boundary favours the larger ethnic group, when numbers also give this group control of the machinery of state.

The Canadian situation is more or less in the middle. Quebec's Law 101 of 1977 was intended to bring Canada nearer to the Swiss model. French was declared the language of administration and business, and the English school system was doomed to progressive extinction, since only the children or the brothers and sisters of those who had themselves been educated in English in Quebec were entitled to schooling in English. The federal Charter of Rights and Freedoms of 1982 has partly reopened the border that Quebec had sought to close, by extending to all Canadian citizens educated in English, whatever their province of origin, the right to English schooling for themselves and their children. The new consitution will likely hinder Montreal's passing from model J to model K and thus prevent the Québécois ethnic group from surrounding itself with solid and protective linguistic boundaries.

If we accept the risks of extrapolating Fisher's observations on physical frontiers, and applying them to ethnic groups, we should expect the politics of the central Canadian government to keep Quebec in its state of ambivalence between separatism and dependence, while the politics of the Parti québécois government (1976–85) could have led it toward either Norwegian-style independence, or acceptance of Swiss-style federation, the latter solution being the more probable.

From typology to the prediction of separatism

Apart from the particular case of Quebec, the different models we have just presented should allow us, in accordance with Fisher's observations, to formulate the hypothesis of a curvilinear type of relationship between the degree of territorial homogeneity and the degree of solidity of the linguistic border of a minority group on the one hand and its tendencies toward separatism on the other. When the vital centre and the boundaries are deeply penetrated by the dominant language, the minority ethnic group will be – according to this hypothesis – in such a state of insecurity and discouragement that it will not turn to separatism as a remedy for its distress. On the contrary, when the linguistic minority has a territory of its own, impervious to the linguistic penetration of the dominant group, when it has placed its territory and its vital centre in perfect security, then one of two things will happen. Either the ethnic group, now sure of itself, will seek to separate itself from the dominant group, or (quite the reverse) simply because it is sure of itself it will accept the political status quo. It may accept, for example, the central government's taking the economy in hand to the extent that the group can retain its power of exclusive decision in matters of language and culture. Conversely – still within the logic of Fisher's correlation – separatism more often characterizes the intermediate situations that result from weak to moderate penetration of the minority territory, from being neither master in one's own house nor conquered. In such a situation one would like to be simultaneously dependent and independent. This state corresponds to the situation that Thom, the mathematician, describes as 'catastrophic'; they escape the logic of linear prediction.

Belgium, Switzerland, and Canada are similar in many respects. They are advanced industrial societies, in the Christian tradition – imbued with ideas of non-violence and lovers of compromise. In these three societites, the most virulent form of linguistic separatism has been seen in Quebec, where there is a strong geographic concentration of the minority ethnic group, but where the ethnic boundaries are open. The penetration of the Québécois by the English ethnic group is not so pronounced that it deprives the minority of all hope of retaining control of its territory. But the assimilation of allogenic elements is so slow that the fear of never managing to be master in one's own house becomes an invitation to separatism. In Switzerland, there is no ethnic separatism in the unilingual cantons that fully control their linguistic frontiers, Geneva and Neuchâtel for example, but no separatism either in a canton such as Grisons, where Romansch has been so deeply penetrated by German that the ethnic minority, geographically fragmented, has lost all hope other than surviving here and there in the countryside. Linguistic tensions and separatism are found in the bilingual cantons where there is both a strong geographic concentration and a relatively weak ethnic border, especially in the canton of Berne, from which Vaud and the Jura have separated. In Belgium, the linguistic conflicts and the source of separatism lie less in unilingual Flanders and Wallonia than in the bilingual region of Brussels. In the Soviet Union, separatism is more virulent in Lithuania, where Russian penetration is moderate, than in Latvia, where it is deep. There is only a feeble separatism both in Kazakhstan, which is more than 70 per cent penetrated by Slav immigrants, and in Georgia, where the Russian presence is slight; in contrast, in Ukraine, in a situation of relatively moderate penetration, separatism is thriving.

What yardstick should be used to measure separatism? How can the geographical concentration of a language be measured in the absence of statistics on the language in current use? The imperfect data that I have just presented leave the impression that linguistic conflicts are more likely to assume the aspect of territorial separatism (autonomy or independence) when the minority ethnic group is relatively homogeneous and concentrated in space but is the target of constant infiltration by the dominant group, which it is unable to stem because it does not control its own borders.[6] Switzerland has been wise enough to set up different systems for the control of territorial mobility – different for individuals and for languages, for the economy and for culture. Even while it was becoming more and more integrated in its economy, Switzerland gave its minority linguistic groups enhanced control over their group boundaries. This system allows people, money, merchandise, and manpower to move about freely but does not allow language to follow them. Language is thus firmly anchored to the ground by well-defined and supportive boundaries all around, within which the vital centres of the minorities feel themselves secure.

6 The comparison of 32 ethnic minorities by Church and his colleagues (1978) indicated that there is no correlation between separatism and territorial concentration. However, a re-analysis of the same data (Laponce 1982) shows a curvilinear relation between these two factors, separatism being more frequent in situations of medium penetration of the minority ethnic group by the dominant ethnic group.

6

Language and the rights of man

It is customary to distinguish ethnic minorities according to whether they separate themselves, or are separated, from the dominant group by race, religion, national origin, or language. This distinction is often neglected when it is a question of protecting a minority by means of the 'rights of man' in the universal sense of the term. The two groups – the dominant and the subordinate – are not bound together by the same system of communication on the racial, national, religious, or linguistic levels. As a result, according to the nature of the minority in question, the rights of man have different geographical contexts. There are rights that 'travel' easily, and others that do so with difficulty. The right to marry whom one wishes, to study one's chosen subject, to establish the business or undertaking of one's choice is individual and easily transported. The right to a language, to speak the language of one's choice and be understood, lacks geographical mobility, for it is both an individual and a collective right.

The right to language: neuropsychological and geographical factors

We have seen that most individuals reject bilingualism when it affords no social advantage. If, in a given society immune from exterior influences, everyone were bilingual, one language would disappear before the other or the two languages would coalesce into one. More rarely, each language would become associated with different roles or functions. Bilingualism, common though it may be, is not natural from the neuropsychological point of view. Thus, languages tend to become grouped in physical space in contiguous and homogeneous blocks.

At their points of contact, languages are subject to two contradictory tendencies: the requirements of communication call for bilingualism, while rejection of synonymy leads to unilingualism. A compromise between these two tendencies is struck according to the stratification between the groups in contact; the stronger group determines the attribution of the languages. Sometimes, in pre-industrial societies, two languages intermingling on the territorial level continue to coexist without either one ousting the other, for they are used to separate groups that are intended to be kept apart from each other. These exceptions typically take the following form: a more important group reserves a more important language for itself and isolates a less important group in a less important language. We have already mentioned the Arawaks of the Antilles who before the arrival of the Europeans spoke two languages, Arawak and Carib; the women and children spoke only the former, while only the men spoke both. It was the same with the Yanas of California, since the men and young boys spoke a dialect different from that used for communication between the sexes – a dialect that the women understood but were not permitted to speak. The same situation also obtained in Bolivia in the nineteenth century, when the Spanish colonists forbade the Indians to learn and speak Spanish, a language considered too noble for a primitive society (Roland Breton 1976).

Dominated groups often develop systems of communication that give them partial protection from observation by the dominant group: 'underworld' argots, or schools 'cants'; these esoteric systems of communication are not truly languages, but masks or embryos of languages. More frequently, particularly in industrial societies in which the masses are integrated and mobile, the dominant group will impose its own language rather than accept the cost of bilingualism. The results of the natural tendency for the dominant group either to impose its language as the sole language, or, failing that, to compel the subordinate group to become bilingual, may not be irreversible. The function of many social and political institutions is to constrain or to reverse the natural, but the tendencies that they obstruct are not temporary.

There is no need to explain a society's unilingualism; this is a natural state. However, bilingualism always calls for an explanation – historical, geographical, or social. In this sense language differs from race and especially from religion. The individual and collective costs and benefits of the coexistence of two different languages in a society are not of the same order as the costs and benefits of the coexistence of different races and religions. I do not have to 'pray' or be of the same race as my neighbours, but I do have to 'speak' with them. The costs and benefits of communication between races and religions are of a cultural order; for languages, they are also neuropsychological, involving acquisition, retention, and comprehension.

We have postulated as a general rule that languages in contact, to the extent that they cannot ignore each other, will show stratification. Further, except when the object is to forbid rather than to facilitate communications, the dominant language will tend to become the only language.

In consequence, a minority language must concentrate geographically in order to protect itself. By so doing, it reduces the cost of individual bilingualism (the more one lives in a unilingual milieu the less one needs a sound knowledge of another language). Thus linguistic overlappings are reduced, and hence the number of situations of asymmetrical relationships that benefit the dominant ethnic group. The creation of linguistic strongpoints or ghettoes may well involve regrettable economic costs, which result from bypassing the centres of decision controlled by the more powerful ethnic group. But this is the only tactic that in the long term can protect a minority language.

Is it better to protect one's language or one's economic interests, one's religion or the political ideology of one's preference? We do not have to answer that question, for it has no reasonable answer. Each individual, each society, answers it according to its own values. However, since we are dealing with linguistic rights, it will simplify the argument if we assume – as did Aristotle – that language is a value in its own right, not a simple interchangeable instrument of communication, a value in which the *polis* finds its bonding and its soul. [1] How then protect the linguistic rights of a minority community? In order to answer the question we must first consider the type of linguistic relations that characterize the dominant group and the subordinate ethnos.

Relations between the linguistic minority and the dominant group

In a typology that contains four different descriptors, Louis Wirth (1945) defined the relation between the dominant group and the minority by the way in which the latter reacts to its position of subordination. A minority was assimilationist if it wished to assimilate itself into the dominant group, pluralist if it demanded tolerance of its distinctive culture, secessionist if it wished to achieve emancipation and separate itself from the dominant ethnic group, and militant if it desired to reverse the existing hierarchy for its own benefit. In a more general way in a previous work (Laponce 1960), I distinguished minorities that accepted their minority political status in order to safeguard their cultural values (Jews in the Polish Kahals, Indians on American reserves, French Canadians until recent years) and minorities

1 For an analysis of Aristotelian thought and its application to the case of Canada, see Andrew (1982).

TABLE 34
Schermerhorn's analytical grid

Attitude of the subordinate group	Attitude of the dominant group	
	Centrifugal	Centripetal
Centrifugal	Cultural pluralism	Forced assimilation
Centripetal	Segregation	Integration (whether pluralism or assimilation)

'against their will,' wishing to be assimilated but rejected by the dominant group. Schermerhorn (1970) notes, correctly, that such typologies need to be enlarged to consider the attitude of the dominant group and that of the subordinate group. To do this, he distinguishes four different types of relationship, according to whether the tendencies of each of the two groups are centrifugal or centripetal (Table 34).

Here I make use of and develop Schermerhorn's typology, in order to obtain the detailed grid of Table 35, which allows us to locate linguistic politics and conflicts, as distinct from religious and racial conflicts.[2] Table 35 records the attitude of two groups – the dominant and the minority – according to whether each wishes (a) to be assimilated, (b) to remain neutral, (c) to reject the other ethnic group, or (d) to assimilate the latter.

Let us first consider case 6 in the matrix, which depicts the point of indifference, or non-interference. For race, this situation of indifference leads to rapid fusion, as has happened in countries like Paraguay or Mexico. Since race is not regarded as an important source of cleavage, the different races coalesce into one; soon what one continues to call 'race' describes differences of language and social class. Case 1, reciprocal affection, accelerates the situation which, in the longer term, would be produced by the neutrality of case 6. If all whites wished to marry blacks, and all blacks wished to marry whites, only a few generations would be needed for blacks and whites to coalesce into one homogeneous racial group.[3]

2 See also the typologies of Berry (1979) and Allardt (1979), which link 'territorial concentration' with 'cultural division of work.'
3 For a typology of the phenomenon of assimilation see Yinger (1981), who distinguishes amalgamation (a biological phenomenon), identification (psychological), acculturation (cultural), and integration (institutional).

TABLE 35
Types of relation between dominant and subordinate groups

Wishes of the subordinate group toward the dominate group	Wishes of the dominant group toward the subordinate group			
	To be assimilated into it	To remain neutral	To reject it	To assimilate it
To be assimilated	1	2	3	4
To remain neutral	5	6	7	8
To reject it	9	10	11	12
To assimilate it	13	14	15	16

For national origin, these situations of indifference or reciprocal affection lead rapidly – if the populations are geographically mixed – to the absence of differentiation, as with the many Canadians who prefer to describe their ethnic origin by the term *Canadian* rather than by one of the labels offered them by the census questionnaire – 'English,' 'French,' 'German,' inter alia. For religion, the effect is more difficult to predict over several generations: syncretism, tolerance, elimination of the less prevalent creeds? There is no obvious answer. For language, the case of reciprocal affection is fairly theoretical – if not on an individual level, then at least on the level of societies. The cost of acquisition of the other language is not of the same order as that involved in marriage with a person of another race or another religion. In the two latter cases, in a situation of indifference or reciprocal affection, the cost can be nil. In the case of language, this is never so.

But suppose that the unlikely occurs, and each acquires the tongue of the other; what would happen then? For unwritten and unstabilized languages, a mixture would probably be produced that would lead rapidly to another language. But where at least one of the languages is written and standardized, why – especially in a situation of neutrality – maintain two systems where one would suffice? To differentiate between roles? This is what the Agans of Ethiopia do (Cooper 1977), or the Mestizos of Paraguay (Rubin 1968), who continue to use a distinct language as the family language in order to maintain their ethnic individuality. It is the same with the trilingual Luxemburgers or the German Swiss, who alternate between dialect and classical German. These cases of di- or tri-glossia, which assign different languages to different roles, can stabilize multilingualism in a given society for a long time. But this stabilization presupposes a clear differentiation of roles and generally produces a hierarchy that corresponds to the hierarchy of these roles. In geographically and socially stable traditional peasant societies, the family language will have more prestige and breadth than in urban societies, with their marked spatial and social mobility, where it will be much more difficult for the family language to resist the assimilative pressures of the public language, which has the most universal degree of expression. In strongly integrated societies, with marked internal mobility, the cost of maintaining two linguistic systems where one would suffice will be deemed excessive, if not exorbitant. In this case, as opposed to what happens in the cases of race, religion, or national origin, neutrality is not in fact neutral; it favours the dominant language, the one with the widest field of application and the greatest prestige.

In the frequent case of reciprocal rejection (case 11 in Table 35), the dominant group, like the subordinate, rejects assimilation; both wish to retain their identity. This situation will generally be clearly asymmetrical. The powers and the sphere of action of the dominant group will be wider than those of the subordinate group. If the minority accepts lower position, the asymmetrical relationship becomes stabilized. But what happens if the minority does not accept its inferior status and in the name of human rights demands equality? In the cases of race, religion, and national origin, it is easy to see how the problem can be resolved: by removing discriminatory obstacles to social promotion that keep members of the minority at a disadvantage. The rights of man of the French type of 1789, or the American type in the first amendments to the constitution of 1787, or again those in the Canadian Charter of Rights of 1982 removed such obstacles. These documents place no obligation on the dominant group to marry persons of a minority race or nationality, or to convert to the religion of the weakest community; they simply require the dominant group to close its eyes, to pay no attention to differences of religion, race, or nationality. The solutions envisaged for the problem posed by discrimination are personal. The injunction is simple: treat your neighbour as yourself. This will mean accepting a person of a minority race or religion as a neighbour, or as the head of a business, or as prime minister.

These correctives to situations of social asymmetry by individual non-discrimination are explained by Rawls's assumption about the basis of a contract of justice. How can one organize the ideal society if one does not know, in advance, what one's race, sex, social class, etc, will be? For the American society that it uses as its model, Rawls's assumption admittedly raises problems. Is it reasonable to think that egalitarian solutions can correct acquired asymmetrical situations? Ought one not to correct such situations by granting privileges of admission – into businesses, universities, or parliaments, for example – to underprivileged groups? Put another way, can one rely on individual solutions that are egalitarian in nature to correct group inequalities?

In the case of race, religion, or ethnic origin, the consensus is not clearly in favour of one particular solution rather than another (Van Dyke 1975; Glazer 1978). The case of American Jews, Japanese, and Chinese shows that it is sufficient that the dominant group change its policy of discrimination into one of neutrality; the minority group, while still maintaining its distinctiveness should it so desire, obtains the equality of individual treatment that will restore the imbalance in its favour. For American blacks, however, perhaps because of a different family structure, simple neutrality of the dominant group was not sufficient to correct the effect of previous discrimination. But if for religion, race, and national origin recognizing the equality of individuals may produce egalitarian social situations, for language individual rights are not sufficient. It is easy and reasonable to say, 'You will be admitted or promoted whatever your race or your religion,' without thereby changing anything in the structure of existing institutions. But how could one say the same thing, in the same conditions of status quo, in the case of spoken language? A language, unless it be dead or reserved for private use, has to have speakers able to understand it. Zolberg puts it excellently: the state can play the blind man but not the deaf-mute (Zolberg 1977). To arrange for 30 per cent of Canadian public civil servants to be francophone is one thing; to arrange for this francophone 30 per cent to work in French is another. The recognition of purely individual linguistic rights (of the type in which each person speaks the language of his or her choice) is, and could only be, a recognition of the status quo, and hence of asymmetry, if there is asymmetry. Such recognition is generally merely a disguised or involuntary form of assimilation, which comes from treating language as one treats national origin.

To protect a minority language, not by ineffective individual rights but by group rights, requires territorial rights. To illustrate this phenomenon, let us consider two opposed cases. The first, which occurs frequently in industrial societies (whether liberal, authoritarian, or totalitarian), corresponds to case 12 of the matrix in Table 35: the dominant group seeks to assimilate the minority, while the minority seeks to preserve its distinctiveness. The second case, just as frequent, corresponds to case 3: the minority seeks to abandon its distinctiveness and to assimilate itself into the dominant group, which rejects this request.

Let us consider the second case first and illustrate the differences between language and the other criteria of ethnicity by imagining the hypothetical case of a spy. 'How does one pass unnoticed in an ehtnic group other than one's own, when one belongs to either a different race, a different religion, a different linguistic group, or a group of different national origin?' The answer will vary in accordance with the distance between the dominant and subordinate groups.

Certain linguistic distances – between Slovak and Chinese – may be greater than certain racial distances – between the whites and browns of Brazil, for example. But in terms of the time it takes to pass from one group to another, the cleavage most difficult to overcome is usually racial; typically, several generations are needed in order to 'pass,' as one used to say in the United States. The simplest obstacle, and least demanding in transition time, is generally national origin. A change of name, or of forename, may be sufficient for a Hungarian to become an English Canadian, or for a Moroccan to become French. Language generally lies between race and religion as regards difficulties in 'passing.' Unless one wishes to become a theologian – and unless the religion is one of extreme esotericism or is tied to other criteria of ethnicity such as race, tribe, or caste – then apprenticeship to its beliefs, practices, and symbols will generally be easier than apprenticeship to another tongue. To penetrate a dominant group that opposes such penetration will thus typically be easier by means of language than by race, but less easy by language than by religion or national origin.[4] Penetration by language will generally be very expensive and often cannot be effected in less than two generations.

I do not know whether it is practical in the sphere of espionage to install a first generation of 'sleepers' which penetrates the target society with a view to activating the second generation, which is no longer 'visible' from the linguistic point of view. But our problem of the spy shows once again that the techniques of protection of a minority that wishes to become integrated into a dominant group that denies it this integration would not be the same according to the criterion of ethnicity. To give each person the right to change his or her name cheaply will often be sufficient to wipe out national origin as early as the first generation; to give the right to learn and to speak the language of his or her choice (which is generally automatic – but which the Indians of Bolivia did not enjoy during the colonial era) will often per-

---

4 A historical case of the testing of the foreigner by the language he speaks is presented by the massacre at Bruges in 1302 – the Flemish insurgents identified French soldiers by their faulty pronunciation of 'Schilde en de vriend' ('shield and friend'), a phrase containing phonemes unpronounceable by a francophone (Berghe 1981). The 'sch' or 'sh' sounds thus appear, from biblical times onward, to have had high survival value – see Judges 12:6. I am grateful to Anthony Martin-Sperry for pointing this out to me.

mit 'passing' only in the second generation, which will have learned the language of its hosts from infancy. The individual type of solution to ethnic discrimination – change of name, language, religion, or race, as and when desired (and this solution is largely ineffective in the case of race) – thus takes effect only in the long term in the case of language. Thus in the United States, where discrimination is predominantly racial in nature, the political authorities, by 'favoritism of the disfavored' (affirmative action), have shifted their interpretation of the constitution from the notion of individual rights to that of collective rights.

A problem diametrically opposed to that of the spy is that raised by the conflicting attitudes of case 12 in Table 35. The dominant group seeks to assimilate the weaker group, which rejects assimilation. This is the problem posed by the conservative immigrant oriented toward the past in a liberal host society oriented toward the future. Can this immigrant single-handedly, without the support of a community in his or her own image, maintain a distinctive identity? In the case of national origin, this preservation can be effected at small cost; all that is needed is a few private associations at which people meet to play cards, a few choral societies where the old country songs are sung, a few community centres to which one sends one's children, in country costume, to do clog-dances on the stage. In a border-line situation, it may be sufficient simply to retain one's family name. In the case of race, refusal to accept loss of identity is already a little more difficult but does not call for heavy densities of population. Even in societies in which divorce is usual, the decision to marry and have children is a relatively infrequent individual decision. An ethnic group determined to maintain its racial origins may seek its spouses elsewhere – sometimes thousands of kilometres away – in order to avoid losing itself within the host society. This is what the Chinese on the west coast of Canada did at the beginning of this century; they had come to build the railways but had brought very few women with them.

Like race, religion normally calls for a certain spatial concentration to maintain itself. But in border-line cases it can survive by keeping itself private; this is what the Jewish religion did. Even if it requires certain public buildings – churches or temples – and hence a certain concentration of population, and even if these buildings must be maintained without aid other than from the local community, this community, if it truly wishes to preserve its religion, will find within itself the resources needed to maintain the cult. The minority is not obliged, at least in a libertarian regime, to maintain a religious relationship with the dominant group. It effectively isolates itself by means of its religion, and it can so isolate itself without costs other than those of transmitting its creed – at least in modern societies in which religion is largely dissociated from politics and the economy. In such cases, then, in a liberal society, individual rights – the right to keep one's name, race, or religion, and to pass them on to one's children – will generally be sufficient to protect a minority that refuses to submit to the assimilative pressures of the dominant group. However, it is totally different for language, because it is a means of universal communication. The need to know one's neighbour's language – be he or she a grocer, doctor, foreman, lawyer, or professor – is not of the same order as that to be surrounded by neighbours of the same religion, nationality, or race. This evidence is ignored when, to protect a minority language, one uses solely the technique of individual rights, invented to protect liberty of conscience.

What spatial concentration of population is required to maintain a language? We have already shown that the yardstick cannot be universal but will vary according to the level of economic and cultural development of the ethnic group in question and according to the degree of assimilative pressure of the rival languages. We have estimated that in a modern industrial society, the survival of a minority language as a language in full use, rather than as a museum piece, a hobby, or a recognition sign, calls for the territorial concentration required for the establishment of a university. A further requisite is a density of population that ensures that the members of the ethnic minority will be able to find, in a geographic area of action within reach of communication at reasonable cost, speakers of the same language who satisfy the demands of their different social roles. In other words, the density of the minority population must be such that one does not need to use another language with the grocer, restaurateur, lawyer, or politician. Further, the density of linguistic communication thus defined will vary according to the state of development of the society in question. Certain peasant societies are sparing of words, if not poorly equipped therewith, and their people have remarkable power in initiating and refusing communication. Contemporary cities, in contrast, are speaking societies in which the speaker has lost the peasant's autonomy of words; he or she is much more frequently the receiver of messages than their initiator. This minimal control over the linguistic environment reinforces the necessity of territorial concentration of the minority language.

Linguistic concentration reduces the costs of communication. For a minority afraid of assimilation it also reduces the temptation to 'desert,' The good sense of traditional morality made it clear that one protected oneself against 'bad' associations only by good ones. For a minority linguistic ethnic group, the only good association is that of the same language, since the 'risks' of assimilation are not symmetrical. Tajfel's hypothesis (1974), according to which the acquisition of a foreign language brings closer the ethnic groups that speak this language, must be qualified by the hierarchical factor (Lijphart 1977; Pool 1979). The reduction of distance will be greater if it takes place upward in the social scale rather than downward; it is thus to the advantage of the dominant group.

In summary, let us distinguish the rights of the person that can protect the individual directly from those that can protect this same individual only indirectly, by the instrumentality of the group, and let us contrast easily transported rights with those anchored in institutions that are themselves anchored in geographical space. These two distinctions give us the matrix of Table 36. Linguistic rights of type A apply directly to persons; they ignore the local linguistic context. Here are several examples that we will examine more closely in the next chapter. The canton of Berne gives the right to each of its residents to file his tax return either in French or in German, wherever he resides in the canton, even if he is the sole francophone of his village or town, and even if he is not a francophone. Every Bernese may obtain from his cantonal government a tax form made out in one of the two official languages. Similarly, Article 19 of the Canadian Charter of Rights and Freedoms of 1982 specifies:

(1) Either English or French may be used by any person in, or in any pleading in or process issuing from, any court established by Parliament.

Transportable rights given to groups rather than to individuals (type B) are rare in the linguistic sphere. The Estonian and Lithuanian constitutional laws of the 1920s, which I will analyse in detail in chapter 7, provide the best example of this. These laws gave to linguistic and religious minorities the right to organize themselves after the manner of local governments even though they had no specific territorial base. For example, the Russian minority in Estonia had the right to set itself up as an autonomous community no matter where its members resided, the right to tax these members, and the right to administer their schools.

The Canadian constitution and American jurisprudence recognize the notion of the minority group and are prepared to tip the scales in its favour by the granting of compensatory privileges (affirmative action), but both of them accord privileges to individuals. They do not give groups the right to decide the way in which acknowledged inequality shall be compensated or to determine who shall benefit thereby. American judges and Canadian legislators have in mind the minorities of type 2 or 3 of Table 35, which wish to assimilate or integrate themselves but run up against the neutrality or the hostility of the dominant group. In contrast, the Baltic legislators had in mind the minorities of types 10, 11, 12, which, whatever the attitude of the dominant group toward them – assimilative, neutral, or hostile – desired to keep their distance, to remain separate, at least partially, from the ethnic

TABLE 36
The rights of man according to territorial localization

	Individual rights	Group rights
Transportable rights	A	B
Localized rights	C	D

group that controlled the central state. In order to do this, these ethnic minorities were granted the right to form subordinate governments that were granted specific powers, especially in the areas of language and education.

Type C of Table 36, the localized individual right, is relatively frequent in the sphere of language. It consists of giving speakers of a minority language the right to their language, not over the whole of the territory, but only in the regions or districts where the minority language exists in sufficient concentration. For example, the Czech constitution of 1920 gave the right to address the public authorities in a minority language if this language were used by at least 20 per cent of the inhabitants. In Finland, the bilingual districts, in which Swedish can be used as the language of local administration, are defined by the '10 per cent and 8 per cent rule' (10 per cent to obtain the right to bilingualism, 8 per cent as the minimum before ceasing to have the right). In Canada, the right to use the official minority language in provincial courts is limited to Quebec, Manitoba, and New Brunswick,[5] and the right to public schooling in the official minority language is limited to the areas of a province in which the number of children using the minority language justifies the exercise of this right. The text of the Canadian constitution specifies neither the number nor the percentage, thus leaving the courts as arbiters of the matter. In Finland and India, the rule is more precise. In Finland, a request by 18 children leads to the establishing of a primary class. In India, instruction in the minority language will be offered if it is demanded by 10 students out of 40 in the case of an elementary school, and by 15 students out of 60 in secondary schools. In the United States, the laws on education and bilingual voting notices use the rule of 5 per cent of the population of the district concerned. Thus in certain cases localization of the right is definitive: it applies then to a geographic entity within well-defined limits (Quebec or New Brunswick, for example), while in other cases, localization is subject to the flow of populations as measured by censuses or scholastic registrations.

5 French may be used in Ontario courts, but the right is not protected constitutionally.

Finally, case D concerns localized territorial rights that have devolved onto groups rather than individuals. A typical application of such a right is the territorial division of Switzerland, or Belgium, which we shall describe more fully in the next chapter. Swiss cantons have the right to pass laws either for unilingualism or for bilingualism, in all spheres under their jurisdiction, particularly in education, culture, work, and public administration. In Belgium (with the exception of Brussels) the two major linguistic communities each have their own particular territorial institutions which govern unilingualism in education, culture, and the workplace. Most Swiss and Belgians are thus deprived of the choice of the language in which their children will be educated, since the local authorities determine in fact the language of education in private as well as public schools.

The right given to a sub-governmental group to control its linguistic environment involves severe restrictions on individual rights. Belgian parents who complained that their fundamental rights were violated by regulations that forbade them to choose the language in which their children would be educated at school appealed the matter to the European Court of the Rights of Man. In its judgment, this court decided that if the Belgian authorities were obliged to respect the philosophic and religious convictions of the parents, they had the right nevertheless to impose, in their education, the language of their choice. In Switzerland, several judgments of the Federal Tribunal have established that local and cantonal authorities have the right to make exceptions to the constitutional rule of equality of treatment of all Swiss, and to forbid, in their territory, the use of certain official languages, in publicity and education, for example. The Federal Tribunal justifies the right given to the cantons to impose unilingualism in these words, in a ruling dating from the 1930s (Héraud 1974, 247):

The linguistic frontiers of our country, once fixed, must be considered as unchangeable; the certainty for each original segment (*souche*) of the population of the integrity of the territory throughout which its language is spoken and over which its own culture extends constitutes the safeguard of the harmonious relationships of the various parts of the country; and the right of each of these to forestall any encroachment must be recognized.

In the same way, the tribunal rejected in 1965 the complaints of a francophone association that sought to have the language of the school recognized as an individual right; it thus confirmed the linguistic frontier in its role as protector of the ethnic minorities (Héraud, 1974): 'The risk of foreign immigration ... is controlled only by the linguistic assimilation of the immigrants ... and it is there that the school has an important role to play; it becomes its duty to communicate to its students the knowledge of the language of their new home.'

The 1982 Canadian Charter of Rights runs counter to the Swiss legislation when it forbids provincial authorities to impose on Canadian citizens from other provinces an official language of instruction other than their own. Article 23 specifies:

(1) Citizens of Canada
   (a) whose first language learned and still understood is that of the English or French linguistic minority population of the province in which they reside [This paragraph, unlike the ones that follow, is subject to ratification by Quebec before coming into effect.], or
   (b) who have received their primary school instruction in Canada in English or French and reside in a province where the language in which they received that instruction is the language of the English or French linguistic minority population of the province,
   have the right to have their children receive primary and secondary school instruction in that language in that province.
(2) Citizens of Canada of whom any child has received or is receiving primary or secondary school instruction in English or French in Canada, have the right to have all their children receive primary and secondary school instruction in the same language.
(3) The right of citizens of Canada under subsections (1) and (2) to have their children receive primary and secondary school instruction in the language of the English or French linguistic minority population of a province
   (a) applies wherever in the province the number of children of citizens who have such a right is sufficient to warrant the provision to them out of public funds of minority language instruction; and
   (b) includes, where the number of those children so warrant, the right to have them receive that instruction in minority language educational facilities provided out of public funds.

The contrast between this article and article 15 of the same charter is revealing. In the case of race, national or ethnic origin, colour, religion, sex, and age, the new Canadian constitution recognizes a principle of exception to the rule of equality, since it permits the favouring of persons belonging to minority groups; but the same constitution excludes language from the right to enjoy unequal rights in the form of affirmative action. Following the logic of its article 15, it could, in article 23 of the charter, have given to the francophone minorities, but not to the anglophones, the right to determine the language of instruction throughout their cultural territories; by so doing, the constitution would have allowed Quebec to adopt a territorial unilingualism of the Swiss type.

That the Canadian constitution did not adopt for language the principle of compensatory inequality that it adopted in other areas well illustrates the specificity of linguistic ethnic groups. As regards religion or national origin, the principle of compensatory privilege, one translated into individual rights, has an assimilative effect; its aim is to remove a cleavage that is a source of political tensions. As regards language, the same principle, applied in matching fashion to collective rights, would reinforce existing cleavages. The difference between article 15 and article 23 of the Canadian Charter of Rights is thus logically in keeping with a legal instrument that seeks to centralize the state and homogenize society. History will record whether or not it is easier to integrate, in one and the same political system, linguistic groups that are mixed on the territorial level (this is the Canadian optional solution assumed by the Charter of 1982) rather than groups that are kept separate, *chacun chez soi*, to each its own house, as in Switzerland and Belgium. The sociology of the relationships between languages in contact, which identifies an effect of inevitable stratification between the dominant language and the minority language, leads one to the conclusion that the Canadian solution works to the advantage of the dominant group. Equal rights given to unequal languages could not produce egalitarian situations.

7

Problems of the multilingual state: personal and territorial solutions

The territorial solution to the problems of the multilingual state is basically one of intra-state frontiers, while the personal solution is basically one of rights that are portable over the whole territory of the state. The utility of either of these solutions depends on the objective of the political group that has adopted it. Depending on whether this objective is the assimilation of the minority into the dominant linguistic group or preservation of ethnic pluralism, and whether this objective is short term or long term, different policies should be followed. To avoid repetition, I shall consider the problem – as in the previous chapter – from the sole point of view of a linguistic minority whose existence is to be protected and survival ensured.

Personal solutions

Personal solutions seek to establish language as a right equally as portable as the right to vote or the right of religious expression. We shall consider the right under various headings: the right to speak, the right to understand and be understood, the right to education, and the right to ethnic identity.

The right to speak

In the modern state, the right to speak the language of one's choice is nearly always subject to strong social constraints. The virulence of these constraints shows up in the behaviour of schoolchildren of different languages; the minority language is speedily driven back into the individual memory, where it hides and atrophies, unless the children form separate linguistic groups in their games as well as their studies. These social constraints play a determinant role in societies in which laissez faire is considered as equality.

I shall deal here, however, only with legal guarantees and constraints and will limit myself to giving a few examples. Article 23 of the Belgian constitution specifies that regulation of the use of languages shall not affect the private sphere. But it is the law which defines this sphere, determines the language of the school and of the official records kept by boards of directors, whether of public or of private enterprises. Despite these encroachments by the legislator, there still remains a vast area of social relationships in which the right to speak the language of one's choice is protected by the law. If this law forbids road signs in French in Flanders, it does not forbid Flemish merchants to speak French to their customers. Article 13 of the Egyptian constitution of 1923 stipulated most precisely that no restriction should be imposed on the right to the language used in private communication, business, religion, the press, and public meetings.

Such provisions are rare. Either the public authority assumes that the use of language in the private sphere is at the individual's choice, or it lets things slide, since freedom works to the advantage of the dominant ethnic group's language. Regulation of the language admitted into the public domain is more frequent. Some constitutions give members of parliament the right to use their own language in the state assemblies. This is what the Sardinian constitution of 1848, which became the constitution of the kingdom of Italy, did for French and Italian; this is what the British North America Act of 1867 does for French and English in the federal parliament and in the Quebec assembly. Sometimes this right is extended to the judiciary. The Canadian constitution of 1867 provides for the use of both French and English before the federal courts and before the provincial courts in Quebec.

In addition to parliamentary assemblies and courts of justice, the right to use a minority language is also sometimes guaranteed in the public administration, in particular, for correspondence between the public services and members of the public. The Estonian constitution of 1920 allowed Russians, Germans, and Swedes to use their own language when dealing with the central administration. Similarly, the Canadian statute on official languages guarantees the right to use either French or English when dealing with federal government offices. The same holds good in Switzerland for French, German, and Italian; in Finland, for Finnish and Swedish; and in South Africa, for Afrikaans and English. However, it is rare to find guarantees as generous as those contained in the Austrian constitution of 1867: 'The State recognizes the equality of the various languages in the offices of the Government and in public life,' a generous guarantee which promised the impossible. In more realistic fashion, the Czech constitution of 1920 restricted the right to address public authorities in German to those

districts in which at least 20 per cent of the inhabitants were germano-
phones. Similarly, Swedes in Finland were permitted to use Swedish in their
dealings with local authorities only in those districts in which they formed at
least 6 per cent of the population.[1]

The right to understand and be understood

It is sometimes enough to give the minority the right to speak without giving
it the right to be understood. When the Italian élite spoke French, or at least
understood it universally, the Sardinian constitution of 1848 could limit
itself to stipulating that the elected representatives of francophone districts
had the right to speak in French and that if they exercised this right they
must be replied to in that language (Dodd 1909). Until simultaneous translation was introduced into the Canadian parliament in 1959, the right
granted to francophone elected members to speak their own language meant
in fact that they had the right to choose not to be understood; conversely,
the anglophones of Quebec, who had the reciprocal right to use their language in the provincial parliament, were in a similar position vis-à-vis their
francophone colleagues as were the Franco-Italians in nineteenth-century
Italy.

Most of the time, the right to be understood implies the existence of a
simultaneous-translation system of the type used in parliaments in Belgium,
Cameroon, Canada, India, Madagascar, Pakistan, Singapore, Swaziland,
Switzerland, and Yugoslavia (see Appendix). Application of the right to be
understood varies according to the function of the institution for which
multilingualism is being legislated. An organ of co-operation will accept the
use of several languages more easily than an organ of command or control.
In nineteenth-century Austro-Hungary even after Hungarian was placed on
an equal footing with German, the latter remained the language of the
army; the emperor refused to allow his troops to be commanded in a language other than his own. In Belgium, the army was one of the last institutions to move from French monolingualism to French/Dutch bilingualism.
In Canada, despite a policy of promoting systematic bilingualism during the
1970s, the language of command – and in particular that of the high command of the armed forces – is still English. The 1979 Royal Commission of
Enquiry into the state of the Canadian Armed Forces received practically no

---

1 For a comparative study of legal and constitutional provisions concerning the right to
language, see Laponce (1960) and *Minorités linguistiques et interventions* (1978). For the
text of constitutions of the ninenteenth and early twentieth centuries, see Dareste
(1928–34) and Peaslee (1950).

briefs in French from officers who were described as francophones, so strong was the view that English was the only really military language.

It cannot however be laid down as a general rule that institutions of command such as that of the armed forces will always be more impervious to multilingualism than those of co-operation. In Switzerland, for example, the armed forces have an avowed function of national integration, more than any other government institution; thus the practice of bilingualism will be pushed to the hilt there. In Belgium also the army is used now as an instrument of national integration – not at unit level, where personnel are mustered in unilingual regiments, but at the command level, where a good working knowledge of the two languages is required from the rank of major upward.

The European Community

The administrative system faced with the most complex linguistic problems is that of the European Community in Brussels. Since the entry of Denmark, Greece, Spain and Portugal into the community, the system must operate in nine different languages: French, English, German, Italian, Dutch, Danish, Greek, Spanish, and Portuguese. There is one level where these languages are equal: the dissemination of texts and official regulations for the use of member states. A regulation of the community must be understood by interested parties in each member state. No compromise is possible at this level. However, an informal meeting between officials or ministers of member states needs a lingua franca. Without simultaneous-translation facilities, the system inevitably tends toward adoption of a dominant language.

At official meetings of the Council of Ministers in Brussels, all languages are used, although Greek and Danish pose considerable difficulties, for there are not enough translators whose mother-tongue is Danish who know Demotic Greek (adopted as the official language after the fall of the junta). It is thus often necessary for translation from Greek to Danish to be done through the medium of another language, German or French, for example; the Danish translator will then put into Danish the translation of the Greek that has been done by a German or French colleague. When ministers continue their discussions in informal committee, typically during the meals they take together, they bring their translators along with them; but on those occasions the understanding is that only three languages will be used in the discussion – French, English, and German.

Further linguistic simplification takes place at the level of the permanent bureaucracy that administers the Community from Brussels or Luxemburg.

The permanent ambassadors of the member states customarily use only French, English, and German. In EC offices only two languages – French and German – were used as lingua francas before Britain became a member. Since Britain's entry, two languages have been dominant – French and English. Of these two, French has the advantage in both areas, written and spoken – 60 per cent of the documents submitted for translation are written in French, 30 per cent in English, and 10 per cent in other languages.[2] When a Community official phones another official whose preferred language he or she does not know, he or she will typically initiate the conversation in French.

The dominance of French in the permanent administration is largely explained by the fact that Brussels is a predominantly francophone city. The official who takes a post there lives in French surroundings and a French atmosphere. But these locational reasons alone would not be enough to make French the dominant language; French is also a lingua franca in western Europe. For this reason, it is in a better position in Brussels, in the EC, than it is in Paris, in UNESCO. But in Paris, as in Brussels, linguistic simplification has been achieved, and effective communication within the organization is carried out mainly in two languages – English and French.

The right to education in one's own language

The rights to speak, to understand, and to be understood would be limited in scope if they were not underlain by the right to educate and to be educated in one's mother-tongue. These rights take two main forms, teaching of the minority language and teaching in that language. None of the provinces of Canada undertakes teaching in Chinese; but none of them places any obstacle in the way of that language's being used in night schools or weekend courses. Every province makes it a legal obligation for Chinese children to receive their normal education, whether in private schools or in state schools, in one or other of the two official languages. France in the 1980s is following a policy of promoting regional languages in its secondary schools, but with minor, almost negligible exceptions, these are 'taught' languages, not 'teaching' languages.

The teaching of one's language is usually an unacceptable substitute for teaching in one's language. The teaching of Ukrainian in the Faculties of Letters and Philosophy at the University of Kiev does not satisfy national-

---

2 According to unpublished data from the Translation Service. By contrast, at the United Nations, 80 per cent of documents originate in English, 12 per cent in French, and 8 per cent in other languages.

ists who would like Ukrainian to be the 'teaching' language in all the faculties, including Science and Medicine. Between teaching of and teaching in the minority language lies so-called bilingual teaching – e.g. English/ Ukrainian in Manitoba – which consists of teaching some subjects in the curriculum in one language and others in another, or even repeating the teaching of each subject in the other language. Then the equation 'language and school subject' can be varied. The minority language need not be systematically linked to minority subjects, which would happen in Canada if, for example, high-prestige subjects such as the sciences were taught in the language of the dominant group, while design, the humanities, and the social sciences were kept for the minority language. However, a bilingual school system generally has only the appearance of equality. Even when it is balanced at the level of the courses it is in fact unbalanced in favour of the dominant language which dominates the environment outside the school. Bilingualism in education is thus generally a bilingualism of transition, which in the long run facilitates linguistic assimilation with the dominant group. Article 19 of the Austrian constitution of 1867 stipulated that in electoral districts populated by various ethnic groups, educational institutions would be organized in such a way that linguistic minorities could receive education in their own language without being compelled to learn a second language.

The right to language as identity

The problems posed by language as an identity, in relation to the right to speak, the right to understand, the right to be understood, or the right to teach, are more easily resolved than are those posed by language as an instrument of communication. A language as an identity, which is often reduced to being scarcely more than a rallying, 'flag' language, makes do with very little: crèches or kindergartens in the language of the ethnic group of origin, bilingual cheques, bilingual administrative forms or notices, sermons or speeches in the minority language. It is obligatory in Canada – even in the provinces in which French is less widespread than in Italy – to use both official languages on the labels of all food products sold in shops.

One hopes that these marks of politeness toward a minority language reduce the negative effects of a subtractive bilingualism (see p. 49). The minority will more willingly agree to use the language of the dominant group if it finds its own native tongue treated with respect on all sides. This native tongue, when an identity-language, lends itself more readily to solutions of the personal type than does language as an instrument; it is more easily accorded portable rights. As a result, language as an identity is not unlike religion but is entirely different in character from language as an instrument; it is symbolic and has almost no need to be spoken, and thus can be content with the territorial dispersion that every individual-type solution seeks to encourage.

Personal solutions of the collective type

Personal solutions, a few examples of which we have just mentioned, assume the aspect of rights of the individual over the political powers that be. There is another form of personal solution, in which power is delegated by higher political authority for the benefit of a subordinate linguistic community defined in non-territorial fashion; the object here is the establishment of a sort of ethnic-based personal federalism. A solution of this nature, applied to the multilingual state, draws its inspiration from practices as long-standing as the Polish Kahal or the Turkish Millet, which delegated administrative and governmental power to non-territorial communities (Laponce 1960). Originally, the object of these practices was to protect and conciliate minority religious communities – Jews in Poland; Christians, Jews, and Orthodox in the Ottoman Empire. Polish Kahals were basically local Jewish governments within territorial boundaries; but each one nominated delegates to a national council that had two functions – to act as the Polish king's agent and to govern the Jewish community established in Poland. This Jewish government had power to levy taxes and to administer its own institutions – in particular, its schools. In the Ottoman Empire, the Millet established solutions even more clearly dissociated from the ordinary territorial administration. Minority religious communities had the right to legislate on every matter which, for the Moslems, came under the jurisdiction of the Sharia; education was one such matter – and hence the language of instruction. In the Millet's sphere of competence, minority individuals had no direct personal relations with the Turkish administration; they dealt perforce with the minority's courts, schools, and other authorities. The Millets, originally set up on a religious basis, were thus often multilingual. This was a source of frequent internal conflict which saw, for example, the Serbs opposing the Bulgarians and the Greeks who wished to impose their language in church as well as in the schoolroom. These tensions – which were not always displeasing to the Ottoman authorities – reached such a level that it was finally decided to divide up the original religious Millets on a linguistic basis; the 3 Millets of the fifteenth century had become 14 by the twentieth.

The most systematic recent examples of application of the principle of personality for the benefit of linguistic communities were provided by the Baltic states in the period between the two world wars. An Estonian law of 1925 enabled every ethnic group of at least 3,000 souls to establish itself as a recognized minority as of public right (Aun 1940). The definition of the ethnic group was entirely voluntary. If he so wished, a germanophone could have his name included in the list of the German minority; or, if he preferred, he could declare himself an Estonian. Conversely, an Estonian – even if he spoke no German – could have himself included in the German list, if he so desired. Children under the age of 18 automatically took the nationality of their parents. These inclusions in minority lists were not permanent. It was always possible to move from one list to another – with the reservation, however, that the minority authorities could refuse to reinstate an applicant who had cancelled his original membership.

In order to obtain recognition as of right, a minority in Estonia had to satisfy the following requirements: have at least 3,000 people in its list of members; obtain the enrolment of at least half the adults of the minority, the total population thereof being taken as the figure determined by the most recent census; have a cultural council elected by at least half the listed electorate of the minority; have requested minority status by a vote of at least two-thirds of its cultural council. The instrument of government of the minority consisted of this cultural council, whose powers included education. The minority had the right to organize its private schools as it wished, equally with its public schools, though the public schools had to be organized in agreement with the central state authorities. The Ministry of Education had the authority, if necessary, to settle any disputes that arose between the minority's cultural council and the local authorities.

The financial resources of Estonia's minority communities came from two different sources – the state budget and the taxes imposed on its members by the cultural council. The rate and assessment of minority taxes, like those of local governments, had to be approved by the central government. The minority administration had the right to issue edicts having the force of law on the members of the minority. In short, minority linguistic communities ranked as local authorities, except that they had no territory of their own. The minorities most strongly concentrated from a geographical point of view – the Russians and the Swedes – were not organized as minority communities; their desire for autonomy was satisfied by their control of a few local governments. In contrast, the territorially dispersed minorities, the Jews and the Germans, profited by the system of personal cultural federalism that was offered them.

Territorial solutions

Territorial solutions stem from the principle that languages in contact should be separated as much as possible by means of fixed frontiers that give a feeling of security. An example of a sub-state frontier controlled by the central authority is provided by the Soviet Union. Change of residence is not freely permitted and the movement of population between each of the republics is decided by the central authorities; thus control of passage across the boundaries surrounding the principal linguistic minorities is in the hands of the dominant ethnic group. The Russians decide – based on reasons that are of course only partly linguistic – on the passage of the country's main internal frontiers and the frontiers of the minority languages. The dominant group can thus use the existing boundaries either to protect the minority or to protect itself.

Unlike the Russian Empire, the Soviet Union has not followed a policy of systematic Russification. Its policy is selective and varies according to the times and nationalities. But the ultimate objective can always be discerned – promotion of Russian at the expense of other languages, especially its sister languages, Ukrainian and Belorussian. This promotion of Russian is carried out simply, by denying the minority languages the ability to penetrate Russian territory; there are no Ukrainian schools or universities in Russia, and minority languages are not used in the central administration. Russians established in the other republics (particularly in the slavic republics) are able to use their own language in the schools and in the administration. This asymmetry works to the advantage of Russian, the linguistic frontiers of which permit exit but forbid entrance. According to Caro (1982) 98.5 per cent of Russians settled in Ukraine retain their language, while only 42.5 per cent of the Ukrainians settled in Russia do so. The retention rate of Russian by Russians is at its lowest in Lithuania, where it 'falls' to 92.8 per cent, while the highest retention rate of Ukrainian by Ukrainians outside their republic occurs in Moldavia, where it is only 79.4 per cent.[3]

An example of partial frontier control granted to a minority group is provided by the 1979 agreement between Quebec and the federal government of Canada, which gave Quebec control over immigration originating outside Canada. This control is not extended to internal migration. Indeed, freedom of *internal* migration is characteristic of every multilingual democratic state. There are linguistic and administrative frontiers in Belgium, Switzerland, Italy, and Spain; but none of these states places any obstacle in the way of citizens who wish to cross these internal frontiers and establish

3 Data on the evolution of linguistic equilibrium in the Soviet Union are supplied by Ornstein (1959), Goldhagen (1968), Guboglo (1972), Silver (1974a, b; 1975), Ashworth (1977), Carrère d'Encausse (1978), Hodnett (1978), R.A. Lewis (1976), Dostal and Krippenberg (1979), Pool (1980), Brunner (1981), Bilinsky (1981), Kreindler (1982), Benningsen (1982), and Caro (1982).

themselves in a linguistic area other than their area of origin, and in none is crossing the linguistic border accompanied by any political discrimination. The Italian who wishes to settle in Val d'Aosta, the Andalusian who moves to Catalonia, the Fleming who moves to Wallonia, and the Bernese who settles in Geneva are in no way deprived of the right to vote in national or regional elections, even in Switzerland, where national citizenship can be obtained only through citizenship at the local government level.

However, freedom to choose one's place of residence does not automatically include the right to import one's language. If Switzerland and Belgium feel they can leave their linguistic internal boundaries open to all provided they are resident within the state, these states have substituted control of linguistic behaviour for control of those crossing the boundary. More precisely, they have established strict control over the use of language within their territory. In a unilingual Swiss canton, for example Geneva, the language of public usage – whether in politics, administration, education, or at work – is exclusively French.[4] In this respect, there is no appreciable difference between Geneva and Paris.

To say that the canton of Geneva and France are unilingual does not of course mean to say that French, and only French, is spoken there. In Geneva, as in France, foreign languages can be learned in private schools, or indeed as a second language in the public school system; but in both the language of instruction in the public schools is exclusively French. In Geneva, as in France, a legal contract must be drafted in French, whether the firm is Swiss or multinational. In Geneva, as in France, correspondence between local and central authorities will be conducted exclusively in French. Further, the visual environment is basically unilingual in both countries. If this is perhaps a little less so in Geneva than in Paris, it is because English rather than German has infiltrated Geneva. If a café waiter or a hotel receptionist speaks German either in Geneva or in Paris, the law does not concern itself; however, in France as in Geneva, the law prevents (with minor and insignificant exceptions) a public secondary school from using any other language than French as the language of education. In Geneva as in France, one must receive one's education in French; and if education at university level is permitted in Geneva in a language other than French, this language will be English rather than German.

The consequences of territorial unilingualism may seem absurd and petty if taken out of their political and sociological context, if one forgets that the object of unilingualism is to prevent the overlapping of languages, which is

4 However, at a high level of decision – a board of directors, for example – the language used for oral communication may be different from the language of the territory; typically, the former language will be that of the head office or headquarters of the company.

always to the advantage of the dominant language. The Flemish postman who returns a letter to Wallonia because the address was written in French instead of in Dutch is making a gesture of defence which, multiplied many times by other gestures of the same kind, is contributing to the maintenance of the linguistic frontier that separates Dutch from French.

The recent history of Louvain University illustrates the dynamics of the principle of territoriality. Once adopted, this principle does not suffer exceptions gladly. At first Latin, then francophone, Louvain University became bilingual, first when some of the courses were given in Dutch, and then when two parallel branches were set up, one French, the other Dutch. But a partly francophone university was operating in Flemish territory. Louvain's bilingualism was merely a transitional phase that led to the forced hiving-off of francophone students and professors, together with part of the books and the laboratories, onto the other side of the linguistic frontier, into Wallonia. An institution of universal appeal, a university, had proved unable to withstand the astringent and exclusive force of the principle of territoriality.

In this connection, it will be interesting to follow the evolution of Canadian bilingual universities such as Laurentian and Ottawa. These universities are now in the unsystematic phase of language planning (some courses in one language, some courses in the other language, still other courses in both languages) experienced by Louvain a generation ago. Will they stay like that, with French dominant in the literary subjects and the social sciences, and English in the natural and biological sciences? The experience of Louvain shows such a mixture to be unstable. The Franco-Ontarian Association has for years been demanding exclusively francophone universities in Ontario – just as the Flemish did in Belgium a generation ago; but – unlike the Flemish – they have found it hard to justify their demand in the absence of a linguistic boundary that would officially separate French from English.

The territorial division of a country into unilingual zones implies the limitation of bilingualism to the national organizations of co-ordination. On this point, let us examine the two appreciably different solutions adopted by Switzerland and Belgium. The first has been set up for some time and has been well tested; the second is still seeking a balance that has not yet been achieved.

The Swiss model

The linguistic minorities of Switzerland have, de facto if not de jure, accepted the preponderance of the majority language in the central federal institutions as a set-off against rigid linguistic internal frontiers that allow cantonal unilingualism.[5] The working language in Bern is almost never Italian, and rarely French. Ninety per cent of documents intended for publication are written originally in German.[6] Between 1975 and 1980, out of 360 draft bills submitted to parliament by the Federal Council, only 14 per cent were originally written either in French or in Italian. And among the 18 most important of these drafts, which involved revision of the federal constitution, only one (5 per cent) was originally written in French.[7] The percentage use of French varies considerably according to the ministry. In Foreign Affairs, some offices prefer to operate in French – those that deal with France, francophone Africa, or the European Community. In Finance, French is scarcely used except as the language of official communication with the French-speaking cantons.

Generally speaking, the more important and urgent is the written word used internally in a central Swiss ministry, the more likely it is to be in German. Two francophone officials who speak to each other in French over the telephone will often write to each other in German, for the written word always has a wider potential spread than the spoken. To obtain the desired attention and influence, one must write in the dominant language. To write in French is to court delays and the hazards of translation, even when the translation is carried out – as it usually is in Switzerland – by colleagues conversant with the technical terminology, rather than – as in Canada – by professional translators lacking the appropriate jargon. Further, francophone officials in Bern often grumble that they spend too much of their time doing or revising translations, a task many of them consider difficult, boring, and relatively unimportant.

The dominance of German in Bern easily is explained: only about 20 per cent of central officials are francophone, and Bern is a German city, although French has been there for a long time and still is to a certain extent a language of culture of the élite. In consequence typists and secretaries usually have a somewhat inadequate knowledge of French. Then again, the administrative and political élites of German Switzerland, particularly the latter (McRae 1984), no longer have the all-embracing knowledge of French characteristic of previous generations. French has lost its role of universal lingua franca, in favour of English. The francophone official who gets a

---

5 On the question of languages in Switzerland, see, among others, Hegnauer (1947), Hughes (1954), Codding (1961), Moulton (1962), McRae (1964; 1975; 1984), Sauser-Hall (1965), Siegfried (1969), Dunn (1972), Steiner (1974), Lijphart (1976), Rubattel (1976), Esman (1977b), Colloque de Montreux (1980), Hunt (1980), and Raffestin (1982).

6 According to data from an investigation carried out in 1979 by the Ministry of Finance

7 According to unpublished data supplied by the Ministry of Finance

plum posting to Bern goes there with no illusions – he or she will have, with few exceptions, to operate in German.

Every now and then this general dominance of German causes protests, regrets, and debates, for example, in this written question in 1978 from a member of the federal parliament, Mr Delamuraz: 'German is in fact slowly becoming the sole official language, at least in several department and federal services in Bern; such a situation is unacceptable to the linguistic minorities, whose influence is becoming abnormally reduced.' The inquiry that followed confirmed the parliamentarian's fears; with few exceptions, the francophone official in Bern could not carve out a career in French – his or her working language had to be German; hence it was difficult to keep francophones in Bern when they were offered the possibility of transferring to their own language region, either as a public official or in the private sector. An exception made in 1981 to the principle of territorial unilingualism in public schools allows the opening of a French primary and secondary school in Bern for use by francophone officials, but this will probably have little effect on the present state of affairs; from the linguistic point of view, the francophone in Bern is in a foreign country.

Now this situation is not entirely displeasing to French cantons. The counterpart to the dominance of German in Bern is the exclusive use of French on the French side of the linguistic frontier, in Geneva and Neuchâtel in particular. Further, the considerable growth in the powers of the central state, especially its economic powers, has not been accompanied by proportional growth in the central bureaucracy. There are only 8,000 federal officials in Bern, including secretaries and ushers. The principle of administrative federalism, under which the centre carries out its administration through the corresponding cantonal ministries, largely avoids the danger that the growing interventionism of the federal state might bypass linguistic minorities. Even when the central ministry has no equivalent at cantonal level – in particular the armed forces and the railways – local administrative offices that offer multilingual services are forced, by the effect of the linguistic boundaries that divide the country, to work essentially in the dominant language of the region.

The Belgian model

In one linguistic crisis after another, Belgium has stressed the principle of territoriality more and more strongly. The country is evolving from a unitary into a federal state but, in contrast with Switzerland, has found it impossible to adopt relatively simple solutions of territorial linguistic federalism. Separating of the country into two linguistic regions, one French and one Dutch, clashes with the problem of Brussels, where the two languages meet and mingle in the capital city, which is at least two-thirds and perhaps as much as 80 per cent francophone but situated in Flemish territory.

The problem of Brussels is one of the underlying causes of the most complicated systems of linguistic balance in the world. Belgium of the 1980s is governed through three levels of institutions: that of the nation, that of the community, and that of the region. For its organs of government, the national level has retained its traditional institutions as a unitary state: king, parliament, and executive. Parliament consists of two chambers, a chamber of representatives, with members elected by direct nation-wide vote, and a senate, the elected members of which are also members of the community councils (Covell 1985). The members of these councils are none other than the members of two regional councils, one of Flanders and the other of Wallonia, sitting together with elected representatives of the Brussels council (half francophone, half Flemish). The small German-speaking minority of Wallonia is represented within the council of Wallonia.

Belgian senators are thus typically members of three different institutions – the senate and the regional council, to which they are elected by direct vote, and the community council, of which they are ex officio members – except that the Dutch speakers, who make up 57 per cent of the population of Belgium, decided in 1980 (when this new three-stage system was brought into being) to amalgamate the regional and community levels. The francophones have retained the three-stage system, on account of the Brussels enclave.

Each level of government (national, community, and regional) has its own powers (Belgian administrative terminology distinguishes between a national law, a community statute, and a regional decree). Powers pertaining to language and culture are granted on community authority. This is a compromise (though perhaps only temporary) between personalism and territorialism, a compromise imposed by the case of Brussels. The Flemish and the Walloons, thanks to their control of the respective sections of the community council, maintain unilingualism on each side of the linguistic border, while in Brussels the services charged for cultural matters are grouped into linguistic entities. The Brussels council, to which three cultural commissions are attached – one Dutch-speaking, one francophone, and one joint commission for common affairs – is itself divided up into unilingual sections. Election to the council calls for the electorate to vote for unilingual lists, either French-speaking or Dutch-speaking, in order to avoid, not always successfully, having francophone electors help elect Dutch-speaking candidates favourable to the cause of the francophones.

The system is complicated; the powers of the newly formed governmental authorities (regional and communal) remain hazy, in particular their financial powers (Brassinne 1981). But beneath this complication, beyond the fog of compromise, implication, and misapprehension, a simple principle can be discerned: the separation of languages in contact. When these languages are already separated on the territorial level, application of the principle produces some simple solutions: in Flanders and Wallonia unilingualism is the rule in government, administration, and everyday life. But when the languages are intermixed on the territorial level, and when the territorial framework used to analyse the problem is not the same (the Flemish think of Flanders while the francophones think of Brussels), application of the same principle leads to extremely complex situations, since the Brussels institutions have not been given a unilingual territorial base like the rest of the country.

Apart from Brussels, the agreement about the two languages does some small violence to the principle of territoriality along the linguistic dividing line. The most unfortunate concerns the little village of Les Fourons, which was given to Flanders as a result of a 'compromise' (one might almost say 'horse-trade') of an electoral rather than a linguistic nature.

The case of Brussels, where purely territorial solutions fail to work (see the linguistic maps of Frognier et al 1982), shows the importance of administrative boundaries and the period in which these boundaries were established. Brussels had a Flemish majority in the middle of the nineteenth century – it was not until the beginning ot this century that the majority was francophone. The francophones who controlled the Belgian state at the time could no doubt have set the linguistic frontier to the north of Brussels, had they adhered to the principle of linguistic federalism. This is no longer possible, now that the majority of the Belgian parliament is Dutch-speaking.[8]

As is normal in a unitary state, the Belgian central administration weighs heavily on local authorities with both its powers and the number of its officials. However, Belgium cannot solve – as Switzerland has done – a large part of its linguistic problems by delegating administration of central decisions to outlying unilingual regions. Despite the declaration of equality between the two official languages, French retains the advantage – far less, however, than German in Switzerland. But if the francophone Swiss have resigned themselves to the dominance of German in Bern, the Flemish are

8 Among studies on Belgian linguistic problems, see Héraud (1963), Lorwin (1966), Herremans (1967), J.A. Lefebvre (1970), Dunn (1972), Coppieters (1974), Lijphart (1976), Schneiderman (1976), Zolberg (1977), Levy (1978), Vilrokx (1978), Wilwerth (1980), Quix and Nelde (1981), and McRae (1984).

less and less content to be almost the only people in Belgium to be truly bilingual. The difference in numbers is enough to explain the difference in attitude – Dutch-speaking Belgians form the majority of the population, while Swiss francophones are only a fifth of the Swiss nation. The desire of the Flemish to administer themselves in their own language and the slowness of the francophones to learn Dutch leads to a system of administration by parallel linguistic networks.

The theory of the Belgian government and administration is illustrated by the regulation that ensures that a career as a public official is subject to precisely defined linguistic requirements (Wilwerth 1980). Rules and regulations governing admission to the public service lay down that 40 per cent of the officials shall be francophones, 40 per cent Dutch-speakers, and the remaining 20 per cent shall be divided equally between French-dominant bilinguals and Dutch-dominant bilinguals. These percentages are not simple overall figures; they apply to each grade of the service. There are thus two big networks within one of which an official makes his career: one Dutch-speaking and one French-speaking. The theory also requires that unilingual officials (80 per cent of the total) shall work only in their own language; if they have to use the other language to communicate with colleagues or the exterior world, they will do so – so the theory has it – with the help either of bilingual officials or, more simply, of passive bilingualism (which supposes that each side understands the language of the other but uses only its own).

A theory that calls for 40 per cent of the officials to work in French and 40 per cent in Dutch leads inevitably to the creation of parallel administrative networks. A department head who is required to work in French will prefer surrounding himself with francophone officials and will use the bilinguals for translation and communication with Dutch-speaking personnel. Repeated at every level of the administration, the creation of unilingual offices should inevitably lead to a sort of de facto linguistic federalism, with minor differences (either planned or tolerated) depending on whether the rules and regulations are applied in French by francophone personnel or in Dutch by Dutch-speakers. The fact that so many francophones do not speak Dutch, or do so badly, must increase the tendency.

What in fact does happen? The situation varies with the ministry. The Ministry of National Education is split into two separate ministries, one French-speaking, the other Dutch-speaking. These two ministries apply the same rules and regulations in areas governed by national norms, but (though detailed studies on the subject are lacking) it would be surprising if the application and interpretation of these rules and regulations were the same. Like separate courts of law, the two ministries probably follow different practices, different 'case-law.' Another ministry, that of the Interior, which controls local administration (concurrently with the 'regional' ministers) without being officially split into two, operates according to geographical boundaries which, in so far as they separate Flanders from Wallonia, correspond to linguistic boundaries.

In other ministries the separation between the two languages is not so clearly marked. Where separation exists, it is within the framework of smaller units, at the level of a director and his or her immediate assistants and advisers or an office within which linguistic dominance will change according to the ethnicity of the occupant. It is not generally possible to identify, as can be done in the case of National Education, the separate linguistic threads that run from top to bottom of the hierarchy. It is more a case of linguistic 'pockets' the existence and relationship of which are not institutionalized. So what stops other ministries from following the example of National Education? Fear, no doubt, lest divided ministries should turn into ethnic pressure-groups, and also the fact that the Flemish are prepared to use French, even when they are Dutch unilinguals by career. The more reluctance they show in this matter, the greater will be the tendency to create parallel administrative networks.

The Belgian case allows us to confirm a normal consequence of bilingual administration. When languages are intermingled at the level of services, one language establishes itself as the dominant language. The most effective way of ensuring equal use of the two languages is to create parallel unilingual networks – as is the case in National Education, and to a lesser degree in the Ministry of the Interior.

During the 1960s South Africa carried out an experiment which, by its failure, confirmed the merits of the Belgian model. A system of mandatory alternation between the two official languages was introduced for internal communication within some ministries – one month English, the next month Afrikaans, and so on in sequence. The experiment was abandoned when it was realized that officials were frequently withholding replies and initiatives until their preferred language was the language of the day. In the absence of strict rules, the South African practice reverted to what it had been before the experiment: the language used for internal communication was the dominant language of the office or the ministry involved, though endeavour was made to answer in the language in which the question, note, or memorandum was couched. In actual fact, Afrikaans is the dominant language in almost 90 per cent of internal communication.

The Yugoslav model

In Yugoslavia, territorial and personal solutions have been intermingled. Personal solutions act as a corrective to absolute territorialism (Ulrich-Atena 1976). In Slovenia, which is homogenous from the linguistic point of view, the small Italian and Hungarian minorities (3,000 and 10,000 people respectively) nevertheless have equality with Slovene in the local administration, as of right. Further, these minorities have the right to education in their own language in the areas where they are concentrated. Within the framework of the system of local self-government and in pursuance of the international agreements that govern the status of Trieste, two different educational systems have been set up there, one for Italians, the other for Hungarians – schooling in Italian for the Italians, bilingual primary schooling (Hungarian/Slovene) for the Hungarians. For the latter, bilingualism has a double function – first, to reinforce the linguistic identity of the minority by the use of its mother-tongue in the primary schools and, second, to encourage the student who pursues studies beyond the primary level to do so in the language of the dominant group.

The two autonomous regions of Vojvodina and Kosovo, which form part of the republic of Serbia, offer another example of partial application of territoriality. In these two regions the Turkish and Hungarian minorities have the right to use their mother-tongue in the primary schools. The result is a divergent bilingualism in which – as in Slovenia – the mother-tongue is used, in the primary school, to reinforce the identity of the ethnic minority. However, in the secondary school and the university, Serbian is established as the language of national integration and rising social status.

Although the other small linguistic minorities of Serbia – Slovaks, Romanians, and Turks, for example – have no administrative areas specifically assigned to them, they too have the right to primary school education in their own language, at least in the regions where these minorities are sufficiently concentrated. The largest minority of Serbia, the Albanians of Kosovo, have a much more extensive educational system of their own – from primary school to university. However, while Serbs rarely acquire the minority languages, many of the educated members of the minorities, even the Albanains, learn Serbo-Croatian (Byron 1985). Yugoslav legislation does not stipulate the minimum percentage of concentration necessary for bilingualism to apply; regional and local authorities and organs of self-government decide whether there are enough parents who wish their children to be educated in the minority language to warrant their being given this right.

Each of the major ethnic groups in Yugoslavia – Serbs, Slovenes, Croats, and Macedonians – has its own autonomous republic. In each of these republics, the dominant principle is that of territoriality. The language of politics, administration, and the workplace is that of the ethnic group dominant in the republic. However, territoriality is not as absolute as in Switzerland's unilingual cantons, since other ethnic groups can, by means of territorial concentration, obtain control of some organs of local government where they could establish their own language (Falch 1973). Such upsetting of the existing linguistic divisions of the country can, with reason, be feared by the more economically prosperous republics, Slovenia in particular, since they attract labour from less-developed regions (Paternost 1985).

Within the central organs of the Yugoslav administration, Serbo-Croatian dominates. The Slovenian or Macedonian official in Belgrade has, of necessity, to work in the dominant language.[9]

The Finnish model

Finland makes Swedish, the minority language, one of the two official languages of the state, and thus of parliament, the administration, and the judiciary. But since the number of Swedish Finns has fallen to less than 10 per cent of the total population, Finnish has become almost exclusively the working language of the central administration. The Swedes have a right to public services in Swedish only in those communities in which Swedish residents reach either 3,000 people or 8 per cent of the total population. This is merely a temporary territorial protection, for there is nothing immutable about Finnish internal linguistic borders; unlike the Belgian or Swiss linguistic boundaries, the Finnish boundaries are subject to modification after each census and never guarantee territorial unilingualism to the minority.[10]

Formerly the language of the élite and the lingua franca of Scandinavia, Swedish is losing its importance and status in Finland – except in a few

9 Among studies of linguistic rights and practices in Yugoslavia, see Mackey and Ver-doodt (1975), Ulrich-Atena (1976), Byron (1979; 1985), Tollefson (1981), Radovanovic (1983), and Paternost (1985). See also Karlovic (1982, 296) for the debate concerning the definition of Serbian and Croatian as similar or as separate languages. In 1954 the Croat authorities acknowledged in the Agreement of Novi Sad that there was a single 'Serbo-Croatian' literary language. In 1967, prominent Croatian intellectuals, including high-ranking party members, sought to repudiate the agreement and to proclaim Croatian a separate language. Amendments were proposed to the constitution of Croatia guaranteeing the linguistic rights of Serbs in Croatia. By implication, this would have established Croatian as a distinct language. The proposal came to naught. The federal authorities forbade the diffusion of a distinct Croatian grammar.

10 A community becomes bilingual if the minority reaches 12 per cent; it becomes unilin-gual when the minority falls below 8 per cent. However, when the proportion lies between 6 and 8 per cent, the government may retain bilingualism. It can even happen, exceptionally, that a community remains bilingual below the 6 per cent limit. On Finnish bilingualism, see Héraud (1963), Holmestad and Lade (1969), Norisiainen (1971), Vries (1973), Nordberg (1976), Havel (1978), McRae (1978), Reuter (1979), and Allardt (1985).

areas, particularly in the Aaland Islands. In these islands, in contrast with what is happening in continental Finland, Swedish is protected by fixed frontiers that result from an autonomous status guaranteed by international treaties. There is a striking contrast between the future of Swedish in Helsinki and its future in the Aalands. Although it was the language of the élite, Swedish in Helsinki is not managing to resist assimilation by the sheer mass of the Finns; yet in the islands the language of shopkeepers, fishermen, and isolated farmers is thriving almost as satisfactorily as in Sweden itself.

Flexible and fixed frontiers

The linguistic boundaries of Finland can change according to the movements of population from one ethnic group to the other. These frontiers encourage bilingualism by territorial superposition. In contrast, bilingualism by spatial juxtaposition assures the security of the minority group by giving it an exclusive home base, thanks to fixed borders. In Belgium and Switzerland, the linguistic frontier has been fixed once and for all; the movements of population from one area to the other do not then affect the territorial separation of the languages; the linguistic frontier at substate level is drawn as though it were a state frontier.

However, in a democratic state, whatever the supposedly permanent character of the frontier, the non-coincidence of the administrative and linguistic divisions will inevitably lead to calls for readjustment. This happened in Belgium in the district of Les Fourons and in Switzerland in some villages outside Fribourg. The minority must thus defend itself not only by the establishment of a fixed frontier but also by the rapid assimilation of immigrants. To this end, control of education by means of scholastic unilingualism is often essential. In the absence of control of intra-state migration, the unilingual school facilitates the assimilation of newcomers in less than a generation.

How is a linguistic boundary established or changed?

The most democratic and consequently one of the most complicated methods ever used to establish a linguistic frontier was that used by Switzerland, where the francophone canton of the Jura was created by partition of the former canton of Bern.[11] In 1959 the Jura Rally, a separatist party based on the poor, Catholic, francophone part of the Jura – roughly the northern

---

11 This chronology is drawn from the press cuttings of the Documentation Centre of the Institute of Political Studies in Paris. See also Mayer (1980) and Schmid (1981).

part – initiated a constitutional review calling for the organization of a referendum on the question of the Jura's separation from the canton of Bern. In the canton as a whole, only 22 per cent were in favour of the proposal; 78 per cent opposed. In the Jura itself, the proposal was rejected by 52 per cent, only 48 per cent being in favour. The separatists' lack of success led the Bernese government to reject any suggestion of constitutional reform that would bring the unity of the canton into question.

However, the incidents and tensions that followed the rejection of the plebiscite polarized the population to such a degree that in 1963 the government of the canton of Bern asked the federal authorities to prepare a plan of reform. In 1969 a commission called 'The Wise Men' published its report, which proposed decentralizing the administration of the canton and granting the Jurassians the right to self-determination. The Swiss constitution said nothing about any such right, except that the number of cantons in the federation was written into the constitution itself, and hence the addition of a new canton implied that the citizen of the federation should be consulted and should approve the necessary constitutional amendment. The Wise Men proposed that their suggested reform be submitted separately to the Jurassians and to the rest of the canton of Bern; and if the Jurassians approved the plan for decentralization (and even more so if they rejected it), they should be offered the choice between the status quo and separation.

The statute of autonomy prepared by the Bernese government was submitted to the Bernese parliament in 1973. As amended by that parliament, the electoral procedure adopted for ascertaining the views of the public provided for the use of a series of referendums. The first, held on 23 June 1974, asked Jurassians to answer the question: 'Do you wish to form a new canton?' This time, the majority voted yes, by 36,802 to 34,057. At this stage, only the Jurassians had been consulted; and each of the regions of the Jura had had to decide the question without knowing how the other regions would vote. Accordingly, the law laid down that in those electoral districts in which the majority vote had run counter to the vote of the Jura as a whole – which happened in four of the seven districts, one germanophone and three francophone – the electors could, if they so desired, demand a new vote at their district level in six months' time, provided they had collected the signatures of one-fifth of the electors of the district to that effect. In the three districts of Moutier, Laneuville, and Courtelary (all with a francophone majority) the electors made use of this right of appeal.

The Jura assembly tried unsuccessfully to oppose the new vote, claiming that the first referendum had created a single Jurassian public authority responsible for the procedure for self-determination of the minorities. The second referendum, held in the three districts that had demanded it, took place on 16 March 1975 to find out whether the electors wished to remain within the canton of Bern or not. In all three districts, the vote was for the status quo, i.e. to remain part of the canton of Bern. In the districts of Courtelary and Laneuville, the decision taken at this second referendum was not appealed, for in all subdivisions (*communes*) in each of these districts the majority had expressed the same opinion. In contrast, in the district of Moutier, several subdivisions voted contrary to the district as a whole. The voters in these localities then exercised their right to call for a communal plebiscite in the next two months, a vote that allowed them eventually to join the new canton of the Jura. The only other case outstanding was that of the germanophone district of Laufonnais, which had two years to decide whether to join one of the two neighbouring germanophone cantons, Soleure and Bâle-Campagne, provided always that the canton of their choice was willing to accept it. In the event, the status quo was the choice; the district of Laufonnais remains part of the canton of Bern.

This system of referendums in series can work satisfactorily only by virtue of 'normal' geographical distribution not only of the two competing languages but also of the ethnic identities. In fact, the area is characterized by a succession of geographic gradations that run from the north (where the language of common usage and the ethnic identity are French) down to Laufernois (where the language and identity are German), via the southern districts where French dominates as the language of common usage, but German ethnic origin remains a salient feature of a large part of the population.

Of course, other factors played a part in the decision to separate from Bern or to join the new canton of the Jura: economic (the north is poor and mainly agricultural, while the south is industrial and comparatively well off) and religious (the majority of the Jurassians of the south are Protestants, while those of the north are mainly Catholics). These factors also had a coherent geographical distribution that intensified the linguistic and ethnic cleavages and made it possible to use the cascade type of referendum that offered a choice on separation to smaller and smaller territorial entities. However, cases where two populations of divergent characteristics and opinions are more or less equally balanced would be more difficult to resolve, as would those where history and geography do not coincide. These difficulties are exemplified by the town of Moutier, the historical centre of the Jura, where the anti-separatists won by only a few votes.

Will the new Jura, separated from its traditional centre, create a new vital centre, or continue to lay claim to Moutier? In Moutier itself, will the wish to rejoin the Jura become a majority one if the francophones of Germanic origin become more and more frequently definable by their spoken language rather than their ethnic origin? Will the role of religion, which now separates the Protestants of the south from the Catholics of the north, diminish to the point that language becomes the dominant criterion of identity? This is the hope of the separatists of Moutier, who have been trying ever since the creation of the canton of the Jura to destabilize the situation until the longed-for state of tranquillity they seek comes to be regarded as possible only as a result of their joining the Jura. Thus in Switzerland, as in Belgium, ethnic conflicts tend to concentrate along the linguistic frontier. Happily for Switzerland this linguistic frontier does not run through any major cities. Switzerland has no counterpart to Brussels or Montreal; linguistic boundary problems are thus limited to local skirmishes, the destabilizing effect of which can be confined to the outlying areas of the national political system.

Another factor – institutional – allows Switzerland to limit the effects of conflict along its linguistic borders: each of the two major ethnic groups is divided into autonomous cantons. The problem of Moutier has not immediately become a source of disharmony between French and German Switzerland; it is a problem between the two cantons of Bern and the Jura. In contrast, the problem of Les Fourons in Belgium rapidly spread to include Flanders and Wallonia.

There are only 4,500 inhabitants in Les Fourons, stretched out along 17 kilometres. They were incorporated into Flanders in 1962, even though fifteen years earlier, in 1947, the inhabitants of the region had voted by a two-thirds majority in favour of incorporation into Wallonia. There are two reasons for this anti-geographical and anti-ethnic decision. The first is historical: the regional dialect, in former times spoken by everyone, is akin to Flemish. The second is electoral and political: Les Fourons has conservative leanings, while the Liège region has a tendency to socialism. Time alone will tell whether it would have been wiser to respect the wishes of the majority of the population – and to do the reverse in Moutier.

These two contrasting cases, Moutier and Les Fourons, show clearly that absolute territoriality of a language, and segregation of languages by territorial juxtaposition, cannot completely avert linguistic conflict. A frontier offers security, but often also means conflict. However, despite its imperfections, a fixed linguistic boundary enclosing a unilingual territory remains the best and probably the only effective way to protect a linguistic minority in the long run.

Conclusion:
from the classless state to the state without language

The great political theories of the second half of the nineteenth century – at least those that this century has dubbed great – describe the asymmetrical relations between classes or social strata that are said to be in conflict within a state of which the organs of government are either reflections of the conflict or indeed the object thereof. In these theories, ethnicity plays only a minor role; and linguistic ethnicity figures less often than religious or national forces.

The economy is so dominant in contemporary political thinking perhaps simply because the frequency of inventions – from the bicycle to the washing-machine, from the electric light-bulb to the television set – gave the impression of unstoppable and irreversible progress. Political, cultural, and religious change – the polling-booth, a free press, coups d'état, wars, priests in pullovers, gains or losses of territory – did not give this same impression. A thinking animal's attention – indeed, any animal's – is caught by anything that moves. Hence the temptation to base a theory of change on what one knows everyone has observed to be in movement – the economy, of course. Conversely, if a theory of permanence is sought, the temptation is then to deny the relation of cause and effect between economics and politics. One thus bases a theory of permanence on what appears stable – for example, human nature.

Centuries of major changes in the national sphere – the past century, and the present one – have produced important theories about two areas in which change seemed greatest, the economy and the structure of the state. In the debate among Smith, Marx, Pareto, and Weber, which still continues among their disciples, the linguistic role of the state is relegated to the background.[1] Yet if one considers the evolution of a country such as France

---

1 There are of course exceptions, which run from de Tocqueville to Fanon, from Otto Bauer to Stalin.

over the last 150 years, one sees the class structure and the structure of the state to have changed, of course, but less than the ethnic structure. There are still rich people and poor people, still those who govern and those who are governed, but now they nearly all speak French, whereas in 1789 more than half of the French nation did not. The French state has not been so much a means of domination of one class by another, as a means of exclusion of weaker languages by a dominant one. Social classes, even at loggerheads, need one another; they are linked together by the division of labour. Ethnic groups, linguistic ethnic groups in particular, can and often do fight to the death in the bosom of the state in which they are embodied. Between classes, communication is imperative; between ethnic groups, separation is often a perfectly viable alternative; between classes, co-operation, competition, and conflict are inextricably interwoven; between ethnic groups, communication may well be simply a source of conflict.

An ethnic cleavage, linguistic, religious, or racial, is always an obstacle to communication. In the case of religion or race, this obstacle may well arise only in certain strictly limited areas of social life – for example, in marriage or friendship – without obstructing commerce or political action. In the modern state, on account of the dissociation of politics and religion, lack of communication in the latter sphere does not necessarily entail its absence in the former.

A linguistic cleavage, in contrast, is a universal obstacle. Political systems that seek to separate the élite from the masses, or perhaps the different regions of the same country, can accommodate themselves to this obstacle, or even profit from multilingualism by using the difference in language to reduce the access of outlying populations to the centres of decision and control of the state (Alexandre 1967; Armstrong 1982). Political systems that for ideological or economic reasons require from their members a quick assumption of one another's roles accommodate to it poorly. If it is desired that every elector can be elected, that any child can become director-general or commander-in-chief, then quite naturally the state – despite the Swiss example – will be tempted to approach this egalitarian situation by means of unilingualism – a simpler and less costly solution than generalized bilingualism or asymmetrical bilingualism at the expense of the subordinate group.

'Give us your immigrants,' the United States said in effect to nineteenth-century Europe, 'and we will impose English on them.' 'Let us eliminate the barriers between territories,' said France and England in that same century, 'and to do this, let us teach only one language everywhere in the schools.' Not every state followed this strategy. Not only did segregationist states like the Ottoman Empire and Austria-Hungary stand as exceptions, but so also did democratic states like Switzerland, Belgium, and Canada. But military

defeat shattered the Ottoman Empire and Austria-Hungary along their linguistic shear-lines, as would probably have happened to the Soviet Union if
it had lost the Second World war. Switzerland avoided the great wars of the
nineteenth and twentieth centuries; and each time, Belgium and Canada
were on the winning side.

If these smaller multilingual democratic states had suffered the same fate
as the Austrian or Turkish empires, would they too have split up according
to linguistic ethnicity? One cannot say, but it is not unlikely; in any case, it
is a priori more likely than if the state has only one language. Unilingualism
protects a segregative state – or an assimilative one – against the shocks of
History, assuring the continuity of the exclusive bond between a government and a particular territory. Such an objective, however mediocre, is
natural and understandable, since it is abnormal for a ruling élite to set
itself the task of losing territory (unless accepting an outcome that it considers inescapable and giving up what it is about to lose in any event). The
segregative state, then, is caught between the requirements of a firm assurance of survival and the advantages to be obtained from the linguistic isolation of a part of its population. In contrast, by its unilingualism the integrative and egalitarian state satisfies its ideal of individual mobility and at the
same time receives assurance of territorial survival.

Three of the states that have consciously, through the use of institutions
such as territorial or community federalism, obstructed the elimination of
minority languages – Belgium, Canada, and Switzerland – have small populations and little military strength. They practice or tend toward neutrality,
especially when their ethnic groups speaking different languages have different sympathies when their more powerful neighbours are at loggerheads.

The other bilingual states won their independence more recently. Among
them are small states whose borders march with those of far more powerful
neighbours – Czechoslovakia and Afghanistan, for example. Their bilingualism is partly the product of a fear that unilingualism might provoke territorial secessions that would play into the hands of more powerful neighbours. But among these new states that are officially bilingual, one finds
mostly former colonies (e.g. Singapore, India, and Pakistan) that use a
foreign language, the former colonial language, to bind outlying ethnic
groups. These latter prefer their position of inferiority to be with respect to
a language imported from outside rather than a national language. Use of a
universal lingua franca, generally French or English, reduces the pressure of
the language of the dominant linguistic ethnic group (Tagalog in the Philippines, Hindi in India, Chinese in Singapore) on indigenous languages that
are numerically or politically weaker. The position of these states is comparable to that of early medieval France and England when administration was
carried out in Latin.

But however reduced may be the use of a foreign lingua franca, the pressure of the language of the dominant indigenous group continues to weigh on the other indigenous languages, whose power of resistance is, typically, tied to two principle factors – the number of speakers and the degree of territorial cohesion. The major Indian languages other than Hindi, which are protected by the large numbers who speak them, and also by territorial federalism, are better able to resist the pressure of Hindi than the minor subordinate languages of the Philippines are able to slow the progress of Tagalog or its derivative, Pilipino.

In terms of the strategy of communication, the cases cited above bring out two main reasons for the existence of the bilingual state. To impose one single language would in certain cases also mean choosing the camp of a single one of the neighbours one is trying to avoid. In other cases it would mean giving too exclusive an advantage to only one of the indigenous languages, the dominance of which has not been sufficiently well established. Refusal to make these choices is a measure of the weakness of the central government in relation either to its neighbours or to its outlying ethnic groups.

A third reason derives from the evolution of states such as South Africa, Finland, and, to a lesser degree, Belgium. In these states demography and democracy have overturned the ethnic hierarchy; the subordinate ethnic group displaced the dominant group before the latter managed to establish its language. The bilingualism that facilitates the rise of the subordinate ethnic group, and makes the loss of status more acceptable to the ethnic group on the decline, is admirably suited to these historic exchanges of position.

Multilingualism facilitates communication with the outside world and gives it a particular direction. Bilingual Canada is better able than the United States to communicate with France and Great Britain, and with francophone as well as anglophone Africa. The Canadian government can find, more easily and more quickly than its neighbour, businessmen, salesmen, diplomats, artists, priests, and middlemen of all kinds who can establish the desired contacts. It is exceptional to find (as happens with Czechoslovakia) an officially multilingual state where at least one of its languages does not tie it to other, typically unilingual, states (Table 37). If multilingualism facilitates communication with foreigners it will also, inversely (except in the case of diglossia of the Luxembourg type), obstruct internal communication. Often it results in the creation of internal linguistic frontiers; multilingualism then becomes a potential threat to the territorial integrity of the state.

Even if this danger could be ignored, how can a balance be struck between the advantages multilingualism offers for external communication

TABLE 37
Number of foreign states to which a multilingual state is linked by its official languages

Afghanistan*	1	Luxembourg	33 (−4)
Belgium†	29 (−1)‡	Madagascar	28
Burundi	28	Malta	45 (−35)
Brunei	3 (−1?)	Mauritania	47 (−19)
Cameroun	73 (−45)	Norway	0
Canada	73 (−29)	Pakistan	46 (−2)
Cyprus	2 (−1)	Philippines	45 (−1)
Czechoslovakia	0	Singapore	49 (−4)
Finland	1 (−1)	Sri Lanka	47 (−3)
India	46 (−2)	South Africa§	45 (−45)
Ireland	45	Swaziland	45 (−1)
Israel	19 (−19)	Switzerland	35 (−30)
Kenya	46 (−2)	Vanuatu	73 (−29)
Kiribati	45 (−1)	Vatican	1
Lesotho	45 (−1)	Western Samoa	45 (−1)
		Yugoslavia	0

*If Farsi and Dari are treated as mutually intelligible variations of the same language
†30 if Afrikaans is considered a variation of Netherlandish
‡The figure in parentheses indicates the number to be subtracted if one bases the calculations on the sole dominant language of the state considered.
§47 (−45) if Afrikaans is considered a variation of Netherlandish

and the resultant disadvantages for internal communication? The answer could well be found in comparative statistics for external and internal communication in each of the official languages. These statistics should take account of the relative importance of the state's contacts with its various foreign communicants. The more the balance swings in favour of internal communication, and the higher the state ranks in the order of precedence of demographic, political, economic, military, and cultural power, the greater will be the pressure for the reduction, through unilingualism, of the cost of internal communication.

Another equilibrium that seems equally bound up with the evolution of the state places this state in different categories depending on whether the official language is uni-state or multi-state, uni-continental or multi-continental. If we define equilibrium by the similarity of the areas of use of all the official languages of the state, we see from Table 38 that disequilibrium is more prevalent. Czechoslovakia, Norway and Yugoslavia (especially the first two, since Yugoslavia's Macedonian is close to Bulgarian) are in a state of equilibrium, for their official languages have the same area of use, a uni-state area. The same holds good for Cameroon and Canada, whose official languages are, in each case, world languages. Nine of the states in Table 38 are in a state of equilibrium, and twenty-three in a state of disequilibrium.

TABLE 38
Multilingual governments, by area of diffusion of their official languages

Diffusion of the subordinate official language	Diffusion of the dominant official language*		
	World-wide	Regional multi-state	Single state
World-wide	**Canada** Cameroun Mauritania Vanuatu§	**Switzerland**† Brunei‡	**South Africa** Israel Malta Vatican‖
Regional multi-state	**Belgium** India Pakistan Singapore Kenya Sri Lanka	**Cyprus**	**Finland**
Single state	Burundi **Ireland** **Luxembourg** Kiribati Lesotho Madagascar Philippines W. Samoa Swaziland		**Afghanistan#** **Czechoslovakia** **Norway** **Yugoslavia****

*The dominant language is that which is predominant in the central administration of the state. The states with names in boldface are those where all the official languages are native (mother-tongue) languages within the state.
†Considering only the two major official languages. If Italian is included as well, Switzerland appears in both the 'regional/world-wide' and the 'regional/regional' category.
‡Assuming Malay to be the dominant official langugage
§French and English are the only two official languages considered here. If Bichlamar is included among the official languages, Vanuatu should appear in the 'world-wide domin-ant/single-state subordinate' category.
‖Assuming Italian to be a single-state language. If it is classified as a regional language, the Vatican should be in the 'world-wide/regional' category.
#Provided Dari is considered distinct from Farsi
**Provided Macedonian is distinguished from Bulgarian

Regional equilibrium or regional dominance appears only rarely in this table. There is no case that brings a dominant regional language into con-tact with a subordinate uni-state language. Only Switzerland brings a domi-nant regional language into contact with a subordinate world language; and Cyprus is the only state where two regional languages are official languages.

Because Cyprus has ceased to be truly bilingual since partition, then Switzerland becomes a remarkable exception.

A more accurate categorization than that of Table 38 would take into account the passive comprehension of a language and its status as a first language or a second. Norwegian is spoken only in Norway but is understood in Sweden and Denmark; Slovak is spoken only in Slovakia but is understood by Czechs and Poles. Macedonian is specific to Macedonia but very close to Bulgarian. These languages thus have an area of regional comprehension more extensive than that of Serbo-Croatian. In assessing the equilibrium between internal and external communication, we must also consider whether a world language is the mother-tongue of the state that uses it in government. This distinction, first noted in Table 26, is partly repeated in Table 38, which separates from other states those in which all the official languages are also the mother-tongues of their populations. This categorization shows Canada, Belgium, and Ireland as exceptional – especially Canada, the only state whose official languages are both world languages and mother-tongues.

Comparison of the first and third columns of Table 38 shows that if a world language can dominate another world language as completely as it dominates a regional or a national language, the converse is equally true. A uni-state language can dominate a world language as completely as it dominates a language of lesser spread. All the states in the first column of Table 38 – except Belgium and Luxembourg – are former colonies or possessions of France, Britain, or the United States. The third column, where the dominant language is uni-state, is more varied; it includes states established before the First World War and more recent states, European states, and a former colony. However, in this third column European states predominate. Such a contrast suggests that perhaps our geographical classification covers a historical phenomenon that would lead states to pass more frequently from a dominant world language to a dominant regional or national language before passing from bilingualism to unilingualism. In other words, they evolve in such a way that they pass from the left of Table 38 to the right, rather than the other way around.

If to Table 38 we added a fourth column, in which we would place officially unilingual states, four of the nine states in the third column would probably pass in one or two generations into this fourth category. These four are Israel – if a Palestinian Arab state were created, which would attract the Arab minority out of the Jewish state; Malta – because of the rapid growth of Maltese in internal administration; Finland – by progressive attrition of the Swedish minority; and Norway – by linguistic unification of the two spoken and written languages, which are already very close to each other. One state in the second column, Cyprus, has already become a juxta-position of two independent and unilingual territories.

Finally, among the states in the first column, where a world language is dominant at present, a regional or national language may well gain the upper hand in Kiribati, Lesotho, Madagascar, and perhaps even Swaziland – countries in which one single indigenous language is the mother-tongue of the population as a whole. In the longer term, the same evolution could pos-sibly take place in the Philippines (if democratization produces a sufficient decline of English among the ruling classes). Morocco, Malaysia, and Somalia show how relatively quickly a government can pass from a foreign language to an indigenous one, provided that the latter clearly dominates other local languages that could compete with it. Such linguistic decoloniza-tion would affect the influence and prestige of English and French, and especially of French, which 'owns' only one single unilingual state in which the first language of more than 90 per cent of speakers is the language of their government.

Although assured of a territory that is really its own, in which the social memory, unifying symbols, and affective and intellectual communication are all unilingual, an ethnic group will often need another language to express semantic associations that the vocabulary of its own language does not permit it to express, because the words either do not exist or lack the degree of diffusion needed for effective communication. According to the Brazilian linguist Antonio Houaiss[2] it must have taken more than ten cen-turies for the major languages of civilization to expand from 4,000 to 90,000 words. Four thousand words is very likely an underestimate, but Houaiss is right on the essential: a major language cannot be an instant creation. Ottawa's terminology-bank, a bank of French/English equival-ents maintained by the Terminology Directorate of the Secretariat of State, contains more than 800,000 French concepts. Technical terms can pass quickly from one language to another, either by direct 'borrowing' or by translation. Japanese is a good example of this; a century ago, this language lacked much of the vocabulary of science or modern technology, but it rapidly borrowd what it needed from the languages of the West. Malay, which added some 170,000 words to its technical vocabulary in one genera-tion, is another example (Milne and Mauzy 1986, 72).

However, a literary vocabulary cannot be built up so quickly. Must ten centuries of written literature elapse – as Houaiss thinks – before a diction-ary comparable to Webster or Littré can appear? The big American dic-tionary contains about 4 million references taken from some 80 million con-

2 Quoted by the *Christian Science Monitor* of 7 December 1981

sulted. The semantic level of some languages is not up to the scientific, philosophic, or literary needs of a society. If Frédéric Mistral had been a chemist instead of an early twentieth-century poet, it is not very likely that he would have taken it into his head to write in Provençal. And many French chemists who used to write their articles in French in Mistral's day now write them in English – not only to reach a wider readership but also, sometimes, to be able to express themselves better and to be better understood.

Thus, even among states with firm control of their linguistic frontiers and no minority language, few will dispense with the use of a foreign language for internal use. To the geography of the borders that separate languages must be added a linguistic geography of artistic, religious, economic, and political decisions and creations, and the diffusion of influence of these decisions and creations must be measured. If a society needs Islam and the Koran, it needs Arabic; if it needs the latest in medicine, it needs English, Russian, Japanese, French, or German. The specific need for a foreign language is so usual that for most countries it goes without saying. The Norwegian, Danish, and Dutch élites have resigned themselves to this. However, the foreign language they must acquire in order to participate in the economic, cultural, or political life of Europe and of the world remains compartmentalized in special spheres; it becomes a step-ladder language used from time to time but not 'part of the landscape' of the ethnic identity.

Garfield (1981) rightly draws attention to this: the penetration of the social and physical spheres of one language by another does not necessarily put the former in danger. But he is wrong when he likens France to Norway: it is entirely true that even if all French scholars wrote their scientific articles in English, French would be no more threatened, within France, than if those same scientists wrote in Latin, as their ancestors did. The English of nuclear physics would be unlikely to affect the French of an ordinary conversation, a political speech, or a joke and might even only slightly affect scientific discussions between colleagues in the same laboratory.

The borrowing of foreign words which pains the purist so deeply more often enriches than disintegrates a language. The problem does not lie there. Unlike Norwegian, French is a world language, at grips all over the world with other widespread languages, English in particular. French scientists who use English in France will of course continue to buy their croissants in French, for French is their mother-tongue. But they will give Brazilian or Vietnamese scientists, and more generally the élite of countries in which French is not an indigenous language, yet another reason to learn English, not only as the language of science but as an everyday language – an English of universal usage rather than a French of limited application.

The language of chemistry spoken in Paris has no immediate effect on the language of instruction in the lycées of Paris or Lyons; but it does affect the language taught as a foreign language in Beirut, or Hué or São Paulo, and hence on la Francophonie in general. Hence it affects indirectly the ethnic community of France, which may or may not, depending on circumstances, be pushed further down the slope of isolationism. To maintain itself as the language of science, a world language like French needs to offer its 'consumers' the 'products' they require without unacceptable delays.

There are areas in which a language is better if it is old; there are others where it is no good unless it is new. On this subject, Rossi-Landi (1975) suggests using the idea of linguistic 'capital,' which would have a fixed asset (the language) and a variable asset (the speakers). These two assets of the global 'capital' would have a reciprocal effect. The semantic quality of a language is bound up with the number and variety of the individual and collective projects of the society that speaks that language. If these projects are not renewed, and do not widen in scope, then the linguistic 'capital' tends to remain stable. The society will accommodate easily to this stability, but its language will be unable to satisfy the requirements of another society with projects of wider scope. A language that does not grow is the equivalent of a capital that brings in no interest; a language that grows or adapts too slowly is an investment whose interest payments will appear too late. To maintain itself amid competition, a language must meet the needs of its users, their needs for signs and symbols.

Language as a means of co-operation and as a cause of conflict

The concept of linguistic 'capital' or product cannot be pushed too far. When it is the first language, often when it is only the second, a language is so intimately bound up with identity that it cannot be grasped and understood outside the matrix of the interrelationships of collaboration, conflict, and competition that constantly create and destroy political hierarchies.

Seliger (1977) notes certain analogies in the contacts between languages and those between animals of different species. Their relationships boil down to four main types: specialization, parasitism,[3] dominance (when different species occupy the same area), and proximity (when they are separated by more or less firm boundaries). Territorial separation reduces conflict, and each language has its own public (which corresponds to each animal having its own source of food). In so far as it is firmly established, the frontier reduces conflict and facilitates collaboration. When one knows

3 As in biology, the term parasite has neither positive nor negative a priori implications.

where everybody is, good neighbourly relations do not automatically spring into being, but they do become easier to establish. The frontier area can then become – as Strassoldo (1970) and House (1980) have pointed out – a zone of exchange, while still remaining a zone of defence.

When languages are intermingled within a territory, the distinction between their parasitic, symbiotic, or hierarchic relationships is not generally absolute, for these vary with circumstances. A few examples will illustrate this. Anglophones in Canada and the United States derive only the smallest linguistic benefit from the presence among them of small communities of Doukhobors, Hutterites, or Amish. These communities are self-sufficient, hold themselves aloof from their host society, and take little part in the international and national communication systems. These small linguistic minorities, grafted onto the economy of their surroundings, but holding themselves separate as regards culture and politics, have survived thanks to their geographic and social isolation and the ideological paralysis of the dominant group when faced with a community that is primarily religious rather than linguistic.

However, even in the case of these 'parasitic' minority groups of only a few thousand members, the dominant group tolerates their isolation only on condition that they accept at least partial linguistic assimilation and keep their numbers small. Like the Hutterites, the Amish speak English more and more frequently. In the 1950s, in British Columbia, the Sons of Freedom – a small sect of Doukhobors who refused to be taught English, for fear of becoming contaminated by a culture they considered too materialistic – saw their children forcibly removed and placed in schools reminiscent of concentration camps (Laponce 1960). In the same period, Saskatchewan passed a law forbidding the establishment of new Hutterite villages near existing ones, to prevent appropriation of large areas of adjacent lands, which would facilitate Hutterite communication and control, normally the prerogatives of local and provincial authorities.

Symbiotic relations between different languages take the form of specialization of tasks; each language needs the other in the orchestration of the various roles of an individual or a particular group. Diglossia permits passage from one language to another when the context changes. The citizens of Luxembourg change from the Luxemburgian dialect to German and from German to French, when they shift from family conversation to reading a newspaper, and from there to administrative correspondence. The German Swiss will likewise pass from dialect to High German depending on whether they are talking to friends or speaking to foreigners. The Catholic priest who, a generation ago, could not have said in his mother-tongue the prayers that he knew how to say in Latin, could not have delivered his Sunday sermon in Latin. Such individual specializations correspond to social specializations – for example, those under which a society trains interpreters for internal communications as well as for external. Specialization does not imply the setting up of a hierarchy; but it is rare for one to take place without the other.

Standardized languages often replace dialects when a slow-moving local civilization is replaced by one that is universal and swiftly progressive. True, there are cases of exceptional resistance. Though standardized French has almost annihilated the francophone patois of French Switzerland, German dialects have maintained themselves well vis-à-vis literary German; they made progress even when Switzerland wished to keep its distance from a Nazi Germany regarded as hostile and hateful. However, in the long run, the language with the widest social spread usually wins over the family languages and, with the help of movements of population, nibbles away gradually at the strongholds of the less prestigious language. In the end, local speech becomes a simple 'recognition' language, a symbolic rallying call.

The greater the difference in rank among individual roles or among linguistic ethnic groups, the greater the assimilative pressure of the dominant language. The dominant language is the one associated with the most prestigious social sphere (work, family, the church, as the case may be) and also with the ethnic group in power, which shifts the cost of bilingualism onto the shoulders of the weaker ethnic groups. When a subordinate group lives in a state of bilingualism for long periods, this sometimes gives a false impression of stability. In fact, the languages used in a given state are waging a war in which the number of speakers (demography) and the control of strategic social positions (economy, culture, politics) plays a determining role. Even in Switzerland, where the minority is protected by a rigid linguistic frontier, the dominant language, German, is progressing gradually in relation to the other languages.

Novicow (1893) thought that the key to the understanding of society, as of nature, lay in the study of micro-phenomena, and the reason sociology was lagging behind other sciences was its neglect of these details. In the war of languages, the key to evolution sometimes lies in areas outside micro-phenomena – for example, a law that requires that the education of children or the training of military recruits be carried out in an imposed language. But the micro-phenomena – the foreign language one decides to learn at school, the friendships one makes thanks to this second language, the voyages and the marriages, the choice of a tradesman, or doctor, or lawyer – these millions of small events, and the millions of daily decisions they involve, contribute every day to the pressure toward the unilingualism of sovereign states and the bilingualism of subordinate élites who are not championed by the dominant state or group of states whose language commands attention as a world or regional lingua franca.

The creation of numerous independent states during the last twenty-five years has allowed many languages, such as Malay and Swahili, to climb back up the slope down which colonialism was pushing them. But over the world as a whole the tendency has been for minor languages to be eliminated. After the period of the 'village' language came that of the state language, and then the continental language; New Guinea, Europe, and the Americas, respectively, exemplify these three ages of humanity. The period of thousands of spoken languages was succeeded by that of a few dozen written languages and four or five international languages. The former languages are struggling for exclusive control of specific ethnic territories; while the latter strive to win the allegiance – secondary, at least, if not primary – of local élites compelled by the necessities of inter-state communication to use a language of wide distribution.

In this pitiless struggle – it is rare for a near-dead language to take on a new lease of life, and no dead language has ever been revived – between ethnic groups, between states, and between continents, English is the best-placed language at the moment. English has acquired many unilingual territories, spread over several continents, is by far the most widely spread international language, and is the strongest by the numbers of its businessmen, politicians, writers, and armed forces. Its dominance stems less from its past and its rich literature than from the military, economic, and political strength of the great states that have carried it across the span of history. Linguistic strength is basically political strength. Lyautey used to say that a language is a dialect that has a navy. Whether with the help of sailors, airmen, or atomic bombs, languages assert themselves by force, even when this force is not actually used. A major state that champions a language is usually particuarly intolerant of linguistic diversity; its history is typically one of progressive absorption of peripheral languages and minorities.

The modern state, especially the state that strives for the geographic and social mobility of its citizens, does not willingly put up with multilingualism. Unless it establishes institutional obstacles, the most powerful of which is the linguistic frontier, it will follow a natural evolution that will lead to unilingualism, in which language ceases to be a source of internal cleavage, ceases to divide the state, as, for Marx, classes would cease to divide society. But, if the classless society is still to come, the 'languageless' state has many times been reached and is here to stay. Marxist and Marxian reflections on the role of the state, in so far as they stuck too exclusively to the phenomenon of class and favoured too exclusively the idea of conflict as opposed to the ideas of communication and co-operation, have obscured a major role of the state in the nineteenth and twentiety centuries. This role was less that of being the instrument of the domination of one class over another; most frequently it was first and foremost an instrument of linguistic assimilation. Marx's 'classless society' drew the veil of an impossible dream over the actions of a glossophagic state.

APPENDIX

Domain of use of the official languages of multilingual states

States	Official languages	Stamps	Passports	Currency	Text of laws
Afghanistan	Dari	x	x	x	x
	Pashto	x	x	x	x
Belgium	French	x	x	x	x
	Dutch	x	x	x	x
Brunei	Malay	x	x	x	x[2]
	English	x	x	x	x
Burundi	French	x	x	x	x
	Kirundi		x	x	x
Cameroon	French	x	x	x	x
	English	x	x	x	x
Canada	English	x	x	x	x
	French	x	x	x	x
Cyprus[4]	Greek	x	x	x	x
(Greek zone)	Turkish	x	x	x	x
Czechoslovakia	Czech	x	x	x	x
	Slovak	x	x	x	x
Comoro	French	x	x	x	x
Islands	Arabic	x	x	x	
Djibouti	French	x	x	x	x
	Arabic	x	x[5]	x	x
Finland	Finnish	x	x	x	x
	Swedish	x	x	x	x
India	English	x	x	x	x
	Hindi	x	x	x	x
Ireland	English	[7]	x	x	x
	Gaelic	x	x	x	x
Israel	Hebrew	x	x	x	x
	Arabic	x		x	x
Kenya	English	x	x	x	x
	Swahili	x	x	x	x
Kiribati	English	x	x	x	x
	Kiribati		x	x	
Lesotho	English	x	x	x	x
	Losotho		x	x	x

Debates in parliament	Dominant language at cabinet meetings	Dominant language of the civil service[1]	Oral translation of debates in parliament	Oral translation at cabinet meetings
x x	x	x	no	no
x x	x?	x?	yes	yes
x	x?	x?	no	no
x x	x?	x	no	no
x x	x	x	yes	no
x x	x	x	yes	yes[3]
x	x	x		
x x	x	x	no, not necessary	no, not necessary
x	x	x	no	no
x	x	x	no	no
x x	x	x	no[6]	no
x x	x	x	yes	no
x 8	x	x	partial: from Gaelic to English	no
x x	x	x	partial: from Arabic to Hebrew	no
x x	x	x	no	no
x[9] x	x?	x	no[10]	no
x[11]	x?	x	no	no

States	Official languages	Stamps	Passports	Currency	Text of laws
Luxembourg[12]	French	x	x	x	x
	Luxemburgian		x	x	
	German				
Madagascar	French	x	x	x	x
	Malagasy	x	x	x	x
Malta	English		x	x	x
	Maltese	x	x	x	x
Mauritania	French	x	x	x	x
	Arabic	x	x	x	x
Norway	Bokmal	x	x	x	x
	Nynorsk	x	x	x	x
Pakistan	English	x	x	x	x
	Urdu	x	x	x	x
Papua–New Guinea	English	x	x	x	x
	Motu				
	Pidgin				
Philippines	English	x	x	x	x
	Pilipino	x	x	x	
Seychelles[13a]	English	x	x	x	x
	French	x	x		
Singapore	English	x	x	x	x
	Malay			x	
	Mandarin			x	
	Tamil			x	
South Africa	Afrikaans	x	x	x	x
	English	x	x	x	x
Sri Lanka[14]	Sinhalese	x	x	x	x[15]
	Tamil	x	x	x	x
	English	x	x	x	x
Switzerland	German	x[17]	x	x	x
	French	x	x	x	x
	Italian	x	x	x	x
Swaziland	English	x	x	x	x
	Siswati				
Tanzania	(English)[18]	x	x	x	x
	Kiswahili	x	x	x	x
Vanuatu[19]	English	x	x	x	x
	French	x	x	x	x

Debates in parliament	Dominant language at cabinet meetings	Dominant language of the civil service[1]	Oral translation of debates in parliament	Oral translation at cabinet meetings
x x	x	x	no, not necessary	no, not necessary
x x	x?	x	no, not necessary	no, not necessary
x	x	x?	no	no
x 13	x	x	no	no
x x	x	x	no, not necessary	no, not necessary
x x	x	x	yes	no
x x x	x	x	partial	partial?
x	x	x	no	no
x x	x	x	no	no
x x x x	x	x	yes	no
x x	x	x	no	no
x x x	x?	x?	yes[16]	no
x x x	x	x	yes	no
x x	x?	x	yes?	yes?
x	x	x?	no	no
x x	x	x		

States	Official languages	Stamps	Passports	Currency	Text of laws
Western Samoa	English	x	x	x	x
	Samoan	x	x	x	x
Yugoslavia	Serbian	x	x	x	x
	Croatian	x	x	x	x
	Slovene	(occasionally)	x	x	x
	Macedonian	(occasionally)	x	x	x

SOURCES: Clerks of parliaments and Canadian embassies; for stamps, Scott (1985); for currency, Monestier (1982). The sign ? indicates that up-to-date information could not be obtained.

1 Language of written communication. Measures of oral communication would give, in some cases, different rankings.
2 In the event of a conflict of interpretation, English is authoritative except for the constitution, the regency proclamation, and nationality legislation, where the Malay text prevails.
3 Since 1979 there is, technically, the possibility of providing immediate translation, but the system is not always used.
4 Unverified partial information.
5 For religious laws only
6 Speeches in Swedish are summed up in Finnish. A written summary in Swedish is provided for Finnish speeches. It is estimated that approximately 25 per cent of the Finnish members of parliament do not understand Swedish.
7 Rarely English
8 Rarely Gaelic
9 The discussions are usually in Kiribati.
10 In 1982, however, there was translation provided for the minister of justice, who was not fluent in Kiribati.

Debates in parliament	Dominant language at cabinet meetings	Dominant language of the civil service[1]	Oral translation of debates in parliament	Oral translation at cabinet meetings
x		x	yes	no
x	x			
x	x	x	yes	no
x	x	x		
x				
x				

11 There is an English written translation of the proceedings.

12 Since 1984, Luxemburgian is the only 'national' language. The function of the other two languages is specified by the law of 24 February 1984. It was expected, in 1985, that Luxemburgian would be used on stamps.

13 French is the language of debates used normally, in the absence of immediate translations.

13a Creole has recently been given official status. It is widely used in parliamentary debates.

14 Strictly speaking, Sinhalese is the only official language – for that reason Sri Lanka appears on the Berdoulay et al map (1980) as unilingual. English was made a national language in 1983 with the intention of keeping it as a bridge between Sinhalese and Tamil.

15 The Sinhalese text is authoritative.

16 Parliamentary reports are provided in the three languages, but the Hansard prints the speeches in the sole text of the original. Immediate translation facilities are available but not always used. Speakers frequently sum up their Sinhalese or Tamil speeches in English.

17 The name of the country is in Latin.

18 The text of the laws is written exclusively in English. The explanations are given in Kiswahili although, strictly speaking, Kiswahili is the only official language.

19 Partial, unverified information

References

Abler, R., J.S. Adams, and P. Gould 1971 *Spatial Organization: The Geographer's View of the World* Englewood Cliffs: Prentice Hall

Abou, S. 1962 *Le bilinguisme arabe-français au Liban* Paris: PUF

Adamson, C. et al 1974 'The Unpublished Research of the Royal Commission on Bilingualism and Biculturalism' *Canadian Journal of Political Science* 709–20

Adler, M. 1966 *Business Languages of the World* London: The Institute of Marketing

– 1977 *Collective and Individual Bilingualism* Hamburg: Helmut Buske

Afendras, E. 1970 'Diffusion Processes in Language: Prediction and Planning' Quebec: Centre international de recherche sur le bilinguisme, Publication B-16

Agnew, J.A. 1981a 'Language Shift and the Politics of Language: The Case of the Celtic Languages in the British Isles *Language Problem and Language Planning* 1–10

– 1981b 'Political Regionalism and Scottish Nationalism in Gaelic Scotland' *Canadian Review of Studies in Nationalism* 45–130

Alatis, J. ed 1970 *Bilingualism and Language Contact: Anthropological, Linguistic, Psychological, and Sociological Aspects* Washington: Georgetown University Press

Albert, M., and L. Obler 1978 *The Bilingual Brain: Neurophysiological and Neurolinguistic Aspects of Bilingualism* New York: Academic Press

Alexandre, P. 1967 *Langues et langage en Afrique noire* Paris: Payot

Allardt, E. 1979 *Implications of the Ethnic Revival in Modern, Industrialized Society: A Comparative Study of the Linguistic Minorities in Western Europe* Helsinki: Societas Scientiarum Fennica

– 1985 'Bilingualism in Finland: The Position of Swedish as a Minority Language' in W.R. Beer and J.E. Jacob ed *Language Policy and National Unity* Totowa, NJ: Rowman and Allanheld

Allardt, E., and K.J. Miemois 1982 'A Minority in Both Center and Periphery: An Account of the Swedish-Speaking Finns' *European Journal of Political Research* 265–92

Allen, S. 1978 *Vox Latina: A Guide to the Pronunciation of Classical Latin* Cambridge: Cambridge University Press

Alston, W. 1964 *Philosophy of Language* Englewood Cliffs: Prentice-Hall

Ambrose, J.E. and C.H. Williams 1981 'On the Spatial Definition of "Minority": Scale as an Influence on the Geolinguistic Analysis of Welsh' in Haugen, et al (1980) 53–71

Anceaux, J.C. 1961 *The Linguistic Situation in the Islands of Yapen, Kurudu, Nau and Miosnum, New Guinea* S'gravenhage: Nijhoff

Ancel, J. 1939 *Géographie des frontières* Paris: Gallimard

Anderson, A.B. 1979 'The Survival of Ethnolinguistic Minorities: Canadian and Comparative Research,' in Giles and Saint-Jacques (1979) 67–86

Anderson, J.R., and G.H. Bower 1972 'Recognition and Retrieval Processes in Free Recall' *Psychological Review* 97–123

Andrew, E. 1982 'Pierre Trudeau on the Language of Values and the Value of Languages' *Canadian Journal of Political and Social Theory* 143–59

Angle, J. 1976 'Mainland Control of Manufacturing and Reward for Bilingualism in Puerto Rico' *American Sociological Review* 289–307

Anglejan, A. d' 1979 'French in Quebec' *Journal of Communication* 54–64

Annual of Power and Conflict 1980-81 1981 London: Institute for the Study of Conflict

April, R. 1977 'Crossed Aphasia in a Chinese Bilingual Dextral' *Archives of Neurology* 766–70

Arieti, S. 1967 *The Intrapsychic Self* New York: Basic Books

Armstrong, J.A. 1982 *Nations before Nationalism* Chapel Hill: University of North Carolina Press

Arnaud, N., and J. Dofny 1977 *Nationalism and the National Question* Montreal: Black Rose Books

Asher, J.J., and R. Garcia 1969 'Optimal Age to Learn a Foreign Language' *Modern Language Journal* 334–41

Ashworth, G. 1977 *World Minorities* Sunbury, UK: Quartermaine House

Association romande de Berne 1973 *Les minorités linguistiques dans l'administration fédérale 1950-1970* Berne: Association romande

Aucamp, A.J. 1926 *Bilingual Education and Nationalism* Pretoria: J.L. van Schaik

Aun, K. 1940 *On the Spirit of the Estonian Minority Laws* Stockholm: Societies Litteratum Estonia

Aunger, E.A. 1981 *In Search of Political Stability: A Comparative Study of New Brunswick and Northern Ireland* Montreal: McGill-Queen's University Press

Azrael, J.R. 1978 *Soviet Nationality Policies and Practices* New York: Praeger

Bain, B. 1975 'Toward an Integration of Piaget and Vygotsky; Bilingual Considerations' *Linguistics* 5–19

– 1976 'Verbal Regulation of Cognitive Processes: A Replication of Luria's Procedures with Bilinguals and Unilingual Infants' *Child Development* 543–6

Bain, B., and A. Yu 1978 'Toward an Integration of Piaget and Vygotsky: A Cross Cultural Replication (France, Germany, Canada) Concerning Cognitive Consequences of Biliguality' in Paradis (1978) 116–25

Balkan, L. 1970 *Les effets du bilinguisme français-anglais sur les aptitudes intellectuelles* Brussels: Aimav

Banks, A. 1971 *Cross Polity Time Series Data* Cambridge, Mass: MIT Press

Banks, A.S. and W. Overstreet 1981 *Political Handbook of the World* New York: McGraw-Hill

Banton, M. 1977 'Rational Choice. A Theory of Racial and Ethnic Relations' University of Bristol: Working Papers on Ethnic Relations, no. 8

Barik, H.C., and M. Swain 1976a 'A Longitudinal Study of Bilingual and Cognitive Development' *International Journal of Psychology* 251-63

– 1976b 'Primary-grade French Immersion in a Unilingual English-Canadian Setting: The Toronto Study through Grade 2' *Canadian Journal of Education* 39-58

– 1976c 'A Canadian Experiment in Bilingual Education: The Peel Study' *Foreign Language Annals* 465-78

– 1976d 'English-French Bilingual Education in the Early Grades: The Elgin Study through Grade Four' *Modern Language Journal* 3-17

Barik, H.C., M. Swain, and A. Gaudino 1976 'A Canadian Experiment in Bilingual Schooling in the Senior Grades: The Peel Study through Grade 10' *International Review of Applied Psychology* 99-113

Barke, E.M. 1933 *A Study of the Comparative Intelligence of Children by an Object-Fitting Test* Minneapolis: University of Minneapolis Press

Barnett, G.A. 1977 'Bilingual Semantic Organization' *Journal of Cross-Cultural Psychology* 315-30

Barrett, D.B. 1982 *World Christian Encyclopedia* Oxford: Oxford University Press

Bauer, O. 1923 *Oesterreichische Revolution* Vienna: Wiener Volksbuchhandlung

Beardsmore, H.B. 1974 'Development of the Compound-Coordinate Distinction in Bilingualism' *Lingua* 123-7

– 1980 'Bilingualism in Belgium' *Journal of Multilingual and Multicultural Development* 145-53

Beaudoin, G.A. 1979 'Linguistic Rights in Canada' in MacDonald and Humphrey (1979) 197-208

Beaujot, R.P. 1979 'A Demographic View on Canadian Language Policy' *Canadian Public Policy* 16-29

– 1982 'The Decline of Official Language Minorities in Quebec and English Canada' *Canadian Journal of Sociology* 367-90

Bédard, E., and D. Monnier 1981 *Conscience linguistique des jeunes québécois: influence linguistique chez les élèves francophones de niveau secondaire IV et V* 2 vols, Quebec: Conseil de la langue française

Beer, W.R. 1977 'The Social Class of Ethnic Activists in Contemporary France' in Esman (1977b) 143-58

Beer, W.R., and J.E. Jacob ed 1985 *Language Policy and National Unity* Totowa, NJ: Rowman and Allanhead

Beezer, B. 1975 'Bilingual Education and State Legislatures' *Educational Forum* 537-41

Béguelin, Roland, no date *Le Jura des jurassiens* Lausanne: Cahiers de la renaissance vaudoise

Bellavance, M. 1980 'Les structures de l'espace montréalais à l'époque de la Confédération' *Cahiers de géographie du Québec* 363-84

Bender, M.L., J.D. Bowen, and R.L. Cooper 1976 *Language in Ethiopia* Oxford: Oxford University Press

Benderly, B.L. 1981 'The Multilingual Mind' *Psychology Today* March, 9-19

Bennett, M. 1973 'Response Characteristics of Bilingual Managers to Organizational Questionnaires' *Personnel Psychology* 29-36

Benningsen, A. 1982 'Langues et assimilation en USSR' *International Journal for the Sociology of Language* 57-61

Bentahila, A. 1983 *Language Attitudes among Arabic-French Bilinguals in Morocco* Clevedon: Multilingual Matters

Berdoulay, V., M. Morales, and E.M. Tremblay 1980 *Carte des langues du monde* Ottawa: Ministère des approvisionnements et services

Berger, S. 1977 'Bretons and Jacobins: Reflexions on French Regional Ethnicity' in Esman (1977b) 159-78

Bergeron, G., and R. Pelletier 1980 *L'Etat du Québec en devenir* Montreal: Boréal express

Berghe, Pierre van den 1981 *The Ethnic Phenomena* New York: Elsevier

Berne des Bernois no date, Lausanne: Cahiers de la renaissance vaudoise

Berney, T.D., and R.L. Cooper 1969 'Semantic Independence and Degree of Bilingualism in Two Communities' *Modern Language Journal* 182-5

Berry, J. 1979 'Research in Multicultural Societies, Implications for Cross Cultural Research' *Journal of Cross-Cultural Psychology* 415-34

Berry, J.W., R. Kalin, and D. Taylor 1977 *Attitudes à l'égard du multiculturalisme et des groupes ethniques au Canada* Ottawa: Imprimerie du Gouvernement

Berthoz-Proux, M. 1973 'Quelques problèmes de bilinguisme comparé' *Etudes de linguistique appliquée* 51-63

Betts, C. 1976 *Culture in Crisis: The Future of the Welsh Language* Upton: Ffynnon Press

Bever, T. 1974 'The Relation of Language Development to Cognitive Development' in E. Lenneberg ed *Language and the Brain: Developmental aspects* Jamaica Plain, Ma: Neurosciences Research Programme Bulletin

Bilinsky, Y. 1981 'Expanding the Use of Russian or Russification?' *Russian Review* 317-32

Birch, A.H. 1977 *Political Integration and Disintegration in the British Isles* London: George Allen & Unwin

Bird, J. 1977 *Centrality and Cities* London: Routledge & Kegan Paul

Birdsell, J.B. 1973 'A Basic Demographic Unit' *Current Anthropology* 337-56

Bishop, D., and S. Pukteris 1973 'English Translation of Biomedical Journal Literature Availability and Control' *Bulletin of the Medical Library Association* 24-8

Blais, D.D. 1979 'Corpus and Status Language Planning in Quebec: A Look at Linguistic Legislation' unpublished manuscript

Borins, S.F. 1983a 'The Federal Public Service: Some Recent Survey Results' unpublished manuscript

- 1983b. *The Language of the Skies: The Bilingual Air Traffic Control Conflict in Canada* Montreal: McGill-Queen's University Press

Bossard, J. 1945 'The Bilingual as a Person – Linguistic Identification with Status' *American Sociological Review* 699–701

Bourhis, R.Y. 1979 'Language in Ethnic Interaction: A Psychological Approach' in Giles and B. Saint-Jaques (1979) 117–42

- ed 1984 *Conflict and Language Planning in Quebec* Clevedon: Multilingual Matters

Bourhis, R.Y., and F. Genese 1980 'Evaluative Reactions to Code Switching Strategies in Montreal' in Giles, Robinson, and Smith (1980) 335–43

Bourhis, R., and H. Giles 1976 'The Language of Cooperation in Wales: A Field Study' *Language Sciences* 13–16

Bouthillier, G. 1981a 'Aux origines de la planification linguistique québécoise' in Martin (1981b) vol. 2, 2–23

- 1981b 'Eléments d'une chronologie politique de l'action linguistique du Québec pour la décennie 1960–1969, précédée d'un aperçu sur la période 1945–69' in Martin (1981b) vol. 2, 23–42

Bouthillier G., and L. Meynaud 1972 *Le choc des langues au Québec* Montreal: Les Presses de l'Université du Québec

Brabyn, H. 1982 'Mother Tongue and the Brain: A Japanese Specialist's Surprising Discovery' *UNESCO Courier* February, 10–13

Brand, J. 1980 'The Rise and Fall of Scottish Nationalism' in C.R. Foster (1980) 29–43

Brassinne, J. 1981 *Les institutions de la Flandre, de la communauté française, de la région wallonne* Brussels: CRISP

Brazeau, J., 1978 'Typologie sur l'emploi des langues dans l'enterprise privée' in *Centre* 259–78

Brazeau, J., and E. Cloutier 1977 'Interethnic Relations and the Language Issue in Contemporary Canada: A General Appraisal' in Esman ed (1977b) 204–27

Brédinas-Assimopoulous N., and M. Laferrière 1980 *Législation et perceptions ethniques: une étude du contenu de la presse anglaise à Montréal* Quebec: Office de la langue française

Bresnahan, M.I. 1970 'English in the Philippines *Journal of Communication* 64–71

Breton, Raymond 1964 'Institutional Completeness of Ethnic Communities and Personal Relations of Immigrants' *American Journal of Sociology* 193–205

- 1978 'Stratification and Conflict between Ethnolinguistic Communities with Different Social Structures' *Canadian Review of Sociology and Anthropology* 148–57

Breton, Raymond, and G. Grant 1981 *La langue de travail au Québec* Montreal: Institut de recherches politiques

Breton, Raymond, J.G. Reitz, and V. Valentine 1980 *Les frontières culturelles et la cohésion du Canada* Montreal: Institut de recherches politiques

Breton, Roland 1964 *Les langues de l'Inde depuis l'indépendance* Aix en Provence: La Pensée universitaire
- 1965 'La répartition des religions de l'Inde' *Bulletin de géographie d'Aix-Marseilles* 1–23
- 1970 *Les provinces et les ethnies de l'Inde: notes et études documentaires* Paris: 29 quai Voltaire
- 1976 *Géographie des langues* Paris: Presses universitaires de France
- 1981 *Les ethnies* Paris: Presses universitaires de France
Bridge, Susan 1977 'Some Causes of Political Change in Modern Yugoslavia' in Esman (1977b) 343–70
Brosnahan, L.F. 1961 *The Sounds of Language: An Enquiry into the Role of Genetic Factors in the Development of Sound Systems* Cambridge: Heffer
Brown, R., and A. Gilman 1968 'The Pronouns of Power and Solidarity' in Fishman (1968) 252–75
Bruck, M., W. Lambert, and G.R. Tucker 1977 'Cognitive Consequences of Bilingual Schooling, The St. Lambert Project through Grade 6' *Linguistics* 13–32
Brunner, E., jr 1981 *Soviet Demographic Trends and the Ethnic Composition of Draft Age Males, 1980–1995* Santa Monica: Rand
Burghart, A.F. 1971 'Quebec Separatism and the Future of Canada' in R.L. Gentilcore ed *Geographical Approaches to Canadian Problems* 229–33 Scarborough, Ont: Prentice-Hall
Burling, R. 1959 'Language Development of a Garo and English Speaking Child' *Word* 45–68
Burnett, A.D., and P.J. Taylor 1981 *Political Studies from Spatial Perspectives* New York: Wiley
Burney, P. 1966 *Les langues internationales* Paris: Presses universtaires de France
Buxbaum, F. 1949 'The Role of a Second Language in the Formation of Ego and Superego' *Psychoanalytic Quarterly* 279–89
Byron, J. 1979 'Language Planning in Albania and in Albanian Speaking Yugoslavia' *Word* 15–44
- 1985 'An Overview of Language Planning Achievements among the Albanians of Yugoslavia' *International Journal of the Sociology of Language* 59–92
Cahiers de géographie du Québec April 1980 'La problématique géographique du Québec'
Cailleux, A. 1953 'L'évolution quantitative du langage,' *Société préhistorique française* 505–14
Caldwell, G. 1980, *Anglophone Quebec outside of the Montreal Area in the Seventies* Quebec: Editeur officiel du Québec
Calvet, J.L. 1974 *Linguistique et colonialisme, petit traité de glottophagie* Paris: Payot
- 1979 *Langue, corps, sociétés* Paris: Payot
Camara, F.S., and F. Ayala ed 1979 *Concepts for Communication and Development in Bilingual-Bicultural Communities* The Hague: Mouton

Campbell, D.B. 1982 'Nationalism, Religion and the Social Basis of Conflict in the Swiss Jura' in Rokkan and Urwin (1982) 279–308

Cans, R. 1981 'Le français est-il encore une langue scientifique?' *Le Monde* 3 Nov.

– 1985 'L'Europe des dialectes' *Le Monde* 7 Nov.

Caprile, J.P. 1978 'French and African Languages in Central African Republic and Chad' *West African Journal of Modern Languages* 98–105

Caramazza, A., and I. Brones 1980 'Semantic Classification by Bilinguals' *Canadian Journal of Psychology* 77–81

Carlos, S. 1973 *L'utilisation du français dans le monde du travail du Québec* Québec: Editeur officiel du Québec

Caro, P.T. 1982 'Differences in Language Usage between Males and Females in the USSR, 1970' *Soviet Geography* 31–48

Carranza, M., and E. Bouchard Ryan 1975 'Evaluative Reactions of Bilingual Anglo and Mexican Adolescents toward Speakers of English and Spanish *Linguistics* 83–104

Carrère d'Encausse, H. 1978 *L'empire éclaté* Paris: Flammarion

Carringer, D. 1974 'Creative Thinking Abilities of Mexican Youth' *Journal of Cross-Cultural Psychology* 492–504

Cartwright, D.G. 1977 'The Designation of Bilingual Districts in Canada through Linguistic and Spatial Analysis *Journal of Economic and Social Sciences* 16–29

– 1980 *Official-Language Populations in Canada: Patterns and Contacts* Montreal: Institute for Research on Public Policy

– 1981 'Language Policy and the Political Organization of Territory: A Canadian Dilemma' *Canadian Geographer* 205–24

Cartwright, D.G., and C.H. Williams 1982 'Bilingual Districts as an Instrument in Canadian Language Policy' *Institute of British Geographers* 474–93

Caskey-Sirmons, L., and N. Hickerson 1977 'Semantic Shift and Bilingualism: Variation in the Color Terms of Five Languages' *Anthropological Linguistics* 358–67

Castonguay, C. 1976 'Pour une politique des districts bilingues au Québec' *Journal of Canadian Studies* 50–9

– 1979 'Why Hide the Facts? The Federalist Approach to the Crisis in Canada' *Canadian Public Policy* 4–15

– 1982 'Intermarriage and Language Shift in Canada, 1971–1976' *Canadian Journal of Sociology* 263–78

Celio, E., no date *Le tessin des tessinois* Lausanne: Cahiers de la renaissance vaudoise

Centre international de recherche sur bilinguisme 1978 *Minorités linguistiques et interventions: essai de typologie* Quebec: Les Presses de l'Université Laval

Champagnol, R. 1974 'Etude génétique de la reconnaissance bilingue' *L'Année psychologique* 440–54

– 1975 'Organisation sémantique et linguistique dans le rappel libre bilingue' *L'année psychologique* 115–34

Chan, G.K.L. 1976 'The Foreign Language Barrier in Science and Technology' *International Library Review* 317–25

Chappaz, M., no date *Le Valais des valaisans* Lausanne: Cahiers de la renaissance vaudoise

Charis, C. 1976 'The Problem of Bilingualism in Modern Greek Education' *Comparative Education Review* 216–19

Charron, G. 1972 *Du langage: A. Martinet et M. Merleau-Ponty* Ottawa: Editions de l'Université d'Ottawa

Charte des Langues 1969 *Actes de la Commission des Langues de l'Institut Fribourgeois* Fribourg

Chemical Abstracts (annual) Columbus: American Chemical Society

Cherry, F. 1980 'Ethnicity and Language as Indicants of Social-Psychological Status' in Giles, Robinson, and Smith (1980) 141–5

Chin-Chuan, C. 1979 'Language Reform in China in the Seventies' *Word* 45–57

Christaller, W. 1935 *Die Zentralen Orten in Süddeutschland* Jena: G. Fisher

Christophersen, P. 1952 *Bilingualism* London: Methuen

– 1973 *Second-language Learning* Harmondsworth: Penguin

Church, R., C. Bateman, J. Dey, and L. Lowenberger 1978 'Ethnoregional Minorities and Separatism: A Cross-National Analysis' Paper read at a conference held at McMaster University

Clammer, J. 1982 'The Institutionalization of Ethnicity: The Culture of Ethnicity in Singapore' *Ethnic and Racial Studies* 127–39

Clark, R.P. 1980 'Euzkadi: Basque Nationalism in Spain since the Civil War' in C.R. Foster (1980) 75–99

Claude, I.L. 1955 *National Minorities: An International Problem* Cambridge: Harvard University Press

Claude, R. ed 1976 *Comparative Human Rights* Baltimore: Johns Hopkins University Press

Claval, P. 1980 'Le Québec et les idéologies territoriales' *Cahiers de géographie du Québec* 31–46

Clement, R. 1980 'Ethnicity, Contact, and Communicative Competence' in Giles, Robinson, and Smith (1980) 150–3

Codding, G.A. 1961 *The Federal Government of Switzerland* Boston: Mifflin

Cohen, S., R. Tucker, and W. Lambert 1966 'The Comparative Skills of Monolinguals and Bilinguals in Perceiving Phoneme Sequences' *Language and Speech* 159–68

Coleman, T.S. 1966 *Equality of Educational Opportunity* Washington, DC: Office of Education

Colloque de Montreux 1980 *La diversité linguistique de la Suisse dans les collectivités publiques* Berne: Office fédéral du personnel

Colloque de Paris-Orsay 1981 *Le français chassé des sciences* Paris: Cireel

Colotka, P. 1975 'The National Question in Czechoslovakia' in Mackey and Verdoodt (1975) 143–54

Combrink, J. 1978 'Afrikaans: Its Origin and Development' in Lanham and Prinsloo (1978) 69–95

Commission on Foreign Languages and International Studies 1979 *Strength through Wisdom: A Critique of U.S. Capabilities* Washington, DC: US Government Printing Office

Commission on the Restoration of the Irish Language 1963 *Summary, in English, of Final Report* Dublin: Government Publications

Connor, W. 1977 'Ethnonationalism in the First World: The Present in Historical Perspective' in Esman (1977b) 19–45

– 1978 'A Nation Is a Nation, Is a State, Is an Ethnic Group, Is a ...!' *Ethnic and Racial Studies* 377–400

Conseil scientifique pour l'Afrique 1962 *Colloque sur le multilinguism* Brazzaville: CSA

Constable, D. 1974 'Bilingualism in the United Republic of Cameroon: Proficiency and Distribution' *Comparative Education* 233–46

– 1976 'Investigating Language Attitudes: Cameroon' *West African Journal of Modern Languages* 31–40

Cooper, R.L. 1977 'Bilingualism with and without Schooling: An Ethiopian Example' *International Journal of the Sociology of Language* 73–88

Cooper, R.L., and S. Carpenter 1972 'Linguistic Diversity in the Ethiopian Market' in Fishman (1972b) 225–95

Cooper, R.L., and B. Danet 1980 'Language in the Melting Pot: The Sociolinguistic Context for Language Planning in Israel' *Language Problems and Language Planning* 1–25

Cooper, R.L., and L. Greenfield 1969 'Language Use in a Bilingual Community' *Modern Language Journal* 166–72

Coppieters, F. 1974 *The Community Problem in Belgium* Brussels: Institut belge d'information et de documentation

Corbeil, J.C. 1974 'Application du concept de bilinguisme fonctionnel à la situation industrielle du Québec' 203–8 in S.T. Carey ed *Bilingualism, Biculturalism and Education* Edmonton: University of Alberta

Council of Ministers of Education, Canada 1978 *The State of Minority Language Education in the Ten Provinces of Canada* Toronto: Council of Ministers of Education

Covell, M. 1985 'Possibly Necessary but Not Necessarily Possible: Revision of the Constitution in Belgium' 71–84 in K.G. Banting and R. Simeon ed *Redesigning the State* Toronto: University of Toronto Press

Creissels, D. 1981 'Multilinguisme et politique linguistique en Yougoslavie et en particulier dans la région autonome de Voivoidine' in Martin (1981b) vol. 2, 213–36

Critchley, M. 1974 'Aphasia in Polyglots and Bilinguals' *Brain and Language* 15–27

Culbert, S. 1977 'The Principal Languages of the World' *The World Almanac* New York: Newspapers Enterprises

Cummins, J. 1977 'Cognitive Factors Associated with the Attainment of Intermediate Levels of Bilingual Skills' *Modern Language Journal* 3–12

- 1978 'Bilingualism and the Development of Metalinguistic Awareness' *Journal of Cross-Cultural Psychology* 131–50
Cummins, J., and M. Gulutsan 1971 'Some Effects of Bilingualism on Cognitive Functioning' 129–35 in S.T. Carey ed *Bilingualism, Biculturalism and Education* Edmonton: University of Alberta
- 1974 'Bilingual Education and Cognition' *Alberta Journal of Educational Research* 259–69
Dalrymple, E.C., and A. Aamiry 1969 'Language and Category Clustering in Bilingual Free Recall' *Journal of Verbal Learning and Verbal Behavior* 762–8
Darcy, N. 1946 'The Effect of Bilingualism upon the Measurement of the Intelligence of Children of Pre-school Age' *Journal of Educational Psychology* 21–44
- 1953 'A Review of the Literature on the Effects of Bilingualism upon the Measurement of Intelligence' *Journal of Genetic Psychology* 21–57
Dareste, F.R. 1928–34 *Les constitutions modernes* Paris: Sirey
Darlington, C.D. 1947 'The Genetic Component of Language' *Heredity* 269–86
Das Gupta, J. 1970 *Language Conflict and National Development* Berkeley: University of California Press
Dauzat, A. 1922 *La géographie linguistique* Paris: Flammarion
- 1953 *L'Europe linguistique* Paris: Payot
Day, D. 1981 *The Doomsday Book of Animals* New York: Viking
De Bono, E. 1968 *New Think: The Use of Lateral Thinking* New York: Basic Books
- 1981 'The Language of the Mind: On Finding Words for Thought' *Language and Society* 7–10
De Chambrun, N., and A.M. Reinhardt 1981 'Publish (in English) or Perish' 15–20 in *Le français chassé des sciences* Paris: CIREEL
DeFrancis, J. 1972 'Language and Script Reform in China' in Fishman (1972b) 450–75
Delpérée, F. 1978 *L'autonomie locale en Belgique, au Luxembourg et aux Pays-Bas* Louvain-la-Neuve: Cabay
Delruelle-Vosswinkel, N., and A.P. Frognier 1980 *Les problèmes communautaires* Brussels: CRISP
- 1981 *L'opinion publique et les problèmes communautaires* Brussels: CRISP
Deniau, X. 1983 *La francophonie* Paris: Presses Universitaires de France
Denison, J. 1977 'Language Death or Language Suicide?' *International Journal of the Sociology of Language* 13–22
De Silva, K.M. 1977 *Sri Lanka: A Survey* London: Hurst
Deutsch, K. 1953 *Nationalism and Social Communication* New York: Wiley
Dharmadasa, K.N.O. 1977 'Nativism, Diglossia and the Sinhalese Identity in the Language Problem in Sri-Lanka' *Linguistics* 21–32
Didier, R. 1973 *Le problème des choix linguistiques des émigrants au Québec* Quebec: Editeur officiel du Québec
Diebold, A.R. 1961 'Incipient Bilingualism' *Language* 97–112
- 1965 *Psycholinguistics. A Survey of Theory and Research Problems* Bloomington: Indiana University Press

- 1968 'The Consequences of Early Bilingualism in Cognitive Development and Personality Formation' 218-45 in E. Norbeck, D. Price-Williams, and W. McCord ed *The Study of Personality* New York: Holt, Rinehart and Winston

Dietrich, R. 1977 'Auswahlbibliographie zur Psycholinguistik 1974-76' *Zeitschrift für Litteraturwissenshaft und Linguistik* 195-213

Dingwall, W.O. 1981 *Language and the Brain* 2 vols, New York: Garland

Dion, L. 1980 *Le Québec et le Canada: les voies de l'avenir* Montreal: Québécor

- 1981 'L'Etat, la planification linguistique et le développement national' in Martin vol 1, (1981b) 13-36

Dobzhansky, T. 1962 *Mankind Evolving* New Haven: Yale University Press

Dodd W.F. 1909 *Modern Constitutions* 2 vols, Chicago: Chicago University Press

Domingue, N. 1978 'L'usage bilingue dans le centre de Montréal' in Paradis (1978) 229-36

Donneur, A. 1982 'Un nationalisme suisse romand est-il possible?' *Canadian Review of Studies in Nationalism* 201-24

Dornic, S. 1975 *Human Information Processing and Bilingualism* Stockholm: Institute of Applied Psychology

Dostal, P., and H. Krippenberg 1979 'The "Russification" of Ethnic Minorities in the USSR' *Soviet Geography* 197-219

Downs, R.M., and D. Stea 1973 'Cognitive Maps and Spatial Behavior' 8-26 in R.M. Downs and D. Stea ed *Image and Environment* Chicago: Aldine

Drake, G.F. 1980 'The Social Role of Slang' in Giles, Robinson, and Smith (1980) 63-70

Dressler, W., and R. Wodak-Leodolter ed 1977a 'Language Death' *International Journal of the Sociology of Language* Special issue No. 1

- 1977b 'Language Preservation and Language Death in Brittany' *International Journal of the Sociology of Language* 33-44

Dreyer, J.T. 1978 'Language Planning for China's Ethnic Minorities' *Pacific Affairs* 369-83

Dunn, J.A. 1972 'Consociational Democracy and Language Conflict: A Comparison of the Belgian and Swiss Experiences' *Comparative Political Studies* 3-40

Dunn, L.C. et al 1975 *Race, Science and Society* Paris: Unesco Press

Durga, R. 1978 'Bilingualism and Interlingual Interference' *Journal of Cross-Cultural Psychology* 401-15

Eastman, C. 1975 *Aspects of Language and Culture* San Francisco: Chandler

- 1979 'Language Resurrection: A Language Plan for Ethnic Interaction' in Giles and Saint-Jacques (1979) 215-22

Edgerton, R.B. 1971 'Mexican-American Bilingualism and the Perception of Mental Illness' *Archives of General Psychiatry* 286-90

Edwards, H.P., and M.C. Casserly 1976 *Research and Evaluation of Second Language (French) Programs* Toronto: Ministry of Education

Edwards, R.D. 1973 *An Atlas of Irish History* London: Methuen

Elizaincin, A. 1976 'The Emergence of Bilingual Dialects on the Brazilian-Uruguayan Border' *International Journal of the Sociology of Language* 123-34

Ellerl, S. 1978 *A Case Study in Bilingualism: Code-Switching between Parents and Their Pre-school Children in Malta* Cambridge: Huntington

Emeneau, M.B. 1980 *Language and Linguistic Area: Essays (India)* Stanford, Calif: Stanford University Press

Engelbrecht, G., and L. Ortiz 1978 'Guarani Literacy in Paraguay' *International Journal of the Sociology of Language* 53–67

Erikson, E.H. 1974 *Dimensions of a New Identity* New York: Norton

Ervin, S. 1961 'Learning and Recall in Bilinguals' *American Journal of Psychology* 446–51

Ervin-Tripp, S. 1964 'Language and TAT Content in Bilinguals' *Journal of Abnormal and Social Psychology* 500–7

– 1973 *Language Acquisition and Communicative Choice* Stanford: Stanford University Press

Erwin, S., and C. Osgood, C.E. 1954 'Second Language Learning and Bilingualism,' *Journal of Abnormal and Social Psychology* supplement 139–46

Esman, M. 1977a 'Perspectives on Ethnic Conflict in Industrial Societies' in Esman (1977b) 371–90

– 1977b ed *Ethnic Conflict in the Western World* Cornell: Cornell University Press

– 1977c 'A Note on Official Bilingualism in Canada' Unpublished manuscript

– 1982 'The Politics of Official Bilingualism in Canada' *Political Science Quarterly* 233–54

Etiemble, R. 1964 *Parlez-vous franglais?* Paris: Gallimard

Europa Year Book 1982 London; Europa Publications Ltd

Falch, J. 1973 *Contribution à l'étude du statut des langues en Europe* Quebec: Presses de l'Université Laval

Fanon, F. 1961 *Peau noire, masques blancs* Paris: Seuil

Fellman, J. 1973 'Language and National Identity: The Case of the Middle East' *Anthropological Linguistics* 244–9

Ferguson, C.A. 1959 'Diglossia' *Word* 325–40

– 1964 'On Linguistic Information' *Language and Linguistics* 201–8

Fernando, C. 1977 'English and Sinhala Bilingualism in Sri Lanka' *Language in Society* 341–60

Fisher, S., and S.E. Cleveland 1968 *Body Image and Personality* New York: Dover Press

Fishman, J.A. 1966 *Language Loyalty in the United States* The Hague: Mouton

– 1967 'Bilingualism with and without Diglossia; Diglossia with and without Bilingualism' *Journal of Social Issues* 29–38

– ed 1968 *Readings in the Sociology of Language* The Hague: Mouton

– 1972a *Language in Sociocultural Change* Stanford: Stanford University Press

– 1972b *Advances in the Sociology of Language* The Hague: Mouton

– 1978a *Advances in the Study of Societal Multilingualism* The Hague, Mouton

– 1978b 'Positive Bilingualism: Some Overlooked Rationales and Forefathers' 42–51 in J.E. Alatis ed *International Dimensions of Bilingual Education* Washington DC: Georgetown University Press

- 1980 'Bilingualism and Biculturalism as Individual and as Societal Phenomena' *Journal of Multilingual and Multicultural Development* 3–16

Fishman, J.A., R.L. Cooper, and A. Conrad 1975 *The Spread of English* Rowley, Mass: Newbury

Fishman, J.A., C.A. Ferguson, and J. Das Gupta 1968 *Language Problems of Developing Nations* New York: Wiley

Fishman, J.A., and R.H. Kressch 1974 'The Use of Hebrew Loanwords in Spoken German in Two Bilingual Communities' *Linguistics* 69–78

Fishman, J.A., et al 1971 *Bilingualism in the Barrio* The Hague: Mouton

Fortier, D. 1980 'Brittany "Breiz Atao" ' in C.R. Foster (1980) 136–52

Foster, C.R. 1980 *Nations without a State: Ethnic Minorities in Western Europe* New York: Praeger

Foster, G.M. 1962 *Traditional Societies and Technological Change* New York: Harper

Foster, M.K. 1982 'Canada's Indigenous Languages: Present and Future' *Language and Society* 7–16

Frain du Tremblay, J.A. 1703 *Traité des langues* reprinted in 1972, Geneva: Slatkine Reprints

Fredman, M. 1975 "The Effects of Therapy Given in Hebrew on the Home Language of the Bilingual or Polyglot Adult Aphasic in Israel' *British Journal of Disorders of Communication* 61–9

Freedom in the World and Political Rights and Civil Liberties 1986 New York: Freedom House

French, P. 1981 'Comparability of Verbal and Non-verbal Measures of Affective Meaning in Bilinguals' Two Languages' *Perceptual and Motor Skills* 251–4

Frognier, A.P., M. Quevit, and M. Stenbock 1982 'Regional Imbalances and Centre-Periphery Relationships in Belgium' in Rokkan and Urwin (1982) 251–78

Galloway, L.M., and R. Sarcella 1982 'Cerebral Organization on Adult Second Language Acquisition: Is the Right Hemisphere More Involved?' *Brain and Language* 56–60

Gannon, R. 1978 'The French-Language Unit: A Key Instrument in Canada's Official Languages Policy' *Lingvaj Problemoj Kaj Linguo-Planado* 131–9

Gardner, R.C., et al 1975 'Ethnic Stereotypes: The Role of Language' *Journal of Social Psychology* 3–9

Gardner-Chloros, P. 1985 'Language Selection and Switching among Strasbourg Shoppers' *International Journal of the Sociology of Language* 117–35

Garfield, E. 1981 'English vs. Spanish vs. French, vs. ... the Problem of Bilingualism' *Current Contents* 27 July

Garn, S.M. 1965 *Human Races* Springfield: Thomas

Gendron, J.D. 1973 *Rapport de la Commission d'enquête sur la langue française et sur les droits linguistiques au Québec* 3 vols, Québec: Editeur officiel du Québec

- 1975 'Statut des hommes et statut des langues' *Revue de l'Association canadienne d'éducation de langue française* 9–15

- 1976 'La situation du français comme langue d'usage au Québec' *Langue française* 20-39
Genesee, F., G.R. Tucker, and W.E. Lambert 1975 'Communication Skills of Bilingual Children' *Child Development* 1010-13
Genouvrier, E., and J. Peytard 1970 *Linguistique et enseignement du français* Paris: Larousse
Georgeault, P. 1981 *Conscience linguistique des jeunes Québécois* Quebec: Conseil de la langue française
Geschwind, N. 1964 *Development of the Brain and Evolution of Language* Language and Linguistics series, Georgetown: Georgetown Institute of Language
Gesell, A.L., and F.L. Ilg 1949 *Child Development: An Introduction to the Study of Human Growth* New York: Harper
Gibbons, S. 1981 *Stamps of the World* London: Stanley Gibons Publication
Gilbert, G.G. 1969 'The Linguistic Geography of the Colonial and Immigrant Languages in the United States' *Linguistic Society of America* December
- ed 1971 *The German Language in America* Austin: University of Texas Press
Gilder, S.S. 1974 'South Africa: Two-Language Medicine' *Annals of Internal Medicine* 264
Giles, H. 1977a *Language, Ethnicity and Intergroup Relations* London: Academic Press
- 1977b 'Social Psychology and Applied Linguistics: Towards an Integrative Approach' *Review of Applied Linguistics* 27-42
Giles, H., R.Y. Bourhis, and D.M. Taylor 1977 'Towards a Theory of Language in Ethnic Group Relations' in Giles (1977a) 307-48
Giles, H., Robinson, P., and P. Smith ed 1980 *Language: Social Psychological Perspectives* New York: Pergamon
Giles, H., and B. Saint-Jacques ed 1979 *Language and Ethnic Relations* Oxford: Pergamon
Giles, H., D.M. Taylor, and R.Y. Bourhis 1973 'Towards a Theory of Interpersonal Accommodation through Speech: Some Canadian Data' *Language in Society* 177-92
Giordan, H. 1982 *Démocratie culturelle et droit à la différence* Paris: CNRS
Glazer, N. 1978 'Individual Rights against Group Rights' 87-103 in Eugene Kamenka and Alice Erh-Soon Tay *Human Rights* London: Arnold
Goldhagen, E., ed 1968 *Ethnic Minorities in the Soviet Union* New York: Praeger
Gonzales, A., and L. Postrado 1976 'The Dissemination of Pilipino' *Philippine Journal of Linguistics* 60-84
Gottmann, J. 1962 *A Geography of Europe* 3rd edn, New York: Holt Rinehart and Winston
- 1973 *The Significance of Territory* Charlotteville: University of Virginia Press
Gould, C.J., and B.Y. Stern 1971 'Foreign Technical Literature: A Problem of Costs, Coverage and Comprehension' *ASLIB Proceedings* 571-6
Graham, V.Y. 1925 'The Intelligence of Italian and Jewish Children in the Habit Clinic of the Massachussetts Division of Mental Hygiene' *Journal of Abnormal and Social Psychology* 371-6

Grand, S., L. Marcos, N. Freedman, and F. Barroso 1977 'Relation of Psychology and Bilingualism to Kinesic Aspects of Interview Behavior in Schizophrenia' *Journal of Abnormal Psychology* 492–500

Granda, G. de 1981 'Actitudes Sociolinguisticas en el Paraguay' *Revista Paraguaya de Sociologia* 7–22

Grande Encyclopédie Larousse 1976 Paris: Editions Larousse

Gras, S. 1982 'Regionalism and Autonomy in Alsace since 1918' in Rokkan and Urwin (1982), 309–54

Grassi, C. 1977 'Deculturization and Social Degradation of the Linguistic Minorities in Italy' *International Journal of the Sociology of Language* 45–54

Gray, M. 1979 'The Acadians' *Globe and Mail* 19 April

Greenwood, D.J. 1977 'Continuity and Change: Spanish Basque Ethnicity as a Historical Process, in Esman (1977b) 81–2

Greenwood, Davydd 1980 'Castilians, Basques, and Andalusians: An Historical Comparison of Nationalism, "True" Ethnicity, and "False" Ethnicity' Unpublished manuscript

Guboglo, M.N. 1972 'Socioethnic Consequences of Bilingualism' *Sovetskaia Etnografica* 26–6 (English translation in *Soviet Sociology* 1974, N.1-2)

Guiora, A.Z., et al 1972 'The Effects of Experimentally Induced Changes of Ego States on Pronunciation Ability in a Second Language: An Exploratory Study' *Comprehensive Psychiatry* 421–8

Gumperz, J.J. 1958 'Dialect Differences and Social Stratification in a North Indian Village *American Anthopologist* 668–82

– 1962 'Types of Linguistic Communities' *Anthropological Linguistics* 28–40

– 1964 'Linguistic and Social Interaction in Two Communities' *American Anthropologist* 137–53

– 1967 'On the Linguistic Markers of Bilingual Communication' *Journal of Social Issues* 48–57

– 1970 'Sociolinguistics and Communication in Small Groups' Berkeley: Language Behavior Research Laboratory, Working paper number 33

– 1971 *Language in Social Groups* Stanford: Stanford University Press

Haegerstrand, T. 1965 'A Monte Carlo Approach to Diffusion' *Archives européennes de sociologie* 43–67

Hagège, C. 1985 *L'homme de paroles* Paris: Fayard

Haig-Brown, A. 1983 'British Columbia Indian Languages: A Crisis of Silence' *B.C. Studies* 57–67

Haller, H.W. 1981 'Between Standard Italian and Creole: An Interim Report on Language Patterns in an Italian-American Community' *Word* 181–92

Hamers, J.F., and M. Blanc 1983 *Bilingualité et bilinguisme* Brussels: Mardager

Hamers, J.F., and W.E. Lambert 1974 'Bilinguals' Reactions to Non-Language Semantic Ambiguity' 101–14 in S.T. Carey ed *Bilingualism, Biculturalism and Education* Edmonton: University of Alberta

Hancock, C. 1977 'Second Language Study and Intellectual Development' *Foreign Language Annals* 75–9

Hardycz, C. 1978 'Cerebral Lateralization of Function and Bilingual Decision-Processes: Is Thinking Lateralized?' *Brain and Language* 56-71

Harrison, S.S. 1957 *The Most Dangerous Decades: An Introduction to the Comparative Study of Language Policy in Multi-lingual States* New York: Language & Communication Research, Columbia University Press

Haugen, E. 1958 'Language Contact' *Proceedings of the Eighth International Congress of Linguists* Oslo: Oslo University Press

- 1962 'Schizoglossia and the Linguistic Norm' *Languages and Linguistics* 63-9
- 1972 *The Ecology of Language* Stanford: Stanford University Press
- 1974 *Bilingualism in the Americas: A Bibliography and Research Guide* Alabama: American Dialect Society

Haugen, E., and M. Bloomfield ed 1976 *Language as a Human Problem* New York: Norton

Haugen E. et al 1980 *Minority Language Today* Edinburgh: Edinburgh University Press

Havel, J.E. 1972 'Some Effects of the Introduction of a Policy of Bilingualism in the Polyglot Community of Sudbury' *Canadian Review of Sociology and Anthropology* 57-71

- 1975 'Le bilinguisme en Finlande selon les points de vue de la minorité suédoise' Unpublished manuscript
- 1978 *La Finlande et la Suède: une grande minorité, les Suédois de l'Est* Sherbrooke, Quebec: Editions Namaan

Haymond, R. 1974 'Second Language Learning for Survival and Participation: Adult Immigration in a Canadian Setting *Canadian Modern Language Review* 310-17

Heath, H.S. 1972 *Telling Tongues: Language Policy in Mexico* New York: Teachers College Press

Hechter, M. 1975 *Internal Colonialism* London: Routledge and Kegan Paul

- 1977 'Language Loyalty in Theoretical Perspective' *Language Problems and Language Planning* 1-9
- 1978 'Group Formation of the Cultural Division of Labor' *American Journal of Sociology* 293-318

Hechter, M., and M. Levi 1979 'The Comparative Analysis of Ethnoregional Movements' *Ethnic and Racial Studies* 260-74

Hegnauer, C. 1947 *Das Sprachenrecht der Schweiz* Zürich: Schulthess & Co

Henriprin, J., and E. Lapierre-Adamcyk 1974 *La fin de la revanche des berceaux: qu'en pensent les Québécois?* Montreal: Presses de l'Université de Montréal

Héraud, G. 1963 *Peuples et langues d'Europe* Paris: Denoël

- 1974 *L'Europe des ethnies* 2nd edn, Paris: Presses d'Europe
- 1978 'Notion de minorité linguistique' in Centre International ... (1978) 15-38

Héredia-Deprez, C. 1977 'Le bilinguisme chez l'enfant' *La linguistique* 109-30

Herman, S. 1961 'Explorations in the Social Psychology of Language Choice' *Human Relations* 149-64

Herremans, M.P. 1967 *Le problème linguistique en Belgique* Brussels: Institut belge d'information et de documentation

Herrera-Calderon, M. 1979 'Integracion linguistica del Peru' *Lenguaje y Ciencias* 122–34

Heye, J. 1974 'Bilingualism and Language Attitudes in Merano, Italy' *Revista Brasileira de Linguistica* 40–57

Himelstein, P. 1964 'Sex Differences in the Spatial Location of the Self' *Perceptual and Motor Skills* 317

Hochmann, K. 1978 'El bilinguismo en Sucre' *Lenguaje y Ciencias* 77–80

Hodder, I. 1978 *The Spatial Organization of Culture* London: Duckworth

Hodnett, G. 1978 *Leadership in the Soviet National Republics* Oakville, Ont: Mosaic Press

Hoetjes, B.J.S. 1982 'Federalist Ideas and Federalist Developments in the Low Countries, the Netherlands, Belgium and the Netherlands Antilles' manuscript

Hoffmann, F. 1979 *Sprachen in Luxemburg. Diglossie als historisches Schicksal* Wiesbaden: Steiner

Hofman, J.E. 1975 'Language Attitudes in Rhodesia' in Fishman, Cooper, and Conrad (1975) 279–301

Holmestad, E., and A. Lade 1969 *Lingual Minorities in Europe* Oslo: Samlaget

Horn, L.F. van 1975 'Switching to Micmac as an Egalitarian Symbol: The Police Example in a Bilingual Micmac Indian Community' *Anthropological Journal of Canada* 23–5

Horowitz, E.L. 1935 'Spatial Location of the Self' *Journal of Social Psychology* 379–87

Houis, M. 1976 'Propos sur une analyse des situations de bilinguisme' *West African Journal of Modern Languages* 47–52

House, J.W. 1980 'The Frontier Zone: A Conceptual Problem for Policy Makers' *Revue internationale de science politique* 456–77

Hubert, J.J. 1980 'Linguistic Indicators' *Social Indicators Research* 223–55

Huellen, W. 1980 *Understanding Bilingualism* Bern: Crencester

Hughes, C. 1954 *The Federal Constitution of Switzerland* Oxford: Clarendon

Hunt, J.A. 1980 'Education and Bilingualism on the Language Frontier in Switzerland' *Journal of Multilingual and Multicultural Development* 17–39

Husband, C. 1979 'Social Identity and the Language of Race Relations' in Giles and Saint-Jacques (1979) 129–96

Hutchins, W.J., L.J. Pargeter and W.L. Saunders 1971 *The Language Barrier* University of Sheffield: Postgraduate School of Librarianship and Information Science

Ianco-Worrall, A.D. 1972 'Bilingualism and Cognitive Development' *Child Development* 1390–1400

Imedadze, N.V. 1960 'On the Psychological Nature of Early Bilingualism' *Voprosy Psikhologii* 60–8

Index Medicus (annual) Chicago: American Medical Association

Institute of Commonwealth Studies 1976 *The Politics of Separatism* London: Institute of Commonwealth Studies

International Institute for Strategic Studies 1982 *The Military Balance (1981–82)* Cambridge: IIS

228   References

Isma'il Ragi al Faruqu and D.E. Sopher ed 1974 *Historical Atlas of the Religions of the World* New York: Macmillan
Jaakkola, M. 1973 *Sprak-Gränsen en studi i tsasprakighetens sociologie* Stockholm: Alders
– 1976 'Diglossia and Bilingualism among Two Minorities in Sweden' *International Journal of the Sociology of Language* 67–84
Jackson, J. 1974 'Language Identity of the Colombian Vaupés Indians' 50–64 in R. Bauman and J. Sherzer ed *Explorations in the Ethnography of Speaking* London: Cambridge University Press
Jackson, J., and R. Zinman 1976 'Instrumentality vs. Authenticity: A Comparative Study of Language Contact in Tecumseh, Ontario, and Lachute, Quebec' *Papers in Linguistics* 39–91
Jacobovits, L., and W. Lambert 1961 'Semantic Satiation among Bilinguals' *Journal of Experimental Psychology* 576–82
Jakob, Nic 1981 'Sprachplanung in einer Komplexen Diglossiesituation dargestellt am Beispiel Luxemburg' *Language Problems and Language Planning* 153–74
Jakobson, R. 1968 'The Beginning of National Self-Determination in Europe' in Fishman (1968) 585–97
James, C. 1977 'Welsh Bilingualism – Fact and Fiction' *Language Problems and Language Planning* 73–82
Jamieson, E., and P. Sandiford 1928 'The Mental Capacity of Southern Ontario Indians' *Journal of Education Psychology* 313–28
Jensen, J.V. 1962 'Effects of Childhood Bilingualism' *Elementary English* 358–66
Jessner, L. 1931 'Eine der Psychose entstandene Kuntsprache' *Archiv für Psychiatrie und Nervenkrankheiten* 382–98
Johannesson, I.L. 1975 'Bilingual-Bicultural Education of Immigrant Children in Sweden' in *International Review of Education* 348–55
Johnson, G.B. 1953 'Bilingualism as Measured by a Reaction-Time Technique and the Relationship between a Language and a Non-Language Intelligence Quotient' *Journal of Genetic Psychology* 3–9
Johnson, N.A. 1974 'Zombies and Other Problems: Theory and Method in Research on Bilingualism' *Language Learning* 105–33
Joy, R.J. 1967 *Languages in Conflict* Ottawa: published by the author
– 1978 *Canada's Official Language Minorities* Montreal: C.D. Howe Institute
Kalin, R., and J.W. Berry 1982 'The Social Ecology of Ethnic Attitudes in Canada,' *Canadian Journal of Behavioural Science* 97–109
Karlovic, N.L. 1982 'Internal Colonialism in a Marxist Society: The Case of Croatia' *Ethnic and Racial Studies* 276–99
Karno, M. 1966 'The Enigma of Ethnicity in a Psychiatric Clinic' *Archives of General Psychiatry* 516–20
Katz, Z., R. Rogers, and F. Harned ed 1925 *Handbook of Major Soviet Nationalities* New York: Free Press
Katzenstein, P.J. 1977 'Ethnic Political Conflict in South Tyrol' in Esman (1977b) 287–323
Katzner, K. 1975 *Languages of the World* New York: Funk & Wagnalls

Keats, D.M., and J. Keats 1974 'The Effect of Language on Concept Acquisition in Bilingual Children' *Journal of Cross-Cultural Psychology* 80–99

Keech, William R. 1972 'Linguistic Diversity and Political Conflict: Some Observations Based on Four Swiss Cantons' *Comparative Politics* 387–404

Keerdoja, E. 1979 'Son of Washoe Learns to Talk' *Times* 28 May, 17

Kelman, H.C. 1972 'Language as Aid and as Barrier to Involvement in the National System' in Fishman (1972b) 185–213

Kelly, R.C. 1973 'The Decline of Bilingualism in French Gascony in the Last Few Decades' *Linguistics* 19–23

Kershner, J.R., and A.G.R. Jeng 1972 'Dual Functional Asymmetry in Visual Perception' *Neuropsychologia* 437–45

Khleif, B.B. 1979 'Language as an Ethnic Boundary in Welsh-English Relations' *International Journal of the Sociology of Language* 59–74

– 1982 'Ethnicity and Language in Understanding the New Nationalism: The North Atlantic Region' *International Journal of Comparative Sociology* 114–21

Khokle, V.S. 1986 'English: Its Place in the Indian Culture Pattern' Paper Presented at the New Delhi Congress of the International Sociological Association 8–23 August 1986

Kidron, M. 1981 *The State of the World Atlas* New York: Simon & Schuster

Kintsch, W., and E. Kintsch 1969 'Interlingual Interferences and Memory Processes' *Journal of Verbal Learning and Verbal Behavior* 16–19

Klineberg, O. 1975 'The Study of Multinational Societies' in Mackey and Verdoodt (1975) 9–28

Kloss, H. 1967 'Bilingualism and Nationalism' *Journal of Social Issues* 39–47
– 1969 *Grundfragen der Ethno-Politik im 20. Jahrhundert* Vienna: Braumuller

Kloss, H., and G.D. McConnell 1974-81 *Composition linguistique des nations du monde*, Vol. 1 *L'Asie du Sud*, Vol. 2 *L'Amérique du Nord*, Vol. 3 *Amérique du Centre et Amérique du Sud*, Vol. 4 *L'Océanie*, Quebec: Presses de l'Université Laval

– 1978 *Les langues écrites du monde: relevé du degré et des modes d'utilisation* Quebec: Presses de l'Université Laval

Knofie, E.N. 1979 *The Acquisition and Use of French as a Second Language in Africa: Sociolinguistic, Historical-Comparative and Methodological Perspectives* Grossen-Unden: Hoffman

Kolers, P. 1965 'Bilingualism and Bicodalism' *Language and Speech* 122–6
– 1966 'Reading and Talking Bilingually' *American Journal of Psychology* 357–76
– 1968 'Bilingualism and Information Processing' *Scientific American* 78–85

Korhonen, O. 1976 'Linguistic and Cultural Diversity among the Soamis and the Development of Standard Saamish' *Linguistics* 51–66

Krapf, E. 1955 'The Choice of Language in a Polyglot Psychoanalysis' *Psychoanalytic Quarterly* 343–57

Kreindler, I., ed 1982 'The Changing Status of Russian in the Soviet Union' *International Journal of the Sociology of Language* 7–39

Kuo, E. 1974 'Bilingual Pattern of a Chinese Immigrant Group in the United States' *Anthropological Linguistics* 128-41

Kurian, G.T. 1979 *The Book of World Rankings* New York: Facts on File

Kwen Fee Lian 1982 'Identity in Minority Groups Relations' *Ethnic and Racial Studies* 42-52

Labov, W. 1968 'The Reflection of Social Processes in Linguistic Structures' in Fishman (1968) 240-52

Lachapelle, R., and J. Henripin (1980) *La situation démolinguistique au Canada: évolution passée et prospective* Montreal: Institut de recherches politiques

Lacroix J.M., and Yvan Rioux 1978 'La communication non-verbale chez les bilingues' *Revue canadienne des sciences du comportement* 130-40

Lafont, R. 1967 *La révolution régionaliste* Paris: Gallimard

– 1971 *Le Sud et le Nord* Toulouse: Privat

Lagache, D. 1956 'Sur le polyglotisme dans l'analyse' *La psychanalyse* 167-78

Lagoria, C.A., and L.Z. Ballon 1976 'Peru: Institutionalizing Quechua' *Prospects* 424-9

Lahovary, N. 1946 *Les peuples européens* Neuchatel: La Baconnière

Laitin, D. 1977 *Politics, Language and Thought: The Somali Experience* Chicago: University of Chicago Press

Lambert, W.E. 1955 'Measurement of the Linguistic Dominance of Bilinguals' *Journal of Abnormal and Social Psychology* 192-200

– 1961 'Behavioral Evidence for Contrasting Forms of Bilingualism' *Languages and Linguistics* 73-80

– 1967 'A Social Psychology of Bilingualism' *Journal of Social Issues* 91-109

– 1969 'Psychological Studies of the Interdependences of the Bilinguals' Two Languages' 99-126 in J. Puhuel ed *Substance and Structure of Language* Berkeley: University of California Press

– 1978 'Some Cognitive and Sociocultural Consequences of Being Bilingual' *Georgetown University Roundtable on Languages and Linguistics* 214-29

Lambert, W.E., and S. Fillenbaum 1959 'A Pilot Study of Aphasia among Bilinguals' *Canadian Journal of Psychology* 28-34

Lambert, W.E., R.C. Gardner, R. Olton, and K. Tunstall 1968 ' Study of the Roles of Attitudes and Motivation in Second Language Learning' in Fishman (1968) 473-91

Lambert, W.E., H. Giles, and O. Picard 1975 'Language Attitudes in a French American Community' *Linguistics* 127-52

Lambert, W.E., J. Havelka, and C. Crosby 1958 'The Influence of Language Acquisition Contexts on Bilingualism' *Journal of Abnormal and Social Psychology* 239-44

Lambert, W.E., M. Ignatow, and M. Krauthamer 1968 'Bilingual Organization in Free Recall' *Journal of Verbal Learning and Verbal Behavior* 207-14

Lambert, W.E., and C. Rawlings 1969 'Bilingual Processing of Mixed Message Associative Networks' *Journal of Verbal Learning and Verbal Behavior* 604-9

Lambert, W.E., G.R. Tucker, and A. d'Anglejan 1973 'Cognitive and Attitudinal Consequences of Bilingual Schooling: The St. Lambert Project through Grade Five' *Journal of Educational Psychology* 141-59

Lamothe, P.L. 1974 'Semantic Generalization in French and English Bilinguals' *Canadian Journal of Behavioral Science* 414–19

Lamy, P. 1974 'Bilingualizing Civil Services, Politics, Policies and Objectives in Canada' *Journal of Comparative Sociology* 53–70

– 1975 'The Impact of Bilingualism upon Ethnolinguistic Identity' *Social Studies* 172–207

– 1976a 'Language and Ethnicity: A Study of Bilingualism Ethnic Identity and Ethnic Attitudes'' PhD dissertation, McMaster University

– 1976 'Bilingualism in Montreal: Linguistic Interference and Communication Effectiveness' *Papers in Linguistics* 1–14

– 1978 'Bilingualism and Identity' 33–40 in I. Haas and W. Shaffir ed *Shaping Identity in Canadian Society* Scarborough, Ont.: Prentice-Hall

– 1979 'Language and Ethnolinguistic Identity: The Bilingualism Question' *International Journal of Sociology of Language* 23–36

Landry, R. 1972 'Some Research Conclusions Regarding the Learning of a Second Language and Creativity' *Behavioral Science* 309

Lanham, L.W., and K.P. Prinsloo ed 1978 *Language and Communication Studies in South Africa* Capetown: Oxford University Press

Laponce, J.A. 1960 *The Protection of Minorities* Berkeley and Los Angeles: University of California Press

– 1975a 'Relating Linguistic to Political Conflicts: The Problem of Language Shift in Multilingual Societies' 185–208 in J.G. Savard and R. Vigneault ed *Les Etats multilingues: problèmes et solutions* Quebec: Presses de l'Université Laval

– 1975b 'Temps, espace et politique' *Information sur les sciences sociales* 7–28

– 1977 'Bilingualism and the Bilingual City' 199–222 in Candido Mendès ed *Urban Networks: Structure and Change* Rio de Janeiro: Conjunto Universitario C. Mendès

– 1980 'The City Center as Conflictual Space in the Bilingual City: The Case of Montreal' 149–62 in J. Gottmann ed *Center and Periphery* Beverly Hills: Sage

– 1981 'La distribution géographique des groupes linguistiques et les solutions personnelles et territoriales aux problèmes de l'État bilingue' in Martin (1981b), vol. 1, 83–106

– 1982 'A Topology of Ethnic Conflicts' Paper read at the IPSA congress in Rio de Janeiro

– 1983 'Ruling Elites in a Multilingual Society: Quebec within Canada' 39–43 in M.M. Czunowski ed *Political Elites in Social Change* DeKalb: Northern Illinois University Press

– 1984a 'The French Language in Canada: Tensions between Geography and Politics' *Political Geography Quarterly* 91–104

– 1984b 'Nation-Building as Body-Building: A Comparative Study of the Personalization of City, Province, and State by Anglophone and Francophone Canadians' *Social Science Information* 971–91

– 1985 'Multilingual Minds and Multilingual Societies: In Search of the Neurophysiological Explanations of the Spatial Behavior of Ethno-linguistic Groups' *Politics and the Life Sciences* 3–30

Laporte, P. 1974 *L'usage des langues dans la vie économique au Québec: Situation actuelle et possibilités de changement* Quebec: Gouvernement du Québec

Larew, L.A. 1961 'Children v. College Students' *Modern Language Journal* 22–4

Laski, E., and E. Taleporas 1977 'Anticholinergic Psychosis in a Bilingual: A Case Study' *American Journal of Psychiatry* 1038–40

Leach, E.R. 1954 *Political Systems of Highland Burma* Cambridge, Mass.: Harvard University Press

Le Bras, H., and E. Todd 1981 *L'invention de la France, Atlas anthropologique et politique* Paris: Librairie générale

Lebrun, Y. 1971 'The Neurology of bilingualism' *Word* 179–86

Lefebvre, C. 1979 'Quechua's Loss, Spanish's Gain' *Language in Society* 395–407

Lefebvre, H. 1966 *Le language et la société* Paris: Gallimard

Lefebvre, J.A. 1970 'Nationalisme linguistique et identification linguistique: le cas de la Belgique' *International Journal of the Sociology of Language* 37–58

Legault, A. 1975 *Le nationalisme québécois à la croisée des chemins* Quebec: Université Laval, Centre québécois de relations internationales

Lemon, N. 1975 'Linguistic Development and Conceptualization' *Journal of Cross-Cultural Psychology* 173–88

Lenneberg, E.H. 1967 *Biological Foundations of Language* New York: Wiley

Leopold, W.F. 1939–49 *Speech Development of a Bilingual Child: A Linguistic Record* 4 vols., Evanston: Northwestern University Press

Le Page, R.B. 1964 *The National Language Question* London: Oxford University Press

Lerea, L., and R. Laporte 1971 'Vocabulary and Pronunciation Acquisition among Bilinguals and Monolinguals' *Language and Speech* 293–300

Levi, M., and M. Hechter 1980 'The Rise and Decline of Ethnoregional Political Parties: Scotland, Wales and Brittany' Unpublished manuscript

Levitt, J. 1977 'Linguistic Pluralism in Switzerland and Belgium' *Geolinguistics* 57–70

Levy, P.M. 1978 'Linguistic and Semantic Borders in Belgium' *International Journal of the Sociology of Language* 9–19

Lewis, E.G. 1972 'Migration and Language in the USSR' in Fishman (1972b) 310–41

– 1977 'Bilingualism in Education – Cross-National Research' *International Journal of the Sociology of Language* 6–30

– 1978a 'Migration and the Decline of the Welsh Language' in Fishman (1978a) 263–352

– 1978b 'Types of Bilingual Communities' 19–34 in J.E. Alatis ed *International Dimensions of Bilingualism* Washington: Georgetown University Press

– 1981 *Bilingualism and Bilingual Education* Oxford: Pergamon

Lewis, R.A., R.H. Rowland, and R.S. Clem 1976 *Nationality and Population Change in Russia and the USSR: An Evaluation of Census Data 1897–1970* New York: Praeger

Lichtenstein, L. 1977 'Language and Control' *Use of English* 46–8

Lieberson, S. 1970 *Language and Ethnic Relations in Canada* New York: Wiley
- 1972 'Bilingualism in Montreal: A Demographic Analysis' in Fishman (1972b) 231–54
- 1981 *Language Diversity and Language Contact* Stanford: Stanford University Press
Lieberson, S., S. McCabe, and J. Edward 1978 'Domains of Language Usage and Mother Tongue Shift in Nairobi' *International Journal of the Sociology of Language* 69–81
Liepmann, D., and J. Saegert 1974 'Language Tagging in Bilingual Free Recall' *Journal of Experimental Psychology* 1137–41
Lijphart, A. 1973 'Religious vs. Linguistic vs. Class Voting: The Crucial Experiment of Comparing Belgium, Canada, South Africa and Switzerland' *American Political Science Review* 442–98
- 1976 'Fragmentaciones linguisticas, sociales y politicas: Bélgica, Canada y Swiza' *Revista Mexicana de Sociologia* 707–27
- 1977 'Political Theories and the Explanation of Ethnic Conflict in the Western World: Falsifield Predictions and Plausible Predictions' in Esman (1977b) 46–64
Lindstrom, L. 1983 'Language and Political Boundaries in Tanna (Vanuatu)' *Anthropological Linguistics* 387–403
Loman, B., ed 1972 *Sprak och samhälle spraksociologisk problem* Lund: Gleerup
Lopez, M., and R.K. Young 1974 'The Linguistic Interdependence of Bilinguals' *Journal of Experimental Psychology* 981–3
Lorson, P. 1950 'Bilinguisme scolaire en Alsace' *Etudes* 228–34
Lorwin, V.R. 1966 'Belgium: Religion, Class and Languages in National Politics' 147–84 and 409–16 in R. Dahl ed *Political Oppositions in Western Democracies* New Haven: Yale University Press
- 1972 'Linguistic Pluralism and Political Tension in Modern Belgium' in Fishman (1972b), 386–412
Lukens, J.G. 1979 'Interethnic Conflict and Communicative Distance' in Giles and Saint-Jacques (1979) 143–58
Lum, J.B. 1976 'Bilingual Policies in the People's Republic of China' *Studies in Comparative International Development* 88–98
Luria, A.R. 1974–75 'Scientific Perspective and Philosophical Dead Ends in Modern Linguistics' *Cognition* 377–85
Lustick, I. 1980 *Arabs in the Jewish State: Israel's Control of a National Minority* Austin: University of Texas Press
McConnell, G.D., D. Daoust-Blais, and A. Martin 1979 'Language Planning and Language Treatment in Quebec' *Word* 87–104
McCormack, P.D. 1974 'Bilingual Linguistic Memory. Independence or Interdependence: Two Stores or One?' 115–18 in S.T. Carry ed *Bilingualism, Biculturalism and Education* Edmonton: University of Alberta
- 1976 'Language as an Attribute of Memory' *Revue canadienne de psychologie* 238–48

McCormack, P.D., and S.P. Colletta 1975 'Recognition Memory for Items from Unilingual and Bilingual Lists' *Bulletin of the Psychonomic Society* 149-51

McCormack, P.D., and J.A. Novell 1975 'Free Recall from Unilingual and Trilingual Lists' *Bulletin of the Psychonomic Society* 173-4

MacDonald, R.St.J., and J.P. Humphrey 1979 *The Practice of Freedom: Canadian Essays on Human Rights and Fundamental Freedoms* Toronto: Butterworths

McGrath, W.J. 1977 'Bilingual Education in the Northern Territory of Australia' *Linguistic Reporter* 4-5

Mackay, D.G. 1980 'Language, Thought and Social Attitudes' in Giles, Robinson and Smith (1980) 89-96

Mackay, J., and F. Lewins 1978 'Ethnicity and the Ethnic Group: A Conceptual Analysis and Reformulation' *Ethnic and Racial Studies* 412-27

Mackay, J.R. 1968 'The Interactance Hypothesis and Boundaries in Canada: A Preliminary Study' 122-9 in B.J.L. Berry and D.F. Marble ed *Spatial Analysis* Englewood Cliff, NJ: Prentice Hall

Mackey, W.F. 1962 'The Description of Bilingualism' in Fishman (1968) 554-84
- 1966 'The Measurement of Bilingual Behavior' *Canadian Psychologist* 75-92
- 1966 *Le bilinguisme phénomène mondial* Montreal: Harvest House
- 1971 *La distance interlinguistique* Quebec: Presses de l'Université Laval
- 1973 *Three Concepts for Geolinguistics* Quebec: Presses de l'Université Laval
- 1974 'Géolinguistique et scolarisation bilingue' *Etudes de linguistique appliquée* 10-33
- 1978a 'Typologie des interventions dans le domaine de l'enseignement' in Centre international ... (1978) 209-28
- 1978b *L'irrédentisme linguistique: une étude témoin* Quebec: Centre international de recherche sur le bilinguisme
- 1980 'The Ecology of Language Shift' 35-42 in *Sprachkontakt und Sprachkonflikt* Brussels: CRP
- 1982 *Bibliographie internationale sur le bilinguisme* 2nd ed, Quebec: Presses de l'Université Laval

Mackey, W.F., and A. Verdoodt ed 1975 *The Multinational Society* Rowley, Mass.: Newbury House

MacLeod, C.M. 1975 'Acquisition and Forgetting in Bilingual Memory' PhD dissertation, University of Washington, Seattle

Macnamara, J. 1967a 'The Linguistic Independence of Bilinguals' *Journal of Verbal Learning and Verbal Behavior* 729-36
- 1967b 'The Bilingual's Linguistic Performance: A Psychological Overview' *Journal of Social Issues* 58-77

Macnamara, J., and J. Edwards 1978 *Attitudes to Learning French in the English Speaking Schools of Quebec* Quebec: Editeur officiel du Québec

Macnamara, J. and M. Kranthammer 1968 'Language Switching in Bilinguals as a Function of Stimulus and Response Uncertainty' *Journal of Experimental Psychology* 208-15

Macnamara, J., and S.L. Kushnin 1971 'Linguistic Independence of Bilinguals: Input Switch' *Journal of Verbal Learning* 480-7

McRae, K.D. 1964 *Switzerland: Example of Cultural Coexistence* Toronto: Institute of International Affairs

- 1975 'The Principle of Territoriality and the Principle of Personality in Multilingual States' *Linguistics* 33-54

- 1978 'Bilingual Language Districts in Finland and in Canada: Adventures in Transplanting of an Institution' *Canadian Public Policy* 331-51

- 1984 *Conflict and Compromise in Multilingual Societies: Switzerland* Waterloo: Wilfrid Laurier University Press

- 1986 *Conflict and Compromise in Multilingual Societies: Belgium* Waterloo: Wilfrid Laurier University Press

McRoberts, K. 1979 'Internal Colonialism: The Case of Quebec' *Ethnic and Racial Studies* 293-318

Mägiste, E. 1979 'The Competing Language Systems of the Multilingual. A Developmental Study of Decoding and Encoding Processes' *Journal of Verbal Learning and Verbal Behaviour* 78-90

Malherbe, E.G. 1945 *The Bilingual School* London: Longmans

Mallea, J.E. 1977 *Quebec's Language Policies: Background and Response* Quebec: Presses de l'Université Laval

Mansour, G. 1980 'The Dynamics of Multilingualism: The Case of Senegal' *Journal of Multilingual and Multicultural Development* 273-93

Marcos, L. 1976a 'Linguistic Dimensions in the Bilingual Patient' *American Journal of Psychoanalysis* 347-54

- 1976b 'Bilinguals in Psychotherapy: Language as an Emotional Barrier' *American Journal of Psychotherapy* 552-60

- 1977 'Bilingualism and Sense of Self' *American Journal of Psychoanalysis* 285-90

Marcos, L., and M. Alpert 1977 'Strategies and Risks in Psychotherapy with Bilingual Patients: The Phenomenon of Language Independence' *American Journal of Psychiatry* 1275-8

Marcos, L., et al 1973 'The Effect of Interview Language on the Evaluation of Psychopathology in Spanish-American Schizophrenic Patients' *American Journal of Psychiatry* 549-52

Marsh, L.G., and R.H. Maki 1976 'Efficiency of Arithmetic Operations in Bilinguals as a Function of Language' *Memory and Cognition* 459-64

Martin, A. 1981a 'L'expérience de la planification linguistique en Norvège,' in Martin (1981b) vol. 2, 173-212

- ed 1981b *L'état et la planification linguistique* 2 vols, Quebec: Office de la langue française

Martinet, A. 1968 *Eléments de linguistique générale* Paris: Colin

- 1969 *Langue et fonction* Paris: Denoël

Maruyama, M. 1965 'Patterns of Individuation and the Case of Japan: A Conceptual Scheme' in M.B. Jensen ed *Changing Attitudes toward Modernization* Princeton: Princeton University Press

236   References

Marvick, A.R. 1979 *Mauritius: The Development of a Plural Society* Nottingham: Spokesman

Masson, L.J. 1964 'The Influence of Development Level on Learning of a Second Language among Children of Anglo-Saxon Origin' *Canadian Education and Research Digest* 188–92

Maurer, D.W. 1981 *Language of the Underworld* Lexington: Kentucky University Press

Mayer, K. 1980 'Ethnic Tensions in Switzerland: The Jura Conflict' in C.R. Foster (1980) 189–208

Mazrui, A. 1976 *A World Federation of Cultures: An African Perspective* New York: Free Press

Means, G.P. 1974 'Human Rights and the Rights of Ethnic Groups – A Commentary' *International Studies Notes* 12–18

Mear-Crine, A. 1975 'Systèmes d'éducation biligue pour les Indiens du Canada' *Revue des langues vivantes* 528–33

Meccaci, L. 1981 'Brain and Social Cultural Environment' *Journal of Social and Biological Structures* 319–27

Meens, B. 1973 'Societal Bilingualism' *Review of Applied Linguistics* 1–9

Meillet, A., and M. Cohen 1924 *Les langues du monde* Paris: Champion

Meillet, A., and L. Tesnière 1928 *Les langues dans l'Europe nouvelle* Paris: Payot

Meisel, J. 1978 'Values, Languages, and Politics in Canada' in Fishman (1978a) 665–719

– 1981 L'identification du problème linguistique: données sociologiques et commissions d'enquête' in Martin (1981b) vol. 1 57–82

Meisel, J., and V. Lemieux (1972) *Ethnic Relations in Canadian Voluntary Associations* Ottawa: Information Canada

Merton, R.K. 1968 *Social Theory and Social Structure* New York: Free Press

Meynaud, J. 1965 *Rapport sur le problème des langues dans l'administration fédérale helvétique* Lausanne: mimeographed study for the Canadian Royal Commission on Bilingualism and Biculturalism

Micaud, C.A. 1974 'Bilingualism in North Africa: Cultural and Sociopolitical Implications' *Western Political Quarterly* 92–103

Milne, R.S. 1980 *Politics in Ethnically Bipolar States* Vancouver: University of British Columbia Press

Milne, R.S., and D. Mauzy 1986 *Malaysia: Tradition, Modernity and Islam* Boulder: Westview

Milroy, L. 1980 *Language and Social Networks* Oxford: Blackwell

Minorités linguistiques et interventions 1978 Quebec: Presses de l'Université Laval

Mishkin, M., and D.G. Forgays 1952 'Word Recognition as a Function of Retinal Locus' *Journal of Experimental Psychology* 43–8

Moles, J.A. 1974 'Decisions and Variability: The Usage of Address Terms, Pronouns, and Languages by Quechua-Spanish Bilinguals in Peru' *Anthropological Linguistics* 442–63

Monestier, M. 1982 *L'art du papier monnaie* Paris: Editions du Pont Neuf

Morgan, K.O. 1980 *Wales in British Politics* Cardiff: University of Wales Press

Morin, E. 1967 *Commune en France; la métaphore de Plodémet* Paris: Fayard

Morin, F., and G. Pouget 1978 'Langue et identité technique: le cas occitan' Paper read at the tenth congress of the International Association of French-Speaking Sociologists, Toulouse, 5–10 Sept

Morris-Jones, W.E. 1975 *Collected Papers on the Politics of Separatism* London: Institute of Commonwealth Studies

Mougeon, R. 1976 'Bilingualism and Language Maintenance in the Gaspé Peninsula, Quebec' *Anthropological Linguistics* 53–69

Moulton, W. 1962 'What Standard for Diglossia? The Case of German Switzerland' Monograph series on Language and Linguistics: Georgetown, Georgetown University 133–40

Mount, J. 1980 'Problèmes du bilinguisme d'une bibliothèque universitaire dans le nord-est de l'Ontario' *Language Problems and Language Planning* 29–37

Mulcahy, F.D. 1979 'Studies in Gitano Social Ecology: Linguistic Performance and Ethnicity' *International Journal of the Sociology of Language* 11–28

Muller, S.H. 1964 *The World's Living Languages* New York: Frederick Ungar

Myers, S.C., and W. Vry 1977 'Bilingual Strategies: The Social Function of Code-Switching' *Linguistics* 5–19

Nahaylo, E. 1981 '"Ethnocide" in the Soviet Union' *Spectator* 24 Jan

Naroll, R. 1971 'The Double Language Boundary in Cross-Cultural Surveys' *Behavior Science Notes* 95–102

Nayar, B.R. 1969 *National Communication and Language Policy in India* New York: Praeger

Neufeld, G.G. 1977 'Language Learning Ability in Adults: A Study on the Acquisition of Prosodic and Articulatory Features' *Working Papers on Bilingualism* 45–60

Newby, R. 1976 'Effects of Bilingual Language System on Release from Proactive Inhibition' *Perceptual and Motor Skill* 1059–64

Nordberg, B. 1976 'Sociolinguistic Research in Sweden and Finland: Introduction' *Linguistics* 5–16

Norisiainen, J. 1971 *The Finnish Political System* trans John H. Hodgson, Cambridge: Harvard University Press

Nott, C.R., and W.E. Lambert 1968 'Free Recall of Bilinguals' *Journal of Verbal Learning and Verbal Behavior* 1065–71

Novicow, J. 1893 *Les luttes entre les sociétés humaines et leurs phases successives* 2 vols., New York: Garland

O'Barr, W.M., and J.F. O'Barr ed 1976 *Language and Politics* The Hague: Mouton

Obler, L. 1982 'Cerebral Lateralization in Bilinguals: Methodological Issues' *Brain and Language* 40–54

O'Bryan, K., et al, *Attitudes and Behaviour of Members of Non-official Language Groups* Downsview, Ont.: York University, Institute for Behavioural Analysis

O'Cuiv, B. 1969 *A View of the Irish Language* Dublin: Stationery Office

O'Doherty, E.F. 1958 'Bilingual School Policy' *Studies* 259-68

Ohannessian, S., C. Fergusson, and E. Polomé 1975 *Language Surveys in Developing Nations* Arlington, Va.: Center for Applied Linguistics

O'Huallachain, C. 1962 'Bilingualism in Education in Ireland' *Languages and Linguistics* 75-82

Okoh, N. 1980 'Bilingualism and Divergent Thinking among Nigerian and Welsh School Children' *Journal of Social Psychology* 163-70

Olzak, S. 1982 'Ethnic Mobilization in Quebec' *Ethnic and Racial Studies* 253-76

Orbach, J. 1953 'Retinal Locus as a Factor in the Recognition of Visually Perceived Words' *American Journal of Psychology* 555-62

Orleans, L. 1972 *Every Fifth Child: The Population of China* Stanford: Stanford University Press

Ornstein, J. 1959 'Soviet Language Policy: Theory and Practice' *Slavic and East European Journal* 1-25

– 1976 'A Cross-Disciplinary Sociolinguistic Investigation of Mexican-American Bilinguals/Biculturals at a U.S. Border University: Language and Social Parameters' *La Linguistique* 131-45

Ornstein, J., and R.P. Murphy 1974 'Models and Approaches in Sociolinguistic Research on Language Diversity' *Anthropological Linguistics* 141-67

Osgood, C. and S. Erwin 1954 'Psycholinguistics: A Survey of Theory and Research Problems' in C. Osgood and T. Sebeok ed *Psycholinguistics* Baltimore: Waverly

Osgood, C.E., et al 1957 *The Measurement of Meaning* Urbana: University of Illinois Press

Osmond, J. 1980 'Wales in the 1980's' in C.R. Foster (1980) 44-72

Overbeke, M. Van 1972 *Introduction au problème du bilinguisme* Brussels: Labor

Paivo, A., and W. Lambert 1981 'Dual Coding and Bilingual Memory' *Journal of Verbal Learning and Verbal Behaviour* 532-9

Pandit, P.B. 1977 *Language in a Plural Society* New Delhi: Dev Raj Charana Memorial Committee

Paradis, M. 1977 'Bilingualism and Aphasia' *Studies in Neurolinguistics* 65-121

– ed 1978 *Aspects of Bilingualism* Columbia, SC: Hornbeam Press

Paternost, J. 1985 'A Sociolinguistic Tug of War between Language Value and Language Reality in Contemporary Slovenia' *International Journal of the Sociology of Language* 9-29

Paulston, C.B. 1980 *Bilingual Education: Theories and Issues* Rowley, Mass.: Newbury House

Paulston, C.B., and R.G. Paulston 1980 'Language and Ethnic Boundaries' *Language Sciences* 69-109

Peal, E., and W. Lambert 1962 'The Relation of Bilingualism to Intelligence' *Psychological Monographs* number 546

Peaslee, A.J. 1950 *Constitutions of Nations* Concord: Rumford Press

Peck, E.C. 1974 'The Relationship of Disease and Other Stress to Second Language' *International Journal of Social Psychiatry* 128-33

Pei, M. 1960 *The World's Chief Languages* New York: Vanni

239   References

Penfield, W., and L. Roberts 1959 *Speech and Brain Mechanisms* Princeton: Princeton University Press

Perez, A.Q., and A.O. Santiago ed, n.d. *Language Policy and Language Development of Asian Countries* Manila: Pambansang samahan 79 Linggwistikang

Pernthaler, P. 1978 'Modes d'action dans le domaine linguistique' in Centre international ... (1978), 71–83

Petrella, R. 1980 'Nationalist and Regionalist Movements in Western Europe' in C.R. Foster (1980) 8–28

Petrica, E. 1975 'Minority Rights in Yugoslav Municipal Statutes' in Mackey and Verdoodt (1975) 115–24

Petyt, K.M. 1975 'Romania: A Multilingual Nation' *Linguistics* 75–101

Philippart, A. 1967 'Belgium: Languages and Class Oppostions' *Government and Opposition* 63–81

Phillips, D. 1978 *Interest Groups and Intergovernmental Relations: Language Policy-Making in Canada* Kingston: Queen's University, Institute of International Relations

Pieris, R. 1951 'Bilingualism and Cultural Marginality' *British Journal of Sociology* 328–39

Pill, R. 1974 'Social Implications of a Bilingual Policy, with Particular Reference to Wales' *British Journal of Sociology* 94–107

Pintner, R. and S. Arsenian 1937 'The Relation of Bilingualism to Verbal Intelligence and School Adjustment' *Journal of Education Research* 255–63

Pisarers, I. 1966 *The Population of the USSR* Moscow: Progress Publishers

Pi-Sunyer, O. 1980 'Dimensions of Catalan Nationalism' in C.R. Foster (1980) 101–15

Pizzorusso, A. 1967 *Le minoranze nel diritto publico interno. Bibliografia, testi e documenti* Milan: Guiffre

Plastre, G. 1978 'Typologie des interventions dans les services publics' in Centre International ... (1978) 146–75

Platt, J. 1980 'Accommodation and Code Switching in a Multilingual Society' in Giles, Robinson, and Smith (1980) 345–51

Pohl, J. 1973 'Psychologie des francophones de Belgique' *Ethno-Psychologie* 289–95

Polomé, E. 1979 'Tanzanian Language Policy and Swahili' *Word* 160–71

Polomé, E., and C.P. Hill 1980 *Language in Tanzania* Oxford: Oxford University Press

Pool, J. 1972 'National Development and Language Diversity' in Fishman (1972b) 213–30

– 1974 'You Are What You Speak? Language and National Identity' Paper presented at the 8th World Congress of Sociology in Toronto

– 1978 'Elementary Models for Solving the Problem of Linguistic Diversity' manuscript

– 1979 'Language Planning and Identity Planning' *International Journal of the Sociology of Language* 5–21

- 1980 'Whose Russian Language? Problems in the Definition of Linguistic Identity' in E. Allworth ed *Ethnic Russia in the USSR* New York: Pergamon

Potichnyj, P. ed 1974 *Ukraine in the Seventies* Oakville, Ont.: Mosaic Press

Prasad, N.K. 1979 *The Language Issue in India* Delhi: Leedaderi

Premack, D. 1983 'The Codes of Man and Beasts' *Behavioural and Brain Sciences* 125-67

Price, W.D.R., and M. Raminez III 1977 'Divergent Thinking, Cultural Differences and Bilingualism' *Journal of Social Psychology*

Pristinger, F. 1980 'Ethnic Conflict and Modernization in the South Tyrol' in C.R. Foster (1980) 153-85

Problems of Bilingualism 1967 *Journal of Social Issues* 1-135

Quine, W.V.O. 1960 *Word and Object* Cambridge: MIT Press

Quix, M.P., and P. Nelde 1981 'La planification linguistique en Belgique in Martin (1981b) vol. 2, 117-41

Racine, J. 1986 'L'Inde, ou comment gouverner Babel?' *Hérodote* 42, 7-32

Radovanovic, M. 1983 'Linguistic Theory and Sociolinguistics in Yugoslavia' *International Journal of the Sociology of Language* 55-69

Raffestin, C. 1980 *Pour une géographie du pouvoir* Paris: Librairies techniques

- 1982 'Langues et pouvoir en Suisse' Paper presented to IPSA Congress in Rio de Janeiro

Raffestin, C., and P. Guichonet 1974 *La géographie des frontières* Paris: Presses universitaires de France

Rakoska-Harmstone, T. 1979 'The Study of Ethnic Politics in the USSR' in Simmonds (1977) 20-36

Ranaweera, A.M. 'Sri Lanka: Science Teaching in the National Languages' *Prospects* 416-23

Rao, T.S. 1975 *The Bilingual Child* Allahabad: Indian International Publications

Rawkins, P. 1980 'The Politics of Benign Neglect, Public Policy and the Mediation of Linguistic Conflict in Wales' Paper read at the CPSA meeting in Quebec City

Rawls, J. 1971 *A Theory of Justice* Cambridge, Mass.: Harvard University Press

Rayside, D.M. 1977 'Les relations des groupes linguistiques au Canada et en Belgique' *Recherches sociologiques* 95-131

Rees, W.H. 1939 *Le bilinguisme des pays celtiques* Rennes: Maurice Simon

Reid, M. 1981 'Ecologie qwagul et kamatsa rituel' PhD thesis in anthropology, University of British Columbia

Reuter, M. 1979 'Swedish in Finland: Minority Language and Regional Variety' *Word* 171-85

Rice, F.A. 1962 *Study of the Role of Second Languages in Asia, Africa, and Latin America* Washington, DC: Center for Applied Linguistics

Richardson, L.F. 1960 *Statistics of Deadly Quarrels* Pittsburgh: Boxwood Press

Riley, G. 1975 'Language Loyalty and Ethnocentrism in the Guamanian Speech Community' *Anthropological Linguistic* 286-92

Rimet, M., no date *Contacts, interférences ethniques et culturelles* Montpellier: published by the author

Rogers, L., W. TenHouten, C. Kaplan, and M. Gardiner 1977 'Hemispheric Specialization of Language: An EEG Study of Bilingual Hopi Indian Children' *International Journal of Neurosciences* 1-6

Rokkan, S., and D.W. Urwin 1982 *Politics of Territorial Identity: Studies in European Regionalism* London: Sage

Ronjat, J. 1913 *Le développement du langage observé chez un enfant bilingue* Paris: Champion

Rose, R.G., et al 1975 'Bilingual Memory for Related and Unrelated Sentences' *Journal of Experimental Psychology* 599-606

Rosenberg, S., and H.A. Simon 1977 'Modeling Semantic Memory: Effects of Presenting Semantic Information in Different Modalities' *Cognitive Psychology* 293-325

Ross, J.A. 1979, 'Language and the Mobilization of Ethnic Identity' in Giles and Saint-Jacques (1979) 15-26

Ross, W. 1972 *Deutsch in der Konkurrenz der Weltsprachen* Munich: Max Hueber Verlag

– 1979 'Europe's Multilingual Future' *Daedalus* 151-62

Rossi-Landi, F. 1975 *Linguistics and Economics* The Hague: Mouton

Rousey C., P. Holzman, and A. Berger 1967 'Voice Confrontation' *Journal of Personality and Social Psychology* 423-8

Roy, N.C. 1962 *Federalism and Linguistic States* Calcutta: Mukhopadhyay

Rubattel, C. 1976 'Recherches sur les langues en contact' *Etudes de linguistique appliquée* 20-32

Rubin, J. 1968 *National Bilingualism in Paraguay* The Hague: Mouton

Ruiz, E.J. 1975 'Influence of Bilingualism on Communication in Groups' *International Journal of Group Psychology* 391-5

Russ, R., J. Gold, and P. Cherubnik 1975 'Semantics and Structure: A Comparison between Monolinguals and Bilingual Subjects' *Journal of Social Psychology* 163-72

Russet, B., and H. Starr 1981 *World Politics: The Menu for Choice* San Francisco: W.H. Freeman

Ryan, E.B., and H. Giles, ed 1982 *Attitudes towards Language Variation: Social and Applied Contexts* London: E. Arnold

Rywkin, M. 1980 'The Russia-Wide Soviet Federated Socialist Republic: Privileged and Underprivileged?' 179-87 in E. Allworth ed *Ethnic Russia in the USSR* New York: Pergamon

Sabourin, C., and N. Petit 1978 *Langues et sociétés: bibliographie analytique informalisée* Quebec: Office de la langue française

Saegert, J., E. Hamayan, and H. Ahmar 1975 'Memory for Language of Input in Polyglots' *Journal of Experimental Psychology* 607-13

Saegert, J., and R.K. Young 1975 'Translation Errors for Abstract and Concrete Responses in a Bilingual Paired-Associate Task' *Bulletin of the Psychonomic Society* 429

Saer, D.J. 1922 'An Inquiry into the Effect of Bilingualism upon the Intelligence of Young Children' *Journal of Experimental Pedagogy* 266-74

St Clair, R.N. 1978 'The Politics of Language' *Word* 44-62

Salvi, S. 1973 *Le nazioni proibite* Florence: Vallechi

Salzmann, Z. 1980 'Language Standardization in a Bilingual State: The Case of Czech and Slovak, Two Closely Cognate Languages' *Language Problems and Language Planning* 38–54

Sanguin, A.L. 1976 *Géographie politique: bibliographie internationale* Montreal: Presses universitaires du Québec

– 1978 'La territorialité linguistique: l'exemple suisse et le cas du Québec' *Cahiers de géographie du Québec* 79–82

Sanjek, R. 1977 'Cognitive Maps of the Ethnic Domain in Urban Ghana: Reflections on Variability and Change' *American Ethnologist* 603–22

Sankoff, G. 1980 'Multilingualism in Papua New Guinea' in Sankoff (1980b) 95–132

– 1980b *The Social Life of Language* Philadelphia: University of Pennsylvania Press

Sapon, S. 1953 'A Methodology for the Study of Socio-economic Differentials in Linguistic Phenomena' *Studies in Linguistics* 57–68

Sauser-Hall, G. 1965 *Guide politique suisse* Lausanne: Payot

Savigear, P. 1980 'Corsica and the French State' in C.R. Foster (1980) 116–35

Schermerhorn, R.A. 1970 *Comparative Ethnic Relations: A Framework for Theory and Research* New York: Random House

Schlanger, J.E. 1971 *Les métaphores de l'organisme* Paris: Vrin

Schlieberr-Lange, B. 1977 'The Language Situation in Southern France' *International Journal of the Sociology of Language* 101–8

Schmid, C. 1980 'Diversity and Social Relations in Swiss and Canadian Society: A Comparative Study of Attitudes of Young People' *Ethnic Groups* 79–96

– 1981 *Conflict and Consensus in Switzerland* Berkeley: University of California Press

Schneiderman, E. 1976 'An Examination of the Ethnic and Linguistic Attitudes of Bilingual Children' *ITL Review of Applied Linguistics* 59–73

Schrijnen, J. 1933 *Essai de bibliographie de géographie linguistique générale* Nijmegen: N.V. Decker

Scott 1985 *Standard Postage Stamp Catalogue* New York: Scott Publishing Co.

Scotton, C.M. 1972 'Choosing a Lingua Franca in an African Capital' Edmonton: Linguistic Research Institute

– 1977 'Linguistic Performance as a Socio-economic Indicator' *Journal of Social Psychology* 35–45

Seliger, H.W. 1977 'Biological Analogs for Language Contact Situations' *International Review of Applied Linguistics in Language Teaching* 113–26

Senghor, L. 1975 'The Essence of Language' *Cultures* 75–98

Sérant, P. 1965 *La France des minorités* Paris: Lafont

Seybolt, P.J., and G. Kuei-ke Chiang 1978 *Language Reform in China* New York: Sharpe

Shabad, G., and R. Gunther 1982 'Language, Nationalism and Political Conflict in Spain' *Comparative Politics* 443–77

Shaffer D. 1976 'Is Bilingualism Compound or Coordinate?' *Lingua* 69–77

Shaffer, R.D. 1974 'Cerebral Lateralization: The Dichotomy of Consciousness' *International Journal of Symbiology* 7–13

Sharma, P.G., and S. Kumar 1976–77 *Indian Bilingualism* Proceedings of the symposium held under the joint auspices of Kendriya Hindi Sansthan and Jawaharlal Nehru University, February 1976, Agra: Kendriya Hindi Sansthan

Sharp, D.W.H. 1973 *Language in Bilingual Communities* London: Edward Arnold

Sibayan, B.P. 1975 'Survey of Language Use and Attitudes towards Language in the Philippines' in Ohanessian et al (1975) 115–44

Siegfried, A. 1969 *La Suisse, démocratie témoin* Neuchatel: La Baconnière

Siguan, M. 1977 'Usages linguistiques dans une université bilingue: le cas de l'université de Barcelone' *Bulletin de psychologie* 356–63

– 1980 'Education and Bilingualism in Catalonia' *Journal of Multilingual and Multicultural Development* 231–41

Silver, B.D. 1974a 'The Status of National Minority Languages in Soviet Education: An Assessment of Recent Changes' *Soviet Studies* 28–40

– 1974b 'The Impact of Urbanization and Geographical Dispersion on the Linguistic Reunification of Soviet Nationalities' *Demography* 89–103

– 1975 'Methods of Deriving Data on Bilingualism from the 1970 Soviet Census' *Soviet Studies* 574–97

Silverman, S.H. 1969 'The Evaluation of Language Varieties' *Modern Language Journal* 241–4

Simard, L., and D. Taylor 1976 'Attribution Processes and Interpersonal Accommodation in a Bilingual Setting' *Language and Speech* 374–87

Simmonds, G., ed 1977 *Nationalism in the USSR and Eastern Europe in the Era of Brezhnev and Kosygin* Detroit: University of Detroit Press

Simoès, A., ed 1976 *The Bilingual Child* New York: Free Press

Sivard, R.L. 1980 *World Military and Social Expenditures 1980* Lessburg, Va.: WMSE publications

Skelton, B. 1973 'Scientists and Social Scientists as Information Users' *Journal of Librarianship* 138–56

Skinner, E.P. 1973 *Peoples and Cultures of Africa* New York: Doubleday

Skutnabb-Kangas, T. 1976 'Bilingualism, Semilingualism and School Achievement' *Linguistische Berichte* 55–64

– 1981 *Bilingualism or Not: The Education of Minorities* Clevedon: Multilingual Matters

Smiley, D. 1977 'French-English Relations in Canada and Consociational Democracy' in Esman (1977b) 179–203

Smith, A.D. 1979 'Towards a Theory of Ethnic Separatism' *Ethnic and Racial Studies* 21–37

– ed 1976 *National Movements* London: Macmillan

Smith, A.K. 1969 'Socio-economic Development and Political Democracy: A Causal Analysis' *Midwest Journal of Political Science* 95–125

Smith, F. 1923 'Bilingualism and Mental Development' *British Journal of Psychology* 270–82

Soares, C. 1982 'Converging Evidence for Left Hemisphere Language Lateralization in Bilinguals' *Neuropsychologia* 653-9
- 1984 'Left-Hemisphere Language Lateralization in Bilinguals' *Brain and Language* 86-96
Soffietti, J.P. 1955 'Bilingualism and Biculturalism' *Journal of Educational Psychology* 222-7
Soja, E. 1971 'The Political Organization of Space' Washington, DC: Association of American Geographers, resource paper, no. 8
Spencer, J. 1963 *Language in Africa* Cambridge: Cambridge University Press
Spoerl, D.T. 1943 'Bilinguality and Emotional Adjustment' *Journal of Abnormal and Social Psychology* 35-57
Sreedhar, M.V. 1979 'The Functions of Bilingualism in Nagaland' *International Journal of the Sociology of Language* 103-13
Stafford, K., and S.R. van Keuren 1968 'Semantic Differential Profiles as Related to Monolingual-Bilingual Types' *Language and Speech* 167-70
Stalin, J.V. 1951 *On Marxism in Linguistics: The Soviet Linguistic Controversy* New York: King's Crown Press
Steiner, J. 1974 *Amicable Agreement versus Majority Rule: Conflict Resolution in Switzerland* (Trans. from German) Chapel Hill: University of North Carolina Press
Stengel, E. 1939 'On Learning a New Language' *International Journal of Psychoanalysis* 471-9
Stephens, M. 1976 *Linguistic Minorities in Western Europe* Llandysul, Wales: Gomer Press
Stewart, W. 1962 'The Functional Distribution of Creole and French Haitian' *Language and Linguistics* 149-59
Steyn, R.W. 1972 'Medical Implications of Polyglottism' *Archives of General Psychiatry* 245-7
Stoller, P. 1977 'The Language Planning Activities of the US Office of Bilingual Education' *Linguistics* 45-60
Strassoldo, R. 1970 'From Barrier to Junction - Toward a Sociological Theory of Borders' Published by the author
Stuchlik, J. 1957 'Contribution à la psychopathologie de l'expression verbale: les néophasies et les néographies' *Acta neurologica belgica* 1004-30
Sulek, A., and R. Sulek 1978 'Bibliography of Sociological Works Written by Polish Authors and Published in Languages Other than Polish: 1977-78' *Polish Sociological Bulletin* 49-75
Sunny, R.G. 1980 'Georgia and Soviet Nationality Policy' in S.F. Cohen, A. Rabinowitch, and R. Sharlet *The Soviet Union since Stalin* Bloomington: Indiana University Press
Sussman, H.M., P. Franklin, and T. Simon 1982 'Bilingual Speech: Bilateral Control?' *Brain and Language* 125-42
Tabouret-Keller, A. 1972 'A Contribution to the Sociological Study of Language Maintenance and Language Shift' in Fishman (1972b) 365-76

– 1975 'Plurilinguisme: revue des travaux français de 1945 à 1973' *La linguistique* 123–37

– 1976 'Plurilinguisme et interférences' *Guide alphabétique de linguistique* 304–10

Taillon, L. 1967 *Diversité des langues et bilinguisme* Montreal: Edition Atelier

Taiwo, C.O. 1979 'Nigeria: Language Problems and Solutions' *Prospects* 406–15

Tajfel, H. 1974 'Social Identity and Intergroup Behaviour' *Social Science Information* 6–93

Tajfel, H., and J.C. Turner 1979 'An Integrative Theory of Intergroup Conflict' 33–48 in W.C. Austin and S. Worchel ed *The Social Psychology of Intergroup Relations* Monterey: Brooks/Cole

Taylor, C.L., and M.C. Hudson 1972 *World Handbook of Political and Social Indicators* New Haven: Yale University Press

Taylor, D.M. 1980 'Ethnicity and Language: A Social Psychological Perspective' in Giles, Robinson, and Smith (1980) 133–45

Taylor, D.M., J.N. Bassili, and F.E. Aboud 1973 'Dimensions of Ethnic Identity: An Example from Quebec' *Journal of Social Psychology* 185–92

Taylor, D.M., and H. Giles 1979 'At the Crossroads of Research into Language and Ethnic Relations' in Giles and Saint-Jacques (1979) 231–42

Taylor, D.M., R. Meynard, and E. Rheault 1977 'Threat to Ethnic Identity and Second Language Learning' in Giles (1977a) 99–118

Taylor, D.M., and R.J. Sigal 1982 'Defining "Québécois": The Role of Ethnic Heritage, Language and Political Orientation' *Canadian Ethnic Studies* 59–71

Taylor, D.M., and L.M. Simard 1975 'Social Interaction in a Bilingual Setting' *Canadian Psychological Review* 240–54

– 1981 *Les relations intergroupe au Québec et le loi 101: les réactions des francophones et des anglophones* Quebec: Office de la langue française

Taylor, I. 1971 'How Are Words from Two Languages Organized in Bilinguals' Memory?' *Canadian Journal of Psychology* 228–41

Ten Houten, W.D. 1980 'Social Dominance and Cerebral Hemisphericity: Discriminating Race, Socioeconomic Status, and Sex Groups by Performance on Two Lateralized Tests' *International Journal of Neuroscience* 223–32

Tennant, P. 1982 'Native Indian Political Organization in British Columbia, 1900–1969: A Response to Internal Colonialism' *B.C. Studies* 3–49

Teschner, R. 1974 'Bilingual Education and the Material Explosion' *Bilingual Review* 259–63

Thananjayarajasingham, S. 1973 'Bilingualism and Acculturation in the Kuravar Community of Ceylon' *Anthropological Linguistics* 276–80

Thomson, D.C. 1979 'Canadian Ethnic Pluralism in Context' Unpublished manuscript

Tollefson, J.W. 1981 'Centralized and Decentralized Language Planning' *Language Problems and Language Planning* 175–88

Touret, B. 1973 *L'aménagement constitutionnel des Etats de peuplement composite* Quebec: Presses de l'Université Laval

Treisman, B. 1965 'The Effects of Redundancy and Familiarity on Translating and Repeating Back a Foreign and a Native Language' *British Journal of Psychology* 369-79

Trent, J. 1974 'The Politics of Nationalist Movements: A Reconsideration' *Canadian Review of Studies in Nationalism* 157-71

Troll, C. 1964 'Plural Societies of Developing Countries: Aspect of Social Geography' 9-33 in *20th International Geographical Congress* London: Nelson

T'Sou, B.K. 1975 'On the Linguistic Covariants of Cultural Assimilation' *Anthropological Linguistics* 445-65

Tsunoda, Tadanobu 1978 *The Japanese Brain* (in Japanese) Tokyo: Taishuukan

Tsushima, W.T., and T.P. Hogan 1974 'Verbal Ability and School Achievement of Bilingual and Monolingual Children of Different Ages' *Journal of Education Research* 349-53

Tuan, Yi-Fu 1974 *Topophilia: A Study of Environmental Perceptions and Attitudes* Englewood Cliffs: Prentice-Hall

Tubiana, J. 1980 'Les langues et l'Etat: autonomies, indépendances' *Le mois en Afrique* déc. 1980-janv. 1981, 143-8

Tucker, C.R., and W.E. Lambert 1972 'White and Negro Listeners' Reactions to Various American-English Dialects' in Fishman (1972b) 174-84

Tulving, E. 1966 'Subjective Organization and Effects of Repetition in Multitrial Free Recall Learning' *Journal of Verbal Learning and Verbal Behaviour* 193-7

Tulving, E., and V.A. Colotla 1970 'Free Recall of Trilingual Lists' *Cognitive Psychology* 86-98

Turcotte, D. 1981 'Analyse comparée de la planification linguistique en Côte d'Ivoire et à Madagascar' in Martin (1981b) vol. 2, 141-62

Ullrich, H.E. 1971 'Linguistic Aspects of Antiquity: A Dialect Study' *Anthropological Linguistics* 106-13

Ulrich-Atena, E. 1976 'National Linguistic Minorities: Bilingual Basic Education in Slovenia' *Prospects* 430-8

Vaillancourt, F. 1983 'The Economics of Language and Language Planning' *Language Problems and Language Planning* 162-78

Valdmam, A. 1979 *Le français hors de France* Paris: Champion

Valéry, P. 1945 *Regards sur le monde actuel* Paris: Gallimard

Valois, H.V. 1967 *Les races humaines* Paris: Presses universitaire de France

Van Dyke, V. 1975 'Justice as Fairness: For Groups' *American Political Science Review* 604-14

- 1976 'Human Rights without Distinction as to Language' *International Studies Quarterly* 3-38

Varsányi, J. 1982 *Border Is Fate: A Study of Mid-European Diffused Ethnic Minorities* Adelaide: Australian Carpathian Federation

Velikovsky, I. 1934 'Can a Newly Acquired Language Become the Speech of the Unconscious?' *Psychoanalytic Review* 329-35

Verdoodt, A. 1972 'The Differential Impact of Immigrant French Speakers on Indigenous German Speakers' in Fishman (1972b) 376-85

- 1973 *Le problème des groupes linguistiques en Belgique* Louvain: Institut de Linguistique

- 1975 'Ethnic Minorities and the United Nations' in Mackay and Verdoodt (1975) 1–8
- 1982 'Les groupes nationaux et les droits linguistiques' *Langue et société* 17–23
- 1983 'Enterprises et services publics: besoins en langues modernes/étrangères' *Sociolinguistics* 9–16
- ed 1978 'Belgium' *International Journal of the Sociology of Language* 5–8

Verescagin, E.M. 1969 *Psixologisceskaja i metodiceskaja xarakteristika dvujazycija* (bilingvizma) Moscow: IMU

Vickery, B.C. 1968 'Statistics of Scientific and Technical Articles' *Journal of Documentation* 192–5

Vikis-Freibergs, V. 1976 'Abstractness and Emotionality: Value of 398 French Words' *Revue canadienne de psychologie* 22–30

Viletta, R. 1978 *Abhandlung zum Sprachenrecht mit besonderer Berücksichtigung des Rechts der Gemeinden des Kantons Graubünden, Band 1: Grundlagen des Sprachenrechts* Zurich: Schulthes Polygraphischer Verlag

Villgrattner, C. 1975 'Protection of Minorities in Austria' in Mackey and Verdoodt (1975) 155–72

Vilrokx, J. 1978 'The French Elite in an Embattled Situation' *International Journal of the Sociology of Language* 61–70

Voegelin, C.F. 1977 *Classification and Index of the World's Languages* New York: Elsevier

Voinescu, I. et al 1977 'Aphasia in a Polyglot' *Brain and Language* 165–75

Vries, J. de 1973 'A Transition Model of Language Shift in Nine Finnish Cities, 1920–30' *Acta Sociologica* 121–35

Vries, J. de, and F.G. Vallée 1980 *Language Use in Canada* Ottawa: Minister of Supply

Vroede, M. de 1975 *The Flemish Movement in Belgium* Brussels: Flemish Cultural Council

Waggoner, D. 1976 'NCES Survey of Languages' *Linguistic Reports* 5–8

Wakefield, J.A. 1975 'Language Switching and Constituent Structure' *Language and Speech* 14–19

Wald, B. 1974 'Bilingualism' *American Journal of Physical Anthropology* 301–21

Walker, E. 1978 'Current Studies of Animal Communication as Paradigms for the Biology of Language' 203–18 in E. Walker *Explorations in the Biology of Language* Montgomery, Vt.: Bradford Books

Wallace, J.D. 1975 'Bilingualism – South Africa Style' *Canadian Medical Association Journal* 22 March, 1975, 49

Walters, J.L. and R.J. Zatorre 1978 'Lateral Differences for Word Identification in Bilinguals' *Brain and Language* 158–67

Wang, S.L. 1926 'A Demonstration of the Language Difficulty Involved in Comparing Racial Groups by Means of Verbal Intelligence Tests' *Journal of Applied Psychology* 102–6

Wardhaugh R. 1983 *Languages and Nationhood: The Canadian Experience* Vancouver: New Star Books

Watamori, T.S., and S. Sasanuma 1978 'The Recovery Processes of Two English-Japanese Bilingual Aphasics' *Brain and Language* 127–40

Weinreich, U. 1968 *Languages in Contact* The Hague: Mouton

Weinstein, B. 1980 'Language Planning in Francophone Africa' *Language Problems and Language Planning* 55–77

– 1983 *The Civic Tongue: Political Consequences of Language Choice* New York: Longmans

Werner M.W. 1976 'The Politics of Equality among European Linguistic Minorities' in Claude (1976) 184–213

– 1983 *The Civic Tongue: Political Consequences of Language Choice* New York: Longmans

Wexler, P. 1974 'Explorations in Byelorussian Historical Bilingual Dialectology and Onomastics' *Slavonic and East European Review* 481–99

Whebell, C.F.J. 1973 'A Model of Territorial Separatism' *Proceedings of the Association of American Geographers* 295–8

Whiteley, W.H., ed 1968 *Language Use and Social Change: Problems of Multilingualism with Special Reference to Eastern Africa* London: International African Institute, Oxford University Press

– 1974 *Languages in Ethiopia, Kenya, Tanzania, Uganda, Zambia* Oxford: Oxford University Press

Whiteley, W.H., and D. Forde 1971 *Language and Social Change* Oxford: Oxford University Press

Wiens, A., T. Manuagh, and J. Matarazzo 1976 'Speeches and Silence Behavior of Bilinguals Conversing in Each of Two Languages' *Linguistics* 79–93

Williams, C.H. 1979 'An Ecological and Behavioural Analysis of Ethnolinguistic Change in Wales' in Giles and Saint-Jacques (1979) 27–56

– 1981a 'Official-Language Districts: A Gesture of Faith in the Future of Canada' *Ethnic and Racial Studies* 334–47

– 1981b 'The Territorial Dimension in Language Planning: An Evaluation of Its Potential in Contemporary Wales' *Language Problems and Language Planning* 57–73

– 1981c 'Identity through Autonomy: Ethnic Separatism in Quebec' in Burnett and Taylor (1981) 389–418

Williams, G. 1978 *Social and Cultural Change in Contemporary Wales* London: Routledge and Kegan Paul

Williamson, R.C. 1982 'The Problem of Linguistic Survival: A Comparative Study' Paper read at the International Congress of Sociology, Mexico City

Wilton, F. 1974 'Implications of a Second Language Program: The Coquitlam Experience' *Canadian Modern Language Review* 169–80

Wilwerth, C. 1980 *Le statut linguistique de la fonction publique belge* Brussels: Editions de l'Université de Bruxelles

Wirth, L. 1945 'The Problem of Minority Groups' 347–72 in Ralph Linton ed *The Science of Man in the World Crisis* New York: Columbia University Press

Wolck, W. 1973 'Attitudes toward Spanish and Quechua in Bilingual Peru' in

R.W. Shuy and R.W. Fasold ed *Language Attitudes: Current Trends and Prospects* Washington, DC: Georgetown University Press

Wood, J. 1981 'Secession: A Comparative Analytical Framework' *Canadian Journal of Political Science* 107-34

Wood, R. 1977 'Linguistic Organizations in Scotland' *Language Problems and Language Planning* 41-52

– 1979 'Language Choice in Transnational Radio Broadcasting' *Journal of Communication* 112-24

Wurm, S.A. 1979 *New Guinea and Neighboring Areas: A Sociolinguistic Laboratory* The Hague: Mouton

Yinger, M. 1981 'Toward a Theory of Assimilation and Dissimilation' *Ethnic and Racial Studies* 249-64

Young, R.K., and I. Navar 1968 'Retroactive Inhibition with Bilinguals' *Journal of Experimental Psychology* 109-15

Zeltner, L.W. 1975 'Non-Jewish Minorities in Israel' in Mackey and Verdoodt (1975) 269-86

Zolberg, A. 1977 'Splitting the Difference: Federalization without Federalism in Belgium' in Esman (1977b) 103-42

Zuckerman, M. 1964 'Perceptual Isolation as a Stress Situation' *Archives of General Psychiatry* 255-76

Index